CARBODIES

THE COMPLETE STORY

Other Titles in the Crowood AutoClassics Series

AC Cobra	Brian Laban
Alfa Romeo Spider	John Tipler
Aston Martin: DB4, DB5 and DB6	Jonathan Wood
Aston Martin and Lagonda V-Engined Cars	David G Styles
Austin-Healey 100 and 3000 Series	Graham Robson
BMW M-Series	Alan Henry
The Big Jaguars: 3½-Litre to 420G	Graham Robson
Datsun Z Series	David G Styles
Ferrari Dino	Anthony Curtis
Ford Capri	Mike Taylor
Jaguar E-Type	Jonathan Wood
Jaguar Mk 1 and 2	James Taylor
Jaguar S-Type and 420	James Taylor
Jaguar XJ Series	Graham Robson
Jaguar XJ-S	Graham Robson
Jaguar XK Series	Jeremy Boyce
Lamborghini Countach	Peter Dron
Land Rover	John Tipler
Lotus and Caterham Seven	John Tipler
Lotus Elan	Mike Taylor
Lotus Esprit	Jeremy Walton
Mercedes SL Series	Brian Laban
MGA	David G Styles
MGB	Brian Laban
Mini	James Ruppert
Morgan: The Cars and The Factory	John Tipler
Porsche 356	David G Styles
Porsche 911	David Vivian
Porsche 924/928/944/968	David Vivian
Range Rover	James Taylor and Nick Dimbleby
Rover P4	James Taylor
Rover P5 & P5B	James Taylor
Rover SD1	Karen Pender
Sprites and Midgets	Anders Ditlev Clausager
Sunbeam Alpine and Tiger	Graham Robson
Triumph TRs	Graham Robson
Triumph 2000 and 2.5PI	Graham Robson
TVR	John Tipler
VW Beetle	Robert Davies
VW Golf	James Ruppert

CARBODIES
The Complete Story

Bill Munro

First published in 1998 by
The Crowood Press Ltd
Ramsbury, Marlborough
Wiltshire SN8 2HR

British Library Cataloguing in Publication Data

A catalogue record for this book is available from the British
Library.

ISBN 1 86126 127 6

The author and publishers would like to thank the following
individuals and organizations for supplying the photos used
in this book: Michael Applebee; British Motor Industry
Heritage Trust, Gaydon; Department of Transport; Dave
Brown; Mrs A. Duthrie and Bruce Walker; John Dyson,
Railton Owners Club, Early MG Society, Mike Evans, Rover
Sports Register, Derek Green, Stephen I. Halliday, FRPS,
Hulton Getty Picture Library, Imperial War Museum, Peter
James, Roger McDonald ABIPP, Jersey Motor Museum,
Barry Jones, London Taxis International, London Vintage
Taxi Association, Bill Lucas, Museum of British Road
Transport, Coventry, Derek Pearce, R. Pierce Ried, Stuart
Pessok, *Taxi* Newspaper, Public Carriage Office, Updesh K.
Ramnath, Steve Shirley, Brian Smith, Joan Swaine, Triumph
2000, 2500, 2.5PI Register and Mike Webster.

Typeset by Phoenix Typesetting, Ilkley, West Yorkshire.

Printed and bound in Great Britain by The Bath Press.

Contents

	Acknowledgements	6
	Evolution of the Company	8
	Introduction	10
1	The Beginnings of Carbodies	11
2	Holyhead Road	20
3	Wartime	38
4	Post-War Growth	50
5	The FX3	66
6	BSA – The Daimler Years, 1954–59	83
7	The FX4	98
8	BSA Years, 1959–73	110
9	Manganese Bronze Holdings to the Rescue	134
10	A New Direction	150
11	Rover Engines and the Birth of LTI	166
12	Beta, Gamma, Eta, Delta – A Cab for the World	186
	Index	205

Acknowledgements

In writing a book covering a period stretching from the last quarter of the nineteenth century to the present day – thus encompassing virtually the whole of the history of the British motor industry – I have had the privilege of speaking to a huge number of people. It was most gratifying that these people, without exception, have given up their knowledge so freely and generously. In some cases it was knowledge that had been painstakingly researched themselves, and in other cases the recollections of a lifetime's work.

These people can be divided into five distinct groups: the past and present employees of Carbodies, the car clubs, the London cab trade, the motor museums and those who did not fit specifically into any of the above categories but whose contributions, large or small, have been very important. To these people, listed here, I owe a very large 'thank you'.

From Carbodies' past employees: Bill Lucas, Peter James, Grant Lockhart, Joan Swaine, Brenda Troman, G. A. Stevens, Brian and Kath Evans, Walter 'Snowy' Beebe, Mike Edwards, Bill Knight, Len Molesworth, Elsie Cork, Cissy Hartly and Beryl Baker.

From LTI Carbodies' present people: Jamie Borwick, Barry Widdowson, Ed Osmond, Jevon Thorpe, Andrew Overton, Updesh K. Ramnath, and a special thank you to Peter Wildgoose, for help and enthusiasm from the very beginning through to the final chapter.

From the car clubs: Alvis Owner Club: David Culshaw and Malcolm Davey. The Alvis Register: John Burnell. Daimler and Lanchester Owners Club: David Adcock, Chris Clark, Harold Wilson, Arthur Buckley, Adrian Lanchester-Hale, John Ridley and Reg Turner. The Daimler Enthusiasts Club: John Nash, Henry Morgan, Anne Trigg and Maurice Niblett. The Early MG Society: Bill Grudgings, Geoff Radford, Philip Jennings, Jeremy Targett, Rex Coxeter, and Michael Applebee. The MG Car Club: Mike Hawke, Andrea Green, Colin Tièche and Mike Allison. Sunbeam Owners' Club: Bruce Dowell, Mike Collis and Philip Neate. Bentley Drivers Club: Bill Port, Richard Alexander, Oliver Suffield, Noel Pizey, R. Pierce Reid and R. Heginbotham. Rolls-Royce Enthusiasts' Club: Peter Baines, Philip Hall and Bernard King. Rover Sports Register: Mike Evans. Standard Car Club: Roger Morris. Railton Owners' Club: John Dyson, Barrie McKenzie and Stephen Halliday. Invicta Owners' Club: Derek Green and Keith North. Morris Register: Harry Edwards. Austin Counties Car Club: Colin Peck. Ford MkI Consul Zephyr and Zodiac Owners' Club: Neil Tee. Cortina Owners' Club: Tony Cooper. Crayford Convertible Car Club: Barry Priestman and Greg Warley. Capri Club International: Isobel Fairbrother and Cavan Ecclestone. Lea Francis Owners' Club: Robin Sawer. London Vintage Taxi Association: Peter Wheatley, Bob McPhail and Anthony Blackman. Singer Owners' Club: Nigel Hughes. Ford Sidevalve Owners' Club: Andy Main and Ivan Precioux.

From the museums: Barry Collins, Museum of British Road Transport, Coventry; Marie Tièche, National Motor Museum Beaulieu; Sara Bailey and Karam Ram, British Motor Industry Heritage Centre, Gaydon; Marie Lee, archivist, Mann Egerton, Norwich; Ron Staughton, Ford Heritage Centre; and David Fearon, Imperial War Museum, Duxford.

From the London cab trade: Stuart Pessok, editor of *Taxi* newspaper; Roy Ellis and Ray Biggs of the Public Carriage Office; Geoff Trotter MBE, Peter da Costa and Roger Ward.

And special thanks to: Barry Jones, Derek Pearce, Steve Wilson, Mike Jackson, Mike Webster, Buckingham Palace, Roger McDonald, Peter Ludford, Philip Dando of Hoyt Alloys, Charles Griffin, Spen King, Peter Whybrow, Alistair Bryce, Nick Walker and Andrew McCleod of the *Coventry Evening Telegraph*

If I have forgotten anybody, then please forgive me.

Carbodies: Evolution of the Company

1919   Robert 'Bobby' Jones starts a car body-making business within Gooderhams, a Coventry timber merchant.

1921   Jones takes over the body-making side and transfers to West Orchard, Coventry, becoming 'Robert Jones, trading as Carbodies'.

1928   Carbodies moves to Holyhead Road, Coventry.

1939   World War II marks the arrival of a large quantity of machine tools under lease-lend. Carbodies becomes a limited company, with Bobby Jones as controlling director and his son Ernest, previously general manager, as managing director.

1946   Works manager Jack Orr develops a system for converting modern, all-steel saloon cars into drophead coupés, and a contract is signed with London taxi dealers Mann and Overton to build, mount and finish bodies for a new London taxi, the FX3.

1954   Bobby Jones sells out to BSA, and Carbodies comes under the wing of Daimler and the chairmanship of Sir Bernard Docker.

1956   Sir Bernard and Lady Docker are removed from the board of BSA. Work begins on a replacement for the FX3 taxi, the FX4.

1958   The FX4 taxi is launched in London.

1961   Following the sale of Daimler to Jaguar Cars, Arthur Burton is appointed chairman of the new BSA engineering group and appoints Jim Munday as director and general manager of Carbodies.

1969   Jim Munday is moved to Triumph Motorcycles at Meriden. Bill Lucas becomes the new director and general manager.

1971   Carbodies takes over the FX4 chassis manufacturing plant from British Leyland.

1973   With the collapse of the BSA empire, Carbodies is taken over by Manganese Bronze Holdings plc as part of a rescue package engineered by the government to save the British motorcycle industry. Bill Lucas stays on, as managing director.

1976   Carbodies Sales and Service is formed to market the hire car as a limousine and the FX4 following British Leyland's falling interest.

1977   Bill Lucas begins the FX5 taxi project, for a wholly new taxi.

1979   Bill Lucas retires, and is replaced by Grant Lockhart.

1980	Grant Lockhart scraps FX5 and begins the CR6 project, a taxi based on the Range Rover body shell.
1982	Carbodies takes over the intellectual rights to the FX4 from British Leyland, and becomes the complete manufacturers.
1984	Carbodies buys Mann and Overton, and London Taxis International is formed. Production concentrates solely on one single product, the FX4 taxi.
1986	Grant Lockhart leaves, and Barry Widdowson is appointed managing director.
1997	The FX4 ceases production, and is replaced by the new TX1. The name 'Carbodies' is dropped, and the company becomes London Taxis International. Barry Widdowson becomes managing director of MBH's Vehicles Group, and Jevon Thorpe is made managing director of LTI.

Introduction

'I didn't know Carbodies made that!' In researching this book, I heard that comment more times than I can remember. Like the factory itself, tucked away off the Holyhead Road, much of Carbodies' story has been hidden, both to the motor historian and the motor industry. And it is something of an irony that one of the world's most recognizable motor vehicles, the FX4 London taxi, is made by a comparatively obscure company.

This book is an attempt to put the record straight. It traces the company's founding by Robert 'Bobby' Jones, its fortunes under its successive owners – Bobby Jones, BSA and Manganese Bronze Holdings – and in doing so reflects the changes in the British motor industry and London's taxi trade over the years, told through the recollections of past and present employees.

I have been particularly lucky in my research for this book, for throughout the history of Carbodies – or London Taxis International (LTI), as it is now known – there have been people in responsible positions who have understood the importance of photographic records. Bobby Jones's son Ernest was a keen photographer, and he took a great many pictures of his company's products up until 1954. Under BSA, their house publication, Group News, reported on all facets of the companies within the group, sending copies of pictures to the companies concerned. The first managing director under Manganese Bronze Holdings' tenure, Bill Lucas, collected as many pictures as possible, and under Grant Lockhart, chief body engineer Peter James took a great many pictures for the archives. To all these people, the employees, the photographers and picture collectors, I owe a great debt of gratitude.

But perhaps the man most responsible for helping me get this book off the ground is Peter Wildgoose, the sales and marketing director of LTI Carbodies. Sadly, Peter died on 25 February 1998, a short time after the manuscript was finished. He was just 52 years old, and had been fighting cancer since the middle of the preceding year. When I first wrote to Peter with what was initially an idea to produce a short series of magazine articles on British coachbuilders, he responded immediately. 'It looks a fascinating project', he said in his reply, 'and I look forward to helping you with it.' He kept his word, and certainly we shared in the fascination as the story unfolded.

Peter's work for LTI was pivotal in ensuring the company's survival for the foreseeable future. He lived long enough to see the 'new baby', the TX1, reach production, and I remember his obvious pride as he showed me the pre-production vehicles. It is a personal sadness for me that he did not live to see this book, and I have also lost a good friend, a kind, generous man, always ready with a smile, a positive word and a story to tell. Therefore it is my privilege to dedicate this book to his memory.

Bill Munro, West Sussex, March 1998

1   The Beginnings of Carbodies

'Bobby Jones was a Tartar'
     The opinion of many who knew and
     worked for Carbodies' founder, Bobby
     Jones

Smoke and flames rose up into the sky above Coventry's West Orchard district. It was 1923, and Robert – 'Bobby' – Jones' new car body-making business was on the verge of destruction. Only two years previously, in 1921, he had moved into the Hill Street premises once occupied by Thomas Pass & Sons. To some the fire would have been disaster, but Jones was a tough, hard-working man with ambitions to get on in life, and he picked himself up and rebuilt his business from the ashes until it became one of the most enduring companies in the history of the British motor industry.

BOBBY JONES' EARLY LIFE

Bobby Jones came from Bury in Lancashire. He was born there at 46 King Street on the 27 November 1873, the son of John Jones, a rag-and-bone dealer. He gained an elementary education at Edward Street school, and when he was fourteen, enrolled at Manchester Technical College on a two-year engineering course. Bobby claimed later to have made the nine-mile journey to Manchester each way on foot. In 1889 he was apprenticed as a body-maker to the firm of Lawton in Manchester's Oxford Street, a company renowned for building some of the finest carriages in England. Even today Lawton carriages enjoy an enviable reputation for their quality and comfortable ride.

In 1894 little Bobby – he grew no taller than five feet in height – reached his twenty-first birthday and finished his apprenticeship. He continued in the carriage-making trade, aware that he would need a steady income because he was soon to marry: he had met Lillie Bridge, who lived in nearby Heywood. On 6 April 1898, when Lillie was twenty and Bobby twenty-four, they married in Bury Presbyterian chapel and moved into Lillie's family home. The following February Lillie gave birth to their only child, a boy whom they named Ernest.

A START IN THE MOTOR INDUSTRY

As the motor car began to appear on the streets of Britain, it was plain to Bobby that his future lay in this new industry, so in 1904 he went to work for Humber at their factory at Beeston in Nottingham. Humber grew to become one of Britain's biggest pre-World War I car manufacturers. They were also building cars in Coventry, but the Beeston cars were always of better quality, with high class coachwork. It was working on such bodies, including the first closed bodies to be mounted on a Humber chassis, that Bobby Jones gained his first experience in this new and booming industry.

By 1907 Coventry had established itself as

the centre of Britain's motor industry, and Bobby moved there to become the first works manager of Charlesworth Bodies, a company newly formed by Charles Steane and C. Gray Hill in Much Park Street. By this time Ernest was eight years old and needed an uninterrupted education, so it was important for the family to stay in one place for a few years. Charlesworth was to continue building high quality bodies until World War II – but in 1912 Bobby Jones embraced new horizons as general manager with Hollick and Pratt.

Coach Builder Edward Hollick set up a new business in Coventry in 1905 with his new son-in-law Lancelot Pratt. In 1912 they began building bodies for a newcomer to the

motor industry, William Morris, who had set his sights on toppling the American Henry Ford's dominance of the British motor market. Unlike Ford, who made virtually every single item for his cars in his own factory, Morris decided that the way to build his car was from proprietary components, and chose Hollick and Pratt as body suppliers. It was at Hollick and Pratt that Bobby, as general manager, supervised the design of the first two-seater body for the new Morris car. Called the Oxford, it was announced in 1912 and put on sale the following year.

In the early decades of motor manufacture, motor bodies were wood framed, and built by the same labour methods as were horse-drawn carriages. Thus a foreman and his

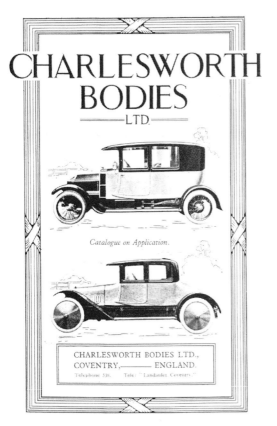

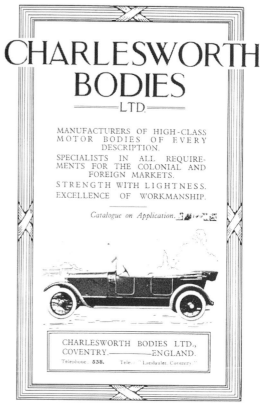

Charlesworth's early catalogue showed some elegant, distinctive styles.

team working within the factory would negotiate with the works manager a price for building a whole body, and that team would build that complete body from start to finish. However, such were the demands placed upon Hollick and Pratt by Morris for a far greater volume of bodies that this practice was replaced by a more cost- and time-efficient method where one man would build, say, a door, another the scuttle and so on; this was a system that Bobby would come to adopt for Carbodies. At Hollick and Pratt he would also have got to know William Morris, who was to provide a useful source of business for him in the future.

Hollick and Pratt were doing well, but later that year Bobby uprooted his family once more, moving them to Liverpool where he was to work as general manager at the coachbuilding department of William Watson. This time the move may have been a little harder on his wife and son, and in later life Lillie recalled that they always seemed to be 'upping sticks and following the work around'. Ernest had been educated in Coventry – he had attended Frederick Bird School and had become a choirboy at Coventry Cathedral – but fortunately by now he had left school. Watson was an early motor-racing pioneer who had set up as a dealer, selling Napier and Berliet cars. He bought a Morris car for his own use, which broke down: William Morris himself came to the rescue, and this so impressed Watson that he took on a Morris dealership. Possibly it was through Morris's reference that Bobby acquired his position at Watson's.

In February 1915, on Ernest's sixteenth birthday, Bobby gave his son a £5 note, a small fortune at the time, and told him to go and make his way in the world. Had Bobby foreseen what was to happen in the next few months he might have delayed that decision, for World War I, which was supposed to have been over by Christmas 1914, was

approaching its second year. The Jones family were still in Liverpool, but no records have been found of what Bobby did during these war years. In 1919, however, he was on the payroll of Mann Egerton and receiving a higher-than-average wage. The aeroplane was becoming a useful tool of warfare. Mann Egerton recruited large numbers of coachbuilders to make them, because they had the skills in working the wood from which these early planes were made. At forty-five years of age Bobby would be liable for conscription. If he was called up it is possible that, with his experience as a works manager in the coachbuilding trade, he may well have been transferred to Mann Egerton to supervise the construction of military aircraft. Some evidence to suggest this comes from the fact that in 1918 Ernest enlisted in the Royal Flying Corps; he might have seen what his father was making and fancied himself as a pilot. However, he never saw active service, as the war ended just months after he joined up.

THE START OF CARBODIES

After the Armistice, Bobby worked at Mann Egerton as coachbuilding manager; but in the later part of 1919 the Jones family returned to Coventry. Bobby joined Gooderham and Co, a local timber merchant's in Foleshill Road; the company wanted to enter the body-making business in the boom years immediately following the Great War, and Bobby set this up for them in Old Church Road. This first building, as Bobby would recall in later times, was not much bigger than two garages put together. Then the opportunity arose to buy out this new side of Gooderham's business, and Bobby decided to take it. One of the earliest employees at Gooderham's was Bill Dawson, a pattern-maker by trade: he and his son

Mick had cycled from their home in Aberdeen to the Midlands to find work. At first Bobby invited Dawson to be a partner, but at the time Dawson did not have the necessary capital; so he approached a man who was to become a sleeping partner for a few years, Mr Tooby Adkins-Soobroy. Bobby's twelve years' management experience stood him in good stead and business began to grow even in the slump of 1920; soon, Bobby needed to move from Old Church Road and find a place of his own.

By 1921 the old-established firm of Thomas Pass had run into serious financial trouble, and their premises in Hill Street became available. Bobby moved in, along with Bill Dawson and the rest of his small workforce, and thus the company known henceforth as 'Carbodies', came into being. It has not been recorded how Bobby decided upon the name of 'Carbodies', but there was a coachbuilder known as Jones Brothers already, so possibly he chose to pick a name that would not cause confusion. (Students of coachbuilding undoubtedly wish that the proprietors of the various companies named Mulliner had each taken a similar decision!)

Some of the men Bobby recruited, like Jimmy Bell, would be doing two or more jobs. He was foreman, designer and draughtsman, but there was only one painter, Mr Molesworth; his sons, Len and Harry, were to take up apprenticeships with Carbodies later on. A talented young sheet-metal worker by the name of Ben Johnson also joined the firm. Wages at the time were not good, especially for the women workers. In 1922 Cissy Reeves joined Carbodies as a fourteen-year-old school leaver, and went to work as a sewing machinist for 2½d (1p) an hour. Cissy fitted in well, but left in order to get married (married women were then not allowed to work); however, she returned to work part-time on motor show cars.

THE FIRST CUSTOMERS

One of Carbodies' first contract customers was the local firm of Crouch, a business which had begun in the motor-car trade building a three-wheeled car, the Carette. For a brief time Bobby supplied them with bodies for their later 8/18 four-wheeled car,

This Sunbeam 3-litre from 1926 carries a boat-tailed racing body by Carbodies. The car's first owner is reputed to have insisted that it be clocked around Brooklands at 100mph before he would buy it! It has been competing in motor sport events ever since.

but Crouch soon began to make their own bodies; they went out of business in 1927. This work, along with a small amount of bespoke building, kept the factory going, and eventually Bobby bought out his partner, establishing the business on his own. Cash was not always plentiful, however: a lifelong employee, Arthur Hughes, would recall much later the time when timber stocks fell so low that the gateposts were cut down to make wheel arches! Very soon, basic designs of body were evolved: an open tourer, a two-seater in either open or doctor's coupé form; saloons, either two- or four-door, each of different appearance; and a boat-tailed racing body. The blueprints for these followed basic designs found in the treatise *Motor Bodywork* by Herbert J. Butler. Although this standard work of reference was published in 1924, it illustrates the contemporary working practice of the immediate post-war years, and gives details of construction as well as line. It clearly influenced the style of many motor bodies of the time.

CONTRACT SUPPLY FOR ALVIS

In 1919 T.G. John, a clever Welsh engineer, bought the Coventry engineering company of Holley Brothers and began making a new design of car which he named the Alvis. The first model, the 10/30, was introduced in 1920, and in the following year John arranged for Carbodies to supply two- and four-seater bodies for this and his second model, the 11/40, at an average of two a week. Most of these were polished aluminium two-seat 'duck's-back' sports bodies. From 1923 Carbodies supplied saloon, tourer and coupé bodies for the model that made Alvis's name, the 12/50. Conventional but very well engineered, the

The Sunbeam's skimpy body just has room for this tiny dicky seat.

12/50 was a tough and reliable car with a sporting potential that was soon realized. Two-seater sports and four-seater tourer bodies followed for the revolutionary front-wheel drive 12/75, and when Alvis decided to build a Grand Prix car – the supercharged front-wheel drive FA 8/15 – Carbodies was asked to supply the bodywork for these five low-slung cars. The work for Alvis was shared with another Coventry firm, Cross and Ellis, who supplied about two bodies for every one from Carbodies, although the prices were competitive. Despite some criticism from Alvis, the quality of Carbodies' work was not to be found wanting; after all, hadn't Bobby served his apprenticeship at one of England's finest coach-makers? Unfortunately, although T.G. John was a good engineer, he was not such a good handler of money and in 1924, Cross and Ellis sued Alvis for £5,000 in respect of monies owed for work, forcing Alvis into receivership. The viability of the 12/50 saved Alvis, surely to Bobby's relief, but he did not resort to court action to recover any money. It may have been that Bobby would not allow debt to build up, and John would only order from Carbodies when he had the money to pay, whereas Cross and Ellis would allow

West Orchard bespoke work: pictured in a typical Warwickshire setting, this 14hp Bean carries a doctor's coupé body.

things to slide. It might be worth noting that in 1922, 1923, 1925 and 1926 (Alvis did not exhibit, for obvious reasons, in 1924) the Alvis entries in the Olympia Motor Exhibition catalogue mentioned Cross and Ellis as the builders of some of the bodies on the stand, but Carbodies' name was not mentioned until 1927 and later.

FIRE IN THE FACTORY

By 1923, more than sixty men were employed at West Orchard and business was beginning to look good – but in the midst of all this, the factory was hit by fire. This was an all-too-prevalent risk, considering that the floor was covered in wood shavings and the highly inflammable raw materials used by the painter were kept on the premises. The place was all but gutted; but practically as they worked, the factory was rebuilt around them, with a new entrance made in Hill Street.

LIFE ON THE SHOP FLOOR

Carbodies quickly gained two reputations: one amongst its customers for good value, and another amongst the tradesmen of Coventry as the last company they'd want to work for: if you had another job to go to, you didn't work for Carbodies – anyone who walked nine miles each way to school as a fifteen-year-old was bound to be a hard master to please. Bobby certainly was, but he would never demand anything in the way of hard work and service that he would not be prepared to give himself. He would open the factory at five minutes before eight o'clock in the morning, and he expected his foremen to be there by that time, too. He also expected punctuality from his men, and he gained the reputation of being a 'Tartar', a tag that would stick with him for all his working days. Nevertheless, Bobby could take a great liking to some people, particularly those who worked well at their job, and he respected those who stood up for themselves; this in turn encouraged fierce loyalty to him and the company on the part of these employees. To those he liked, Bobby was courteous and on occasions even generous, making a small number life-long friends. Many of his staff worked for the company all their life, although those who could not stand Bobby's iron discipline would not last a month.

Although the actual date is unknown, it must have been around the mid-1920s that Ernest Jones joined his father at Carbodies. Ernest was a keen photographer, and some of his earliest known work is from this period.

CONTRACTS FOR MG

The acquaintance with Morris formed at Hollick and Pratt brought Bobby a new and important source of work. Besides making his own cars, Morris also sold them at Morris Garages Ltd in Cowley, Oxfordshire. In 1921 he made Cecil Kimber sales manager there, and in 1922 promoted him to general manager. For a short time in 1921 Morris had offered a sports body in the Cowley shop, and Kimber decided that there was a future in this market; he therefore commissioned aluminium sports bodies, some with distinctive two-tone paint, from both Raworth and Carbodies, and in 1924 ordered a body for an 'MG Sports Special' from Hughes of Birmingham.

The striking polished aluminium body of the Hughes car attracted a lot of attention, especially when taken by its owner, Jack Gardiner, to the home of British motor sport, Brooklands; Kimber saw the sales opportunity and asked Hughes for more just like it. They could not meet the order, however, so Kimber went to Carbodies. He ordered three two-seaters and three four-seaters, and had the specially lowered chassis driven up to West Orchard to be fitted. From this model Kimber developed the Morris Cowley-based MG 14/28. The cars sold well and over 350 bodies – including two seaters, four-seat tourers, coupés, saloons, salonettes and a single racing body – were supplied by

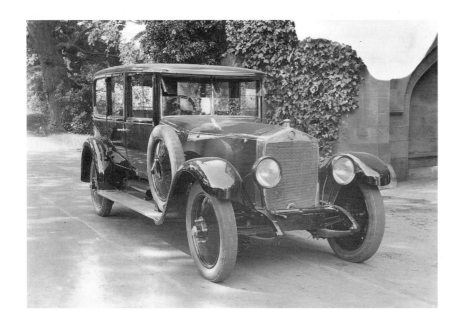

More bespoke: photographed by Ernest Jones at Lord Leigh's estate in Warwickshire, a Lanchester 40hp with an early six light saloon body.

The two-seat sports body on a 'Bullnose' MG 14/28, restored and in use in the late 1990s. The distinctive engine turning on the body sides has been painted over; it simply takes too long to polish!

Carbodies in two years. In late 1926 Morris introduced the new 'Flatnose' Cowley, which became the basis of Kimber's 14/40 specials, eventually replacing the Bullnose cars; these enhanced his reputation even further.

Mention should be made here of FC 7900 – 'Old Number One' – a car that holds a special place in MG history. Cecil Kimber built this one-off car for the Land's End Trial in 1924. It has been generally understood that its skimpy single-seat body was built by Carbodies, and this is stated in *MG by McComb*. However, much as the author would like to verify that claim, MG factory staff have testified to Mike Allison, author of *The Magic of the Marque*, that the body was built by MG themselves.

BURSTING AT THE SEAMS

By the mid-1920s the Alvis 12/50 was selling very well, to Carbodies' benefit. From modest beginnings in 1921 when just forty-nine bodies were made, a high of 483 was ordered in 1927. This 1927 figure included bodies for the new six-cylinder 14.75 chassis, an average of nearly ten a week. Taking into

account the seasonal nature of the motor industry, at its busiest times West Orchard would have nearly thirty bodies under construction at once, including MGs and the occasional bespoke job. Alvis at that time did not have car body-making facilities of their own, and no doubt concerned about the amount of outside work they were having to pay for, T.G. John approached Bobby with the view to having closer ties with, or even buying Carbodies; but nothing resulted from this proposition.

From 1927 the number of orders placed by Alvis with Carbodies began a steady decline;

Elegant engine turning on the sides sets off this 1927 14/28 tourer.

but orders would increase from MG. In 1927 Kimber quickly seized the opportunity to build a small sports car out of a new baby Morris, the Minor: he modified a chassis and sent it to Carbodies, where Bobby had built an all-wood, fabric-covered, two-seat body. Boat-tailed, it had distinctive raked-back doors and a lift-up boot lid which revealed the spare wheel laying flat on the floor. Kimber christened the little sports car the Midget, and gave it the factory type-letter 'M'. Many more MG bodies would be wanted now, because the cheap, fast little Midget could be raced and rallied almost 'out of the box' and found ready buyers. With steady contract work for both Alvis and MG, and bespoke work too, business for Carbodies was booming. West Orchard was bursting at the seams: more room was needed.

A curious body in today's eyes: a 1927 14/28 'Flatnose' chassis carries a two-seat 'ducks back' Sporting Salonette body. Certainly there is some luggage space, and it is an alternative shape to the flat boot supplied on other Carbodies saloons!

An Alvis 12/50 coupé from 1927. Chassis were dispatched from 'The Alvis' in Holyheaad Road over to West Orchard. Very soon they would not have so far to go!

2   Holyhead Road

'What matters is what goes out the bloody door!'

Bobby Jones's view on what
Carbodies should produce

A NEW HOME, AND EVEN MORE WORK

News that factory premises had become available reached Bobby's ears, on a large site opposite the Alvis factory, adjacent to the main Coventry–Nuneaton railway line, between Holyhead Road and Coundon Road. Even though Carbodies was thriving, Bobby needed financial help to move and so he approached the Coventry Economic Building Society which advanced a large sum,

enabling him to buy the land. In addition to the small number of buildings he was to occupy, Bobby dismantled his old woodmill over a weekend, moving it completely from West Orchard to his new premises.

In 1928 Cecil Kimber designed and built his first original model, the big six-cylinder 18/80 and the first car to feature the exclusive MG radiator. Kimber commissioned Carbodies to produce for this car versions of bodies that had already been seen on the 14/40 and 14/28. The 14/40's two-seat sports and Salonette bodies were adapted to suit the 18/80, though the tourer gained four full doors, and a number of special designs were seen, too. Then in 1929 Kimber moved his recently formed MG Car Company into a new factory at Abingdon in Oxfordshire, where he could make many more Midgets to meet the demand. Now both Carbodies and MG were into quantity production, and

MG M-Type Midget bodies were shipped down, three in a crate, to MG's factory, priced at £6 10s each. Here the bodies are already mounted on the chassis at Abingdon. In the background are MkI 18/80 Salonettes.

20

Bobby set up a special part of the Holyhead Road factory, the 'Midget Shop', to make the bodies for the little car. Each Midget body was composed of an ash frame without iron reinforcements, and a plywood skin covered in fabric. The 14/28, 14/40 and 18/80 chassis were driven up to Coventry to be fitted with bodies, and the completed cars were driven back. In their new factory MG could mount the Midget bodies themselves. Completed two-seater and Salonette bodies were shipped out by road – the two-seaters three in a crate at a price of £6 10s each – where they were fitted to the chassis.

OLYMPIA DEBUT

In October 1929 Bobby presented his products at the annual Olympia Motor Exhibition for the first time, the main sources of his work and the range of his products being displayed. There were two cars from his two main contract customers: an ivory-over-green MG 18/80 two-seater sports, possibly the prototype for a new more powerful model, and a new six-cylinder Alvis Silver Eagle with the four-door, four-light 'Atlantic' saloon body; also a six-light 'Pacific' saloon featured on a 16hp Sunbeam chassis, finished in blue cellulose with fabric upholstery and burr-walnut cabinetwork. Afterwards the 18/80, in the end the only MG known to have been fitted with a body of this style, went to the Scottish Motor Show; it then returned to Holyhead Road where it is believed the body was removed, subsequently remounted. In any event, the car was sold in early 1930.

MORE BODIES FOR MG

Cecil Kimber had a MkIII version of the big six-cylinder MG prepared for the Brooklands Double-Twelve race. Named the 18/100 Tigress, it failed to finish, and proved to be too slow to keep up with its intended rival, the Talbot 90. However, the Tigress was rebodied by Carbodies with a four-seat sports-tourer body. It was shown at Olympia in 1930, and in referring to the car in their Motor Exhibition review, *The Autocar* said that Carbodies had 'gained quite a reputation for sports bodies'. Kimber had intended the Tigress for limited production, but in fact no more than five were built, and the remainder of the twenty-five sports bodies ordered from Carbodies for the model were fitted to MkI and MkII 18/80s. The big 18hp cars never sold well, but the Midget was a runaway success – Midgets had won the team prize at the Double-Twelve – and Kimber quickly realized that this was his main market. A special high-performance version of the Midget was built, the C-Type Montlhéry, forty-four in all, carrying a

George Tweedie Walker racing his Bentley at Silverstone in the 1950s. 'Tweedie' bought this 4.5-litre tourer, the only such chassis with Carbodies' coachwork, from its original owner, a Mr R. Squires. The car later underwent a similar treatment to many others of the marque, namely the fitting of a Vanden Plas replica tourer body. Some fourteen Bentleys in total were fitted with Carbodies' coachwork, including twelve 3-litre models and a single Speed Six.

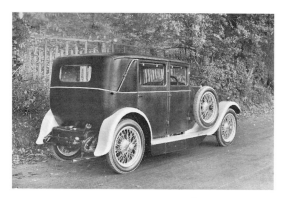

More bespoke coachwork from the late 1920s and early 1930s. This 3-litre high chassis Lagonda carries a version of the fabric-covered 'Alvista' body patented by Alvis. Bodies of this type were built by both Carbodies and Cross and Ellis for Alvis.

This Atlantic-bodied 1932 Delage D6 was ordered in the Wirral, in Cheshire.

little boat-tailed racing body supplied by Carbodies.

ERNEST AND BOBBY

Ernest and Bobby were very different in appearance: Bobby was short and stocky, whilst Ernest was tall, like his mother; his facial features also resembled hers, although

A selection of body styles on the MG 18/80 chassis: A 1930 MkI Salonette,

. . . a 1930 MkI four-seat tourer,

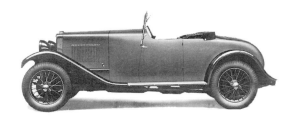

. . . a 1929 MkI two-seater,

the red hair and protruding ears he inherited from his father. As Lillie was never seen at the factory, a rumour spread that Ernest was adopted, but it was just that: a rumour. Bobby had made sure that his only son had attained a high level of skill in his father's

Lord Rothschild's MG18/100 Tigress, one of only five such cars built. The small door was fitted to allow the use of a straight-through exhaust.

trade of coachbuilding, and that he had gained a good grounding in the running of what was in reality 'Robert Jones, Trading as Carbodies'. Ernest's role as the 1930s progressed to what could be described as that of general manager, though Bobby, as the owner, was very much the boss. However, Ernest was also a good salesman, and this complemented his father's tight control of the factory and his hard-headed approach to business.

SMALL PRODUCTION RUNS EQUAL GOOD PROFIT

Bobby soon found that it paid to take on contract work that bigger coachbuilders found uneconomical, because he could adapt any of his small range of bodies to fit other makers' chassis at an economic price. In keeping with this policy, a small number of Pacific and Atlantic saloons were fitted to the Lea-Francis 'Ace of Spaces' and 12/40 chassis in the early 1930s – although Lea-Francis was in financial difficulties at the time, and

would not have been an attractive customer to Bobby. Riley made the majority of its own bodies in the Midland Motor Body Company, but subcontracted Hancock and Warman, another Coventry concern, to build four-light saloon bodies for the new six-cylinder Stelvio. But Hancock and Warman's premises were destroyed by fire around 1930 and they never resumed business; later, some Stelvio models had Carbodies' Atlantic bodies fitted.

Bobby, however, had no time for fancy coachwork designs, and if one of his standard bodies could be used to fulfil a contract, then that is what was used. Only if a customer came to him with an already established design that they wanted making on a limited run basis, would the Carbodies' body-plate be seen on something different. He often said, 'What matters is what goes out of the door': in other words, if it doesn't sell, if it doesn't make a profit, don't waste time with it – he was to see too many of his contemporaries go bankrupt, trying to maintain too complicated a range of models. Bobby would keep things simple. And talking of profits, book-keepers

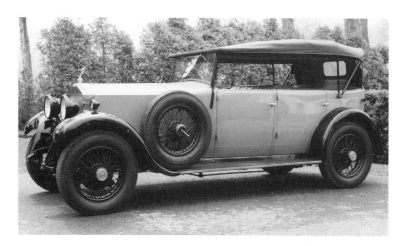

1930 Rolls Royce 20/25 tourer, one of some fourteen Rolls-Royces to carrry Carbodies' coachwork. This is the car's original body, and it was still known to carry it in the late 1980s.

1930 20/25 Rolls Royce with Pacific saloon body. This is a rebodied car, photographed by Ernest Jones in the garden of the home he built in 1932.

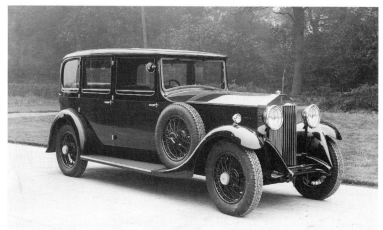

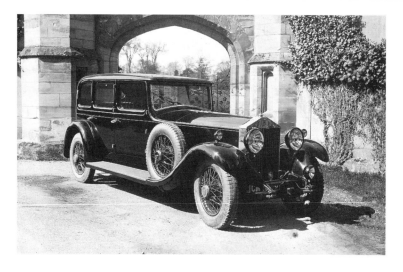

Perhaps the most handsome Pacific body, this Phantom II from 1930 was ordered through Bambers of Southport, Cheshire, for a private customer. Later it was sold on to Glasgow Co-operative Society's funeral department, which once ran the largest fleet of Rolls-Royces in Britain. It was subsequently rebodied as a tourer by Wilkinsons of Derby.

Ernest Jones's handwritten caption on the back of his own picture says 'Saloon body on S. H. Daimler chassis for agent. About 1930/31'. The story in Carbodies at the time was that this Pacific-bodied car was 'for the Queen'. The date suggests that this would be Queen Mary, who was known to have a Daimler saloon for her personal use in the Royal Mews. We may never know the truth . . .

had of course been employed, but as the business grew it was necessary to improve the standard of financial control: G. A. Stevens, known throughout his working life simply as 'Steve', joined the company in 1937, and brought his expertise in accountancy to the firm.

PROSPEROUS TIMES: MARRIAGE, AND THE JONES FAMILIES MOVE HOUSES

As business grew, Bobby and Lillie moved into Heath Close, a large Edwardian detached house just off the Stoneleigh Road with two acres of ground and a landscaped terraced garden. Bobby enjoyed a game of golf when time allowed, but this was not always possible: the business was his life and he continued to work hard, although his big garden allowed him at least to practise his putting skills. In 1932 Ernest married Dorothy Aikin from Finchley in North London. They set up home at Earlsdon in the south-west of Coventry, but immediately bought a plot of land off the Kenilworth Road where they built a large detached house

which they called Broadfield. They moved in as soon as it was completed, and in 1934 Dorothy gave birth to a son, whom they named Barry.

MORE MGS: THE BEGINNINGS OF A CLASSIC STYLE

A tiny four-seat body, a smaller version of that fitted to the Alvis front-wheel-drive tourer, was fitted to the M-Type Midget's later derivative, the 1932 D-Type. In the preceding year Kimber had ventured again to make a slightly bigger sports car, the 12hp F-Type Magna. Carbodies displayed a closed foursome coupé body on the chassis at Olympia that year, and on the F2 version they also supplied the first of what was to become the traditional English sports car design. The four-seat body from the D-Type was shortened to a two-seater, giving room for a rear-mounted slab fuel tank, and two other features gave extra room in the tiny cockpit whilst allowing the body to be mounted lower on the chassis: the tops of the doors were cut away to give the driver much-needed elbow-room, and the now classic

Ernest and Dorothy's wedding day, at Barnet parish church.

Proud parents: Bobby and Lillie at Ernest and Dorothy's wedding.

'humped' scuttle was fitted, allowing the instruments to be mounted higher to give more leg-room.

The Magna was superseded in 1932 by the K-type Magnette, and the K3 version was a powerful racing machine. Kimber decided to enter three Magnettes for the gruelling Mille Miglia road race the following year, and after making some prototypes at Abingdon, he commissioned Carbodies to make a two-seat racing body for the K-Type based on artwork produced for MG, and featured on the front of the catalogue. This body was exhibited on Carbodies' stand at Olympia in 1932, although the bodies subsequently made for the K3s at Abingdon were of lighter construction.

The M- and D-Type Midgets ended their run in 1932. More than 2,000 out of the known 3,225 M-Types made were fitted with the Carbodies' two-seater body, and others with the little two-seat Salonette. The cost of each individual body might have not been great, but it was the biggest single job by far that Carbodies had yet done. In 1932 MG brought out another new Midget, the J-type. The four-seat body supplied by Carbodies for the J1 version was an adaptation of that fitted to the front-wheel-drive Alvis 12/75, and the two-seat J2 and J3 featured smaller versions of the Magna body.

ALVIS AND MG DEPART

In about 1932 William Morris steered Cecil Kimber to Morris Bodies for the new P-type Midget. It was a blow to Carbodies to lose MG as a contract customer, although it was not quite the last time the little sports cars were seen at Holyhead Road. Carbodies also lost Alvis: as well as furnishing Alvis's 12/50 and the later 12/60, Carbodies' coachwork had found its way in saloon and sports form onto the bigger six-cylinder 18hp Silver Eagle – but Alvis had set their sights higher and in 1931 they introduced a new and exciting model, the big six-cylinder Speed 20. Carbodies featured a four-door saloon body for this model for Olympia in 1932. A second saloon and a racing body were built – but then in 1933 Charles Follet arrived as Alvis's new London distributor, and urged the company to look for coachbuilders with prestige names to complement the Speed 20. In 1933 Carbodies built its last contract body for a pre-war Alvis, losing the work to Vanden Plas and Charlesworth, as well as to Cross and Ellis.

HENRY ALLINGHAM, ROVER BODIES AND THE AIRLINE COUPÉ

The Rover Car Company had been turned from disaster in the early 1930s by Spencer Wilks, and the board decided that a wide range of bodies should be made available for the new range of chassis that would establish the company as a maker of solid, quality cars. Coachwork designer Henry W. Allingham was commissioned by Rover to find suitable firms to provide the range of bodies, and Carbodies was one of the nine selected. They were to make the 'Nizam' Sports (all Rover models for that year carried names from the Indian sub-continent) for four chassis in the range. The Nizam was an adaptation of the Alvis 12/50 'beetle-back' body, and the 12hp version was displayed at Olympia in 1931. The Indian names were dropped by Rover for the 1933 season.

In 1933 the 12hp Speed Pilot chassis, with a four-seater sports body featuring a new rounded back and rear-mounted spare wheel, was shown by Carbodies at Olympia. Complementing it in the Rover catalogue was the two-seat sports body from the previous year, looking much better on the low-slung Speed Pilot chassis – but something more lasting was seen at Olympia. In 1932 a Rover Speed Pilot with a handsome two-door saloon body by Charlesworth had won coachwork awards at the RAC Rally in Hastings, Sussex, and for

Henry Allingham negotiated for Carbodies to be one of no less than nine separate coachbuilders to supply bodies for Rover's new range of chassis. This 12hp 'Nizam' sports is in the collection at the British Motor Industry Heritage Centre, Gaydon.

27

The 1935 Rover Streamline coupé (left), and saloon. Both are fully restored examples, photographed at a European rally.

the 1933 season the model, dubbed the Hastings Coupé, was offered in the Rover catalogue. Charlesworth's fortunes were often troubled, however, and perhaps for this reason Rover approached Carbodies, who would be a more reliable, and probably cheaper source of supply for this body. The Atlantic body was therefore adapted to take the small boot, and was made in two- and four-door forms. As mentioned above, the four-door sports saloon appeared on Carbodies' stand at Olympia in 1933, mounted on a Speed Pilot chassis. After 1936 Rover took over all their own body manufacture, simplifying the range, and the Charlesworth design gradually evolved into the classic Rover style that lasted until 1948.

For 1935 two new four-door models appeared for Rover, the streamline saloon and coupé. This particular saloon style is not known to have been fitted by Carbodies to any other make – although Henry Allingham, the man who had set up the original contract between Rover and Carbodies, had designed a 'streamlined' two-seat fixed-head coupé, named the Airline, which bore a close resemblance to the Rover streamlines, and Carbodies was commissioned to supply over forty of these little coupé bodies, of

highly complex internal structure, for three MG models. Most were for the PA Midget from 1934, but there were six for the six-cylinder N-Type MG Magnette in the same year, and just one on the T-Type Midget.

THE FAIRWAY, A FAVOURITE NAME

Ever the golfing enthusiast, Bobby had christened the 1933 Rover four-door sports saloon the 'Fairway', and although Rover never used the name, it appeared twice at Olympia in 1933. For the 1934 model year William Watson ordered a bespoke special fixed-head coupé on a tuned Morris 10/6 chassis, offering either four-light or two-light versions. It was effectively the same body as used on the Hillman Minx Foursome Coupé of the same year, but with a major difference: the Morris was a 'faux' or false, coupé, with a fixed head, its dummy hood-irons and fabric roof covering giving it the appearance of a drophead body. Watson called the model the Fairway Watson Special. These would not be the only occasions that the name Fairway was used, either in Bobby Jones's time, or much later.

A BIG NEW CUSTOMER

Carbodies, geared up for contract work, found an ideal new customer in the form of the Rootes Group. William and Reginald Rootes had started as car dealers in Maidstone, Kent, and in 1925 bought the coachbuilders Thrupp and Maberly. Towards the end of the 1930s they had acquired a substantial holding in Humber-Hillman; their intent was to build a motor-manufacturing empire on the lines of the American giant, General Motors and from 1931 onwards they began developing a comprehensive range of cars. Beginning with the six-cylinder Hillman Wizard and the immediately popular 10hp Minx, they followed with the Humber 12, the Snipe and the Pullman. These cars were well made and engineered but unexciting in their mechanical specification. Standard saloon bodies for the whole range were made by Pressed Steel,

1932 Hillman Minx Sports body, similar in type to the Olympia show car of the same year, from the front . . .

. . . And from the rear, showing the rear-mounted spare and the Carbodies' signature, the louvred chassis valance.

29

but to make the cars more attractive the Rootes brothers decided to follow industry trends and offer a range of sports bodies as well. As Thrupp and Maberly were too small to build special bodies in the volumes expected, Rootes subcontracted out the work; Carbodies was one of a number of additional coachbuilders engaged, along with Holbrook, Martin Walter and Maddox. A two-seat sports, another adaptation of the 'beetle back' with a rear-mounted spare wheel and cutaway doors, featured at Olympia in 1932.

The following year the range for Rootes was much larger. The coachbuilding firm of Salmons had produced a design of coupé de ville head, and Carbodies made use of this design for a new Minx Foursome coupé; this and a sports saloon, a further adaptation of the Atlantic body, appeared on the Humber 12 at Olympia in 1933. By now Rootes had grown to be Carbodies' biggest customer, more than compensating for the loss of MG and Alvis. Carbodies' 1934 Olympia stand was an all-Rootes affair, featuring the Atlantic-derived sports saloon body on the big six-cylinder Hillman 20/70. A Humber 12 drophead coupé and a smart two-door sports saloon, the Cresta, was fitted to the low-chassis Aero Minx, and completing the line-up were three Minxes, two coupés

and a sports tourer. Bobby always referred to the Hillman Minx as his 'bread-and-butter model', and the little car became his choice of motoring with, of course, a body made in his own factory.

By now, Carbodies' styles were beginning to show their age at a time when 'stream-lining' was coming into vogue, influenced by the quest for speed on land, sea and air: something more modern was needed. For the 1936 season Rootes had a new range of models: the Minx was restyled and given the supplementary name 'Magnificent', and the shape of its pressed-steel radiator shell was also seen on the new big Hillman, the Hawk, and on a two-door sports saloon; the first of a new, more modern line appeared on this car at Olympia. This line was also used on a sleek drophead coupé. Carbodies were to specialize in this type of body, and the number of other makers' chassis fitted with the new drophead coupé began to grow.

NOEL MACKLIN'S HIGH PERFORMANCE CARS

Old Etonian Noel Macklin had been buying bodies from Vanden Plas, Mulliner and others for his fast and expensive 4-litre

From the 1933 Hillman catalogue, the Carbodies' Minx foursome drophead coupé.

Almost extinct now, six-cylinder Hillmans from the early 1930s such as this 20/70 were offered with sports saloon body. The rear quarters show its origins in the Atlantic body.

The 1935 Olympia exhibition saw Carbodies first Railton body, effectively an Atlantic saloon with a boot. Behind to the left is a Minx drophead coupé, whilst to the right is a Hillman Hawk sports saloon. Also on the stand, but not seen, is a Humber 12 foursome drophead coupé.

Invicta, built in the grounds of his home at Cobham, near Brooklands race-track in Surrey. However, the slump of the early 1930s brought sales to a virtual standstill and Macklin needed to cut prices quite dramatically – the Cabriolet by Cadogan was an astonishing £1,775 – if he was to survive. He could not do much about reducing the price of the complex chassis which he made himself, or the bought-in Meadows' engines, but he could use cheaper suppliers of coach-work. All of Invicta's records have been lost so it is not clear as to how Macklin came to hear of Carbodies, but he did agree a deal

with Bobby to supply more economically priced bodies for the low-chassis S-type. The four-seater sports model shown on Carbodies' stand at Olympia in 1931 was £887, and when Macklin brought out his 12/45 and 12/90 model, Carbodies supplied the coachwork for these, too.

Macklin's follow-up to the Invicta, the Railton, was much cheaper, and thus commercially more successful, because he pursued a totally different policy. The American Hudson Terraplane was a powerful performer with a 4-litre straight-eight engine, and for his new car Macklin

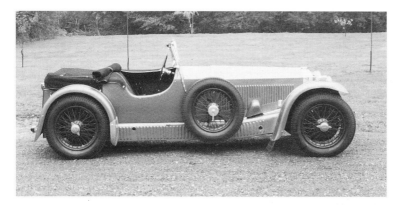

The 1931 S-Type low-chassis Invicta four-seat tourer.

The Holyhead Road body-plate, from the 1931 Invicta. The four-figure number to the left is the actual body number, whilst to the right is the date, in this case 16 April 1931.

negotiated to buy the Terraplane chassis, in the right-hand drive form made for the Empire market; in 1933 he began modifying these at Fairmile, his small Surrey factory.

The car's name was acquired in the following way: Macklin's close friend Reid Railton was chief engineer with the firm of Thomson and Taylor at Brooklands, where he had already made his name with the ERA racing car and Malcolm Campbell's Bluebird land speed record car. Macklin signed Railton as engineering consultant and paid him £5 per car for the use of his name. Railton added André Hartford Telecontrol shock absorbers to the chassis; but contrary to contemporary reports, no Hudson chassis

was ever lowered by the factory.

The high ground clearance, along with the small 16in 'roller-skate' wheels of the Hudson chassis, presented something of a challenge to British coachbuilders. Originally Macklin had his coachwork for the new car designed in-house and bought from Motor Bodies and Berkeley; by 1935, however, he decided that he could get a better price for his standard saloon, and returned to Carbodies. The first of Carbodies' Railton saloons adapted to match Macklin's in-house design was the Atlantic body with a bustle boot added. It fitted the bill as well as, if not better than its predecessor from Coachcraft, and at £598 it was nearly £200

*For the 1936 season,
Railton commissioned
Carbodies to make this
more up-to-date Cobham
saloon, a style which
originated with Coachcraft.
Pictured with the car,
right, is Noel Macklin, the
man responsible for
Railton cars. With him is
Leon Cushman, works
manager at the Fairmile,
Surrey factory where he
had previously overseen the
production of the Invicta.*

*The 1937 Railton Tourer.
This example is the
property of Tim Railton,
son of Reid Railton.*

cheaper than a Stratton University saloon on the same chassis. But the ageing style accentuated the Railton's high ground clearance, and for 1936 Macklin commissioned a new range of body styles. For its first design Carbodies adopted a style from Coachcraft with a sweeping integral boot, named the Cobham, plus a four-seat tourer similar to the design used on the 1933 Rover. Then in 1938 the Cobham name was given to a redesigned Coachcraft saloon with a razor-edged roof line. Carbodies' third design of saloon, the Sandown, was effectively a modernization of the Atlantic, with a boot

similar to the 1935 Hillman Hawk sports saloon grafted on, and lowered over the chassis to give a much reduced ground clearance. Carbodies also featured a new, sleek, drophead coupé body named the Claremont. The range was completed with the tourer along similar lines. Sandown and Claremont bodies were also fitted to the 17hp six-cylinder version of the Railton-Hudson chassis.

Macklin would not join the Society of Motor Manufacturers and Traders, and was therefore not eligible to exhibit at the Olympia Motor Exhibition in his own right.

However, Bobby was happy to exhibit Railton cars, or Railton-Hudsons as they were entitled in Carbodies' catalogue entry, and did so from 1935 until 1938, the last exhibition before the outbreak of war and the first to be held at Earl's Court.

The Sandown was to be the last saloon body in production at Carbodies for almost twenty years. A prototype saloon body was made for Lea-Francis in late 1937, but was not accepted, and subsequently Bobby focused his strategy on going for smaller contracts requiring just one type of body: the drophead coupé.

MORE DROPHEAD BODIES AND POWER-OPERATED HEADS

A medium-sized version of the new drophead coupé body was mounted on a 1937 Singer 12 chassis. Exhibited on Carbodies' stand at Olympia that year, the car was equipped with an electrically operated power system patented by a Frenchman, Maurice Bessoneau. According to the show catalogue, the three-position head could be operated from the de ville position, 'giving "open" or

"closed" positions, without even stopping the car'. This Singer became Bobby's personal transport. By the following year Bobby had purchased the rights to Bessonneau's patents, giving them the now familiar name 'Fairway', and he displayed at Olympia a two-position drophead coupé body on the Humber Super Snipe chassis. (This Humber became Ernest's choice of motoring, promoting, like his father, the firm's products to the full.) Further orders came from Captain John Black, the managing director of Standard Motors, whose policy, like that of the Rootes brothers, was to offer a choice of special bodies from different coachbuilders. He contracted Carbodies to build a drophead coupé body for the new Flying 8, and at the 1938 Motor Exhibition a Standard Flying 14 coupé was on Carbodies' stand.

The foreman of the sheet-metal workshop, John (Jack) Orr, was involved with the adoption of the Bessoneau patents, and he had formed some ideas of his own. He thought the system of lowering the head too complex. In its two-position form the design included the simultaneous telescoping of the forward hood-sticks with the folding of the rear portion of the head. Orr also disliked the fact that in the conventional head

The 1938 Railton Claremont drophead coupé with a manually operated head. This was one of the largest chassis to be fitted with this body.

This Standard Flying 14hp drophead coupé with three-position, manually operated head is similar to the 1938 Carbodies' Earl's Court Motor Exhibition model. Bodies in this style were shown on both Singer 12 (1937) and Lanchester 14 chassis (1938), each with power-operated hood.

design, visibility to the side and rear was virtually nil, and on the Humber fitted a drop quarter-light. He began working on his own modifications to the Tickford three-position head, which also included a bigger back window and a simpler system of power operation than Bessoneau's. These designs would bring dividends to the company, but further into the future than many had anticipated.

1939: THE THRESHOLD OF AN UPHEAVAL

In 1939, a young lady by the name of Joan Harper struggled through pouring rain trying to find Carbodies' entrance in Holyhead Road: she had an appointment for a job interview with Steve Stevens. Her recollections of her first day there give a clear idea of Bobby's factory in those pre-war days:

It was pouring with rain, and I didn't want to go. I couldn't find the place. I turned around – and there I saw the name on the wall. You wouldn't find it. The drive was a sea of mud because Bobby wouldn't spend money on things that weren't going to bring money in. I ploughed up the drive and went into the office which was a poky little place, and said I'd come to see Mr Stevens. He gave me a job in wages and the money I was after. I didn't think they'd pay it because it was a tin-pot little place, but that was the best day's work I ever did. I was very happy there. There were no luxuries. I looked down onto the trim shop and would see the rats which used to run through the trim shop – they liked the upholstery material!

Within months of Joan Harper starting work at Carbodies, Britain was at war, and the motor industry would never be the same. For Carbodies, the war would set in motion a chain of events that would not only affect the difficult years after the war, but the company's survival and future prosperity.

Bobby Jones

If you knew Bobby Jones, you either liked him or hated him – but whatever your opinions, he was a real character. Many stories have been told about him, often repeated over and over again by the different people who knew and worked for him. Here are a few, collected from (in alphabetical order) Elsie Cork, Brian Evans, Peter James, Barry Jones, Bill Knight, Bill Lucas, Len Molesworth, Joan Swaine and Brenda Troman:

Bobby was a very strict, hard man to work for. He had three pet hates: tea drinking, trade unions and smoking. He would never allow anyone to smoke at work – though that wasn't surprising, considering how inflammable the wood shavings on the workshop floor were. Once, on a Sunday, when we were preparing a Motor Show car, Bobby came in and saw a man smoking a pipe in the factory. He went up to him and asked why he was smoking a pipe. The man said, 'What am I supposed to do with it, chew it?'

Bobby would not even allow smoking in the toilets. The toilet block had an entrance at each end, and the waste from the cubicles was carried off in a long trough that ran under each seat. If Bobby thought anyone was skiving off and smoking in a cubicle, he would screw up some newspaper, set light to it, push it along the trough and wait for somebody to shout out in pain!

Bobby allowed tea breaks, but if any man went near the urn even a few seconds before the tea whistle, he would tip the whole urn onto the floor. If anyone brewed up outside of tea-break time, and Bobby saw the billy-can on any of the wood stoves that heated the factory, he would stand beside it until it boiled dry and burned. There is a story of a new panel-beater who when he arrived on his first day, put his hammer and tin mug on his bench. Bobby walked up to him, picked up the hammer and said, 'You won't have much time for tea drinking around here,' and crushed the mug with the hammer!

He watched the pennies very closely, as any guv'nor would, and he hated waste. He used to say that he always ordered a packet of screws for every job, and another packet for the ones that fell on the floor!

Bobby was a man of regular habits. Every single day including Sunday, he would rise at 6am, wash, dress in a suit, collar and tie and boots – never shoes – and be at work before 8am. And he would demand the same degree of punctuality from his employees. Not that he was infallible. The Coundon Road railway station was behind the factory, and six trains a day would carry workers down from Nuneaton and Bedworth to Coventry. One morning just after starting time Bobby saw a man walking through the factory with his coat on and his lunch under his arm; he stopped him and said, 'You're late! Get your cards and go!' The man looked at him and replied, 'You can't sack me!' 'Why not?' demanded Bobby. 'It's my factory, I'll sack who I like!' 'Because,' said the man, 'I work for the Alvis over the road, and I'm using your factory as a short-cut!'

Bobby and Ernie were always having rows. Ernie was pipe smoker. Bobby hated that, and he wouldn't tolerate it in his presence. He had a dog before the war, and wherever that dog was, that's where the boss was! The old office was off the yard, up a flight of steps. One day the dog went up the steps first and sat down outside the office. Now, normally the dog would have gone into the office first, and that gave Ernie the chance to put out his pipe and save an argument.

But this time Bobby walked up the stairs, past the dog and of course found Ernie in the office smoking his pipe. Well, they had a row, Ernie went out of the office, tripped over the dog and as he tripped, kicked it downstairs. He got the sack for that – but in a few days he was back, and Bobby had forgotten all about it.

The Comparative Dimensions Plan

With a standard range of bodies that could be adapted to fit cars as small as the MG Midget and as large as the Railton and Humber Snipe, and to make them at such an economical price, Carbodies obviously had some particularly effective system. It was based on the following: stored away in the archives of the Museum of British Road Transport in Coventry is a large drawing, dated 1946, called a comparative dimensions plan. Specific for cars of 16hp and above, it is in two parts: the upper half is an orthographic outline drawing of a typical saloon car of the period, with dimensions such as wheelbase, track, ground clearance, seat height etc. indicated by dimension lines and key letters. The lower half is a chart, listing down the left-hand column the dimensions marked on the outline drawing. Across the top of the chart, above a row of successive columns, are the names of contemporary cars, in this case mostly American but also showing larger British cars such as Humbers, and Wolseleys and Austins; and in those columns are dimensions that relate to each model.

Thus a whole set of dimensions for each body for each car could be taken easily from this plan and working drawings prepared, so that the chosen body style could be made to fit the chassis exactly.

3 Wartime

'When I warned them [the French Government] that Britain would fight on alone whatever they did, their generals told their Prime Minister and his divided cabinet: "In three weeks England will have her neck wrung like a chicken". Some chicken! Some neck!'

Sir Winston Churchill in a speech to the Canadian Parliament, 30 December 1941

Prime Minister Neville Chamberlain's announcement on 3 September 1939 of Britain's declaration of war on Germany had been expected. War had been imminent in Europe for several years, and Chamberlain's much criticised Munich agreement of 1938, in which he had the promise from Hitler of 'peace in our time', had bought Britain more time to re-arm. As early as 1936 the 'shadow factory' scheme had been set up, whereby new, high-volume aircraft factories, under the control of the major car manufacturers, had been built, located for safety's sake some distance from their main plants.

Although the Ministry of Supply issued contracts for war work to major companies such as Austin, Ford and Lucas, a great deal of the work was carried out on a subcontract basis; this was because the big companies, as in peacetime, had neither the resources nor very often the expertise to produce many of the machines and components required by the country. Initially Carbodies, with its long-standing expertise in wooden body-building, was set to work making lorry and ambulance bodies, mobile field kitchens and personnel and ammunition carriers.

Aircraft made in the shadow factories were assembled from components made in

Army lorries in all shapes and sizes were fitted with wooden bodies, and Carbodies was one of many suppliers. The author's father is seen here in the driving seat of a 4×6 AEC.

factories and small workshops all over the country; this had the advantage of raising production far above that achieved by individual factories, and added flexibility and safety to the system. Also, in the event of complete factories being destroyed, aircraft could still be assembled from outside components at another location, thus avoiding any serious loss in production. Besides, as the specific skills of contractors and sub-contractors became known, they could be called upon quickly in an emergency. One example of this flexibility was the urgent job of building fireproof bulkheads for the Armstrong Whitworth Whitley bomber. Introduced in 1938, the Whitley was outdated in comparison to its far more advanced contemporary, the Vickers Wellington, but the two aircraft were the mainstay of Bomber Command at the outbreak of war. The Whitley was first fitted with Bristol Siddeley radial engines, but from 1940 the MkV Whitley was to be fitted with more powerful Rolls-Royce Merlin

units, and Carbodies was contracted to make fireproof bulkheads for the installation. These consisted of two circular sheets of aluminium about 6ft (2m) in diameter with a sheet of asbestos sandwiched in between, and holes drilled through for oil and fuel pipes and cables. Carbodies' craftsmen and apprentices were called back from home after their Saturday morning shift, and set to work through Saturday afternoon, all through Sunday and on to Monday morning. As one might imagine, the workers coming off that shift on the Monday morning were 'like zombies'!

UNION PROBLEMS

The Sheet-Metal Workers' Union had been very strong, the skills of its members being much needed to make the metal skins for wood-framed bodies; however, its dominance in the motor industry was slowly diminishing as the pressed-steel body was

The Lancaster bomber's huge bomb-bay doors and the nacelles for the engines were among the many aircraft components pressed out at Holyhead Road.

increasingly employed. In 1940 the union called its members in Carbodies out on strike, and the older apprentices, feeling that they were at one with the men, followed. Jack Orr, foreman of the panel-beating and sheet-metal shop, called them back in and told them to do the men's work, but they refused; so Orr told them that if they were not back in work by the following morning, he'd suspend them all for a week. News of this got quickly to the union secretary, and he sent word to Orr that if any apprentice was suspended then that lad would lose his union membership and would be reporting down to the Ministry of Labour for a job; and Orr would be in trouble for dismissing anyone, because under wartime rules nobody could be out of work. Orr would not be pushed, however; although many factory workers were in reserved occupations and therefore exempt from call-up, enough had gone into uniform for the factory to need every remaining man and boy to be working. Len Molesworth, the son of Carbodies' original painter, was apprenticed in 1937 as a panel-beater and was one of the striking apprentices. He recalls:

> The men went on strike in 1940. It was money I suppose, but I can't remember. As an apprentice we weren't allowed to strike. Me and two others, being the elder apprentices, acted big and said, 'We're with the men'. My father had two solicitor's letters written to him, signed by Ernest Jones, which told us to get back to work, or else.

Ernest Jones' letters threatened the apprentices with court action and the cancellation of their indentures, and their parents with a fine of up to £40. Under pressure from their parents, the apprentices had no option but to return to work.

The Sheet-Metal Workers' Union had not finished. In 1941 they demanded exclusivity in Carbodies' body assembly shop, under the same pressure to survive that had prompted the strike the year before. Bobby and Ernest stood firm, however, maintaining that they could not stand in the way of progress, and the union had to back down.

THE BLITZ

In the Autumn of 1940, with the Luftwaffe repulsed in the Battle of Britain, Hitler switched tactics and ordered Operation *Barbarossa*, the German invasion of Russia. In an attempt to take an offensive position, the RAF's Bomber Command under Arthur Harris was authorized to launch an air raid on Berlin, a city which was enjoying a virtually normal lifestyle. Hitler had sworn to the German people that the Fatherland would never be bombed, and outraged at this violation, ordered the Luftwaffe to begin the bombing of Britain: thus began the Blitz. Every major city in the UK became the target for sustained bombing raids, and Coventry, as the centre of Britain's motor industry, was a prime target.

At this time, British intelligence made a breakthrough that gave the Allied forces their biggest boost for ultimate victory: a secret German Enigma code machine, used to decipher enemy messages, was captured and by the autumn of 1940 the code was broken. Much as this news gladdened the heart of the British government, it forced Winston Churchill to make perhaps the hardest decision of his life. One of the first messages the Allies managed to decode revealed plans for a massive German air raid on Coventry, scheduled for the night of 14 November 1940. If Churchill sent enough aircraft and artillery to defend the city, the Germans would surely guess that their code had been broken. Churchill knew he would

Monty's Caravan

Field-Marshal Montgomery's trailer caravan, built on a chassis supplied by the British Trailer Company, is now on display at the Imperial War Museum, Duxford in Cambridge.

When fighting both Italian and German forces in North Africa, the British commander, Lt Gen N. M. Ritchie, saw that his Italian counterpart, General Annabele Bergonzoli, was using a caravan body mounted on Lancia lorry chassis as living accommodation. When Bergonzoli was defeated in February 1941 the caravan was captured and its body mounted on a Leyland chassis, and it was adopted by Ritchie for his own use. When General Montgomery was given command of the British Eighth Army, he took over this caravan for himself.

In May 1943 Monty captured a second Italian caravan when he defeated General Giovanni Messe in Tunisia, and had its body transferred from the original Lancia chassis to an American Mack truck. This second caravan was Monty's home for the rest of the war, including the invasion of Europe, and he rapidly came to value its advantages over a tent in that it could be moved far more quickly, and was much more weatherproof. Moreover, in conducting his campaigns in North Africa, Sicily and Italy, Monty soon recognized that a lorry-mounted office, essentially a map-room, would be a great asset to the swift advance of Allied forces. He therefore asked the Ministry of Supply for such a vehicle, and the British Trailer Company, set up to provide all manner of trailers and caravans for wartime use, was contracted to build it. This company built the chassis, and subcontracted the building of the body to Carbodies to the specifications supplied by Montgomery. It was delivered to Monty on 17 April 1944 at his headquarters at St Paul's School in west London. Seven weeks later the D-Day invasion began, and the office caravan, behind its Fordson tractor unit, went into action.

At the end of the war, all three caravans were taken by Monty to his home in Hampshire and housed in a specially built barn. On his death in May 1976 they were willed to the Imperial War Museum, and put on display at their site at Duxford, Cambs, in 1977.

Information on Montgomery's caravans kindly supplied by The Imperial War Museum, Duxford

A fire-pump trailer, with sheet-metal work supplied by Carbodies. Powered by a Coventry Climax engine, these trailers were used behind civilian vehicles requisitioned for use with the Auxiliary Fire Service. In London, many taxi-cabs were pressed into service with the AFS and towed these trailers, and cabmen who were not eligible for military service were retained to drive them. Their specialized knowledge of London was vital because they could get to the fire quickly when many streets were blocked by fallen buildings.

have to rely simply on what was normally stationed around the city, and to consider the inevitable slaughter as a sacrifice to the greater chance of victory. Alvis, opposite Carbodies in Holyhead Road, were making tanks and aero engines, and they were a high priority target for the Luftwaffe. In the event, almost the entire Alvis factory was wiped out, and Carbodies suffered major collateral damage too.

As a former choirboy, Ernest was moved to tears when he saw the destruction of Coventry Cathedral. He and his young son Barry had attended evensong on the night of 14 November, the last service held there before that fateful night. Incidentally, the first bomb ever to fall on Coventry landed in the back garden of Ernest's house, Broadfield; and interestingly, the one-eighth plate glass in the windows resisted the blast, whilst the windows of the houses next door were completely blown out.

As already mentioned, skilled workers, as were large numbers of Carbodies' staff, were

classified as having 'reserved occupations' and were retained in the factories to make military supplies instead of being called into fighting units; for every man in uniform in World War II, there were probably seven civilians keeping him supplied. A great number of civilians were also recruited into organizations such as the Home Guard or the Auxiliary Fire Service (AFS). Ernest was made captain of Carbodies' AFS unit, and Jack Orr was the captain of the Home Guard unit. Orr was later to be moved to the AFS, a more important force as far as Coventry was concerned at the time. Often these men, along with all their staff, worked long hours during the day and then spent night duty in military service.

PERSONAL MEMORIES

Apprenticed as a panel-beater at Carbodies in 1937, Bill Knight was exempt from military service until he had finished his

The Carbodies' Auxiliary Fire Service Company. Centre front, in civilian clothes, is Ernest Jones; on his left is the commanding officer, Jack Orr. Most of the men in the company would be in reserved occupations because of their skills.

time. However, whilst still indentured Bill was nevertheless in uniform, in the Home Guard. He recalled the dreadful scene on the morning of the 15 November 1940:

We had to report to Carbodies the following morning. You couldn't get there by bus or bike – you had to walk. It would normally take me three-quarters of an hour to walk there, but that morning it took me hours because every street you went down was roped off with barriers; you couldn't go through because of unexploded bombs and debris all over the place. When I got to the factory there was some slight damage so we helped tidy up. There was no water, no electric, nothing. We did what we could, and then returned to our Home Guard units. We went round various sites where there were suspected survivors. I heard various figures mentioned about those that were killed in Coventry, but to my way of thinking it was nowhere near high enough. There was one shelter in the middle of the town near the market place which had been crowded with people, and the only way you had of counting the dead was two arms, two legs and such like. And the smell of it! There was burning as well, and two years after you could still smell it.

The water was off. They put stand-pipes up where they could, and you had a queue a mile long for water to make a cup of tea. You couldn't go to the toilet; you had to take a spade and go out into the field. If you had any coal, you built a fire to boil a kettle on. They rushed a lot of stuff back into Coventry – food, bread, milk – and within a fortnight they got the main services back, which wasn't too bad. It was a closely built town, and when the bombs fell, whole sides of the buildings fell in the road. It took weeks and weeks to clear up, and at first they could only clear enough space for people to walk through. It was a hell of a time.

The 14 November raid is the most infamous, but it was one of many; though in the midst

Dating from 1943, these Craig and Donald presses were some of the first to be installed at Carbodies during the war years.

of the horror there was still the occasional lucky escape, as Bill Knight recalls:

> One day I was up at the railway station by the grammar school when the planes came over and set the place on fire. Then the all-clear went, and we thought 'That's it'; but they'd come over to light the target. There was an old Tiger Moth by the library at the back of the school, and I had been sitting in it with a couple of the lads, acting the fool, shooting the Jerries down. All of a sudden the warning went again – a bomb blast lifted us off our feet and we dived down this underground shelter. When we got out we saw a bomb had fallen right on this old aeroplane!

PRESSES AND PRODUCTION IMPROVEMENTS

Armstrong Whitworth had been making drop-tank pressings at their Wigston factory, and this job was later transferred to Carbodies. Early in the war years, over at a company called Toolmakers and Design based in Clay Lane to the east of the city, a young man was working on secret government work involving a lot of expertise in machining brass. It was part of a plan to have 15in naval guns on the east coast at various intervals, controlled by a called sound-detection system which we now know as radar. The man, Bill Lucas, was returned to the army, but in 1941 he was called back – and although he didn't know it, that call was to set the course of his future. Bill himself recollects the time:

> They'd got themselves in a mess with this job, and although I was very young I got it going. I was on indefinite release – the Ministry of Manpower board, which controlled released army personnel, said I'd got to go back in the army, but 'There's a job we'd like you to go and help, at Carbodies'. I thought, 'God, not Carbodies! Where are they going to send me?' But it was either that

or the army. When I had the interview with Jack Orr and Jack Beresford, the Manpower man from Coventry, Jack Orr said they were trying to make a 40-gallon drop-tank. They had their own foundry and a zinc-based alloy called Kirksite. So the drop-tank was the first job I had to do when I went to Carbodies.

Even after the war Kirksite was to provide Carbodies with opportunities which would ensure the company's survival and prosperity; but at the time it was essential for war work. For all its versatility, Kirksite required very little in the way of sophisticated preparation: the foundry was a simple affair, described by those who knew as almost like the iron foundries of the early industrial revolution. The material's low melting point, just above that of lead, needed very little heat, and the moulds did not have to be expensive items. The Carbodies' team – Freddie Holland the moulder, pattern shop foreman Jimmy Marrs, toolroom superintendent Ken Everett with whom Bill Lucas worked, and chief draughtsman Don Cobb – produced a whole range of pressings using Kirksite tools.

Use of Kirksite enabled parts for aircraft fuselages and wings to be made, such as for the Supermarine Spitfire and the Avro Lancaster; the covers for the nacelles – the engine housings, holding the equally famous Rolls-Royce Merlin engines – for the Lancaster bomber were pressed out on the stretcher press. Press-shop foreman Alf Barker had no large presses to work, and the process wasted a great deal of metal; it also took three days a week of the operator's time. However, it saved hours of hand-work, and the sheet-metal workers had only to finish each part.

Gun turrets were a bomber's defence against enemy fighters, and aircraft manufacturer Boulton and Paul devised their own turret. Boulton and Paul didn't have the capacity to build enough turrets to fit the new Halifax heavy bomber as well as their own Defiant night fighter, so the job was sub-contracted to Joseph Lucas, the car electrical equipment manufacturers. In turn, Lucas sub-contracted the complex work of building the turrets' superstructure to a number of other companies, including Carbodies.

LEND-LEASE

Prior to the USA entering the war, President Franklin D. Roosevelt persuaded a sceptical, not to say hostile, Congress to instigate the lease-lend scheme, whereby everything from machinery to battleships were supplied to aid the Allies' war effort. In April 1943 Bobby moved to make Carbodies a limited company, with himself as controlling director, retaining a 90 per cent stake and Ernest as managing director holding the remaining 10 per cent; R. G. Bland, who replaced Steve Stevens in 1940, was appointed company secretary. It may have been a condition of the lease-lend agreement that industrial equipment went to *bona fide* companies, and not to individuals, because up until then the firm had been 'Robert Jones trading as Carbodies'. Whatever the reason, suddenly machine tools started to arrive at Holyhead Road. The first was an open-sided Stirk planer, with a bed size of 14 x 7ft, (4.2 x 2.1m) and a toolroom had to be built to house both this and the other machines that were to follow. Frank Tomin, a factory builder and a neighbour of Bobby's, was told to convert the shop where army lorry chassis and engines were being delivered to be fitted with wagon bodies. It had to be a high building, high enough to house a crane that could lift up to fifteen tons, half as much again as the weight

Mounted on an Austin K6 lorry chassis, these wooden-framed bodies were used by the RAF as recruiting offices, signal's lorries and laboratories. The units were supplied in left- and right-handed pairs and folded compactly on the chassis, with tables, chairs and access ladders neatly stowed. Each opened out to provide a large covered area, where extended floors and awnings gave protection from the weather. The picture of the two units placed together as they would be in service was taken in Carbodies' yard, probably in the spring of 1944.

A professional portrait of Ernest Jones with his ever-present pipe, taken in 1944 when he was forty-five.

The Jones family, photographed in the garden of Bobby's house, Heath Close, around 1946. Pictured from the left is Dorothy, Bobby, Barry, Lillie with her new grand-daughter Judy, and two members of Dorothy's family.

of the planer. Then a Pratt & Whitney Keller die machine appeared, for producing very accurate press tools: as one part of it traced a wooden pattern, the second part machined a steel casting to its exact profile. Eventually three more planers – a 12 x 5ft, (3.6 x 1.5m) a 6 x 4ft (1.8 x 1.2m) and a 4 x 3ft (1.2 x 0.9m) – joined the large one, along with a second Keller die machine. Carbodies began to build what they were to consider as the finest tool-room in Coventry.

Real progress in Carbodies' war effort could be made, largely because Kirksite's versatility meant that the factory could turn its hands to any job involving sheet metal. Austin's Joe Edwards had heard about this wonderful material and wanted to know more; they were making parts for the American Lockheed Lightning fighters and the Spitfire at Castle Bromwich. He and his tooling specialists, Billy Betford and Geoff Salmons, paid a visit to Carbodies, and as a result set up a contract to cast some Kirksite tools which would enable Austin to produce the pressings for these aircraft far more cheaply and quickly.

As the war changed Britain for good, so it changed Carbodies, eventually for the better. Whereas many of the old-established coach-building firms would never return to the motor industry, the new toolroom offered Carbodies the chance to move on, and to carve itself a unique position amongst both the giants and the smaller subcontractors. But it wasn't an easy path to follow.

Kirksite

Aircraft manufacture during World War II was greatly speeded up with the invention of Kirksite. Developed as a result of a research programme begun in 1939 by J. Paul Kirk, vice president of Morris P. Kirk and Son of California, it is an alloy with a low melting point that is used to make tools for pressing sheet-metal components. It needs only simple open moulds, and produces tools that do not need the final finishing required by the most common tool material, steel.

On cooling in the mould, Kirksite contracts by exactly 1/8 in (3mm) per foot (305mm), and if this contraction is allowed for in the manufacture of the patterns from which the moulds are made, an extremely accurate tool can be made. It has two drawbacks: first, the raw material is expensive to buy; however, as it can be melted down and re-used to make other tools with very little loss, it can be a sound long-term investment. It is also relatively soft, and will wear out much more quickly than steel. However, if the job requires only a short run, this is unimportant. Kirksite comes into its own on a small production run because the user can keep manufacturing costs down to an economical level.

Not surprisingly, American aircraft manufacturers such as Douglas, Boeing, Lockheed and North American were the first to use Kirksite. The Hoyt Metal Company, a subsidiary of the British-owned National Lead Company, took out a licence to manufacture it, and Carbodies is believed to have been the first British user. Towards the end of the war British aircraft manufacturers such as Vickers, Hawker, De Havilland and Fairey started to use it, and continued to do so for many years. In peacetime the use of Kirksite spread to the motor industry, too, adopted by manufacturers such as Ford, Leyland, Austin, Morris and Sunbeam, and suppliers of components and bodies such as Briggs Motor Bodies, Weymann, Mulliner Park Ward and British Light Steel Pressings.

The Hoyt Metal Company were bought out by Darchem Ltd in 1971, and Kirksite continues to be made by them.

Sea Otter Floats

Wing floats for the Supermarine Sea Otter amphibious aircraft were of hand-riveted construction. This was a complex and tricky business because not only did they have to be accurately made, but they had to be water-tight as well. Aluminium was used, and this had to be annealed in a special pickling compound; moreover the effect of this pickling process lasted only a short time before the metal rehardened, and had to be retreated. This made the accurate forming of the skin over the internal skeleton a highly skilled job. During assembly, a special yellow sealant, sticky and difficult to remove from the hands, was used to waterproof the joints.

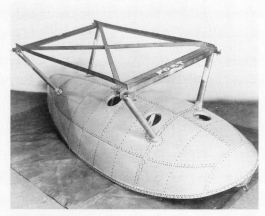

The complete port-side float for the Sea Otter.

A wing float for the Supermarine Sea Otter amphibious aircraft, with the jigs used to assemble each half, and the formers used to shape the skin.

4 Post-War Growth

'If you lasted a month, you were there for life!'
The prospects of a newcomer to
Carbodies

As quickly as the war work had arrived, it disappeared, and the tax man took a huge slice of Carbodies' turnover, claiming the firm had made excessive profits. Out of a net profit in 1945 of nearly £122,000, they had been left with just over £1,200, and they were close to broke. In April of 1946 Ernest applied for a refund of the excess profits' tax. The Ministry of Aircraft Production advised that Carbodies was one of the very few companies that did not grossly overcharge the government for goods supplied in times of national emergency, and eventually the Exchequer returned the sum of £100,000. Carbodies was now able to invest to meet the challenge of the changes that had to take place in the motor industry.

A CONFLICT OF INTERESTS

With the post of controlling director, Bobby was still the boss, and like many who had built their own empire, he maintained that his word was final. He still came in to work every day, at five to eight, his morning routine starting at the press shop where he weighed himself on the weighing machine. Then he would visit each department in the factory and talk to his apprentices (the company had taken on a significant number

in the late 1940s). He would ask them the same questions about their tools and then go into his office, which he shared with Ernest. Nearing seventy-two years of age by the end of the war, Bobby had always held strong views on virtually everything. For instance he would not, on principle, settle any money on his son, because he felt that Ernest should earn his own money, and he wanted him to take firm control of the factory, running it after he – Bobby – was gone.

In fact Bobby himself found it hard to grasp the changes happening in the motor industry. He was a 'wood man', and the mechanization involved in the manufacture of all steel bodies was something that at his age, he was unlikely ever to be able to understand. Ernest did understand the modern methods, but he was a different character to Bobby, and was increasingly putting his trust in Jack Orr's talents and ideas. Orr was a clever man: he had a Bachelor of Science degree, and was an associate member of the Institute of Mechanical Engineers. He would shortly work out a design for the conversion of modern all-steel production saloon cars into drophead coupés, and this was to establish Carbodies in a field on its own. To progress his career, Orr would need an ally in Ernest. Where Ernest was a salesman and a good administrator in the office, and would mix socially with the top people of other companies allied to the motor industry, Orr was a different man entirely; in particular he could see that his engineering talents and his ability to run the shop floor would complement Ernest's sales and administration skills. But Bobby was grieved by Ernest's growing dependence on Jack Orr, and it became a source of friction between father and son, causing some fearful rows.

COMMERCIALS

Whilst motor manufacturers had begun planning their new models in the last months of the war, Carbodies as a subcontractor was still geared up to take on the sort of jobs that were too small for the bigger companies to be interested in, and was therefore dependent on new work coming from these big makers. For example, bodies for Morrison Electricar milk floats, a far cry from the elegant drop-head coupés of the 1930s, kept the much-reduced workforce occupied in the years following the end of the war.

The wartime connection with Austin resulted in Carbodies being asked to make the bodies for the new Austin K8 'Three-Way' van; this was one of a small number of peace-time commercial models that Carbodies was to make. Building the Three-Way brought together both old and new methods of

construction being used at Carbodies: a steel cab pressed over Kirksite tooling and a body of aluminium sheets over a timber frame. When the contract started, every part of the body came in separately from an outside supplier, and these were sorted not into sets of parts for each body, but into identical components; so then a part had to be taken from each pile in order to make complete sets for each van! The 'Three-Way' sold well; it was particularly popular with bakers, whose standard-sized trays could be stacked from top to bottom between its parallel sides.

Rootes restarted production of the pre-war N-type 30cwt van, and through connections established before the war, Carbodies made the bodies for it, offering a variation in door types. Another popular seller in its time, the Commer provided work for the factory until the early 1950s.

BUILDING EXPANSION

Steady profits continued to be made year on year, adding to a growing surplus in Carbodies' bank account. In February 1945

The Austin K8 3-Way van, a mix of pressed steel cab and wood-framed body.

The N-type Commer van with the optional hinged door, and opening windscreen. The forward-control body was an early walk-through type.

A smart, special order body for Home and Colonial Stores, with an extra-wide sliding door, sloping roof and curved back.

the company purchased a Dutch-built river cruiser, the *St Denise*, for an undisclosed sum, and in October 1946 Ernest bought the yacht from the company for £1,960. It was the first of a number of river launches that Ernest was to buy, although his commitment to his job would prevent him from enjoying them. More important to the factory, in April 1946 Carbodies moved to purchase, for £9,750, an adjoining piece of land that once belonged to the Motor Packing Company, thus enabling Frank Tomin to add to the growing number of buildings being developed on the site.

A NEW ALVIS

Some of the old skills were in demand for Alvis, who wanted a drophead coupé body for their first post-war model, the TA14. An upgrade of their four-cylinder pre-war 12/70, large orders had been placed by the car-starved motoring public. Mulliners of Birmingham were to supply a saloon body, and both Tickford and Carbodies were asked to submit a tender for the coupés. Jack Orr had been working to improve the design for the drop quarter-light that Carbodies had fitted to the 1939 model Humber coupé. The new Alvis coupé was to be a full four-seater, and Orr felt that this extra glass would lighten up what was rather dark rear accommodation. Sadly, Alvis declined the design, preferring to have Carbodies make a style similar to Tickford's. Carbodies and Tickford were asked to build 250 coupé bodies each. Superficially Carbodies' cars were different from Tickford's in not having external hood-irons and in having a longer passenger compartment, and there were differences in construction, too. Tickford's

cars were of an all-timber construction, whilst Carbodies used a significant amount of pressed steel, particularly in the doors. This made a considerable difference in price: £1,200 for the Carbodies' model against £1,800 for the Tickford. The majority of customers opted for the cheaper version, and Carbodies finished up by making over 400 coupés of the 500 Alvis originally planned to make. Incidentally, some forty or fifty years on, a number of professional restorers of both models have commented that the craftsmanship of Carbodies' coupés was much better than Tickford's!

A UNIT-CONSTRUCTION CONVERTIBLE

From the pre-war method of building a wood-framed body on a separate chassis, the motor industry had moved to much cheaper, mass-produced all-steel saloons for their main models. In the 1930s some companies such as Morris and Rootes had begun to use pressed-steel platform chassis, and by 1939 the

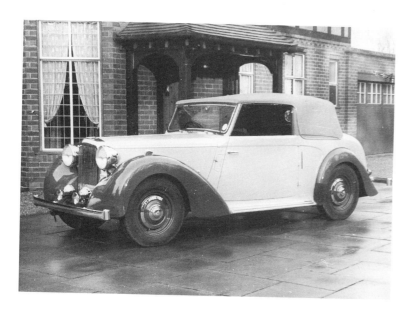

One of the first Alvis TA14 coupés, photographed by Ernest Jones, outside his house in Coventry. Jack Orr's patent large back window is visible.

A Special Car for 'Mrs Ernest'

Dorothy Jones with daughter Judy and the special Alvis TA14 sports saloon.

Freddie Connolly of Connolly Leather was a close family friend of the Joneses. He was a guest at Ernest's and Dorothy's wedding, and he promised them a hide of white upholstery leather as a present. All Dorothy needed was a car for it. She had to wait more than fourteen years for this special model, war notwithstanding, when Ernest commissioned from the company's workshops a close-coupled, two-door sports saloon on the new 14hp Alvis chassis. The pillarless body with drop quarter-lights was adapted from the design Carbodies had used on the 1936 model Hillman Hawk sports saloon. Connolly kept his promise and delivered the hide, in fact a very light tan pigskin. The car was finished in maroon and trimmed in the wedding present hide. Ernest's picture shows Dorothy and their daughter, Judy, at the Château Impney, Droitwich, Worcestershire, around 1950.

After Dorothy sold the car, it was resprayed and in the early 1960s used by a member of the Alvis Owner Club for everyday transport and club rallies. It was damaged extensively in a road accident, and left to rot in a field. It has been rescued by the registrar of the AOC, and has undergone major restoration work.

Phase I Hillman Minx saloon was of unit-construction design, the body and floor being an entire welded unit, with no separate chassis. Where once the car's strength had derived from the chassis, it was now a complete, strong steel shell.

In 1946 the Minx saloon was available again to the public. Moreover Carbodies, with its new presses and tooling facility, was able to follow on from its pre-war work for

Rootes, building the drophead coupé version; and this would fit in well with Carbodies' policy of going for small production runs. Like so much work of the immediate post-war period, this was a mix of pre-war styles and modern technology. A complete body rearward of the scuttle was made up, with all-steel doors, rear quarters, internal structural panels and boot. A full three-position coupé head covered the four seats. Painted

The start of something big . . . a phase III Hillman Minx coupé prototype pictured in Carbodies' canteen It isn't quite complete as the offside door has no quarter-light, but the shadow of one on the passenger side can just be seen.

and trimmed, it was returned to Hillman for the fitting of the mechanical components.

The Minx range received a minor re-style in 1947, with the headlights built into the front wings, but in that year development of the all-new Phase III Minx saloon, a modern unit-construction car styled by an American-domiciled Frenchman, Raymond Loewy, was well under way. Rootes wanted a drophead coupé version of the new car, to help with their export drive, and so a new Minx saloon was brought into the experimental shop for Ben Johnson and his team to work on. With the body held on a jig, the roof and the rear doors were removed and the B pillar moved back by almost 12in (30cm). New front doors and rear wings were made by hand. The windows were made with chrome frames, and two of Orr's pet features, which would enhance visibility in the new car, were built in: a large rear window in the folding head was one important feature, and chrome-framed, drop quarter-lights the other. Extra structural members were added to the floor, and the three position, hand-operated head installed.

Thus Orr had taken an all-new, modern English saloon car body and made an up-to-date American-style convertible. In one

respect Carbodies, a small independent English company, was neck-and-neck in style with the American giants, because the new US models only reached the showrooms for the 1949 season. Carbodies had developed, built, and funded with money returned from the government, their first modern British drophead coupé, and the motor industry was quick to take notice of the initiative. (Note: this type of drophead body was always referred to within Carbodies as the coupé, and although we might today associate the name with closed bodied cars, you will find the Carbodies' term used throughout the rest of the story when referring to open-topped cars.)

Rootes were delighted with the smart little coupé, and they shared the design of the head and drop quarter-light on their Thrupp and Maberly-built Sunbeam Talbot coupés, introduced the same year. With the Minx signed off by Rootes, Carbodies tooled up for production. Rootes allowed Carbodies to exhibit it on their stand at the 1948 Motor Show, the first to be held after the war. Finished in pastel green with brown hide trim, it shared the stand with an Alvis coupé, by now in its third year of production. It was a fascinating comparison between the old and the new.

The 1950 Motor Show stand. The contrast between the lines of the FL1 hire car and the newer Austin Hereford coupé, right, and also the Hillman Minx is stark.

Also on the stand was another brand-new vehicle with very old-fashioned styling: the Austin FL1 hire car, the four-door version of the brand-new FX3 taxi. Here the three strands of Carbodies' production could be seen: the Alvis marked the passing of the old style; the importance of the modern Hillman coupé for the company's future was certainly felt at the time – but it would be impossible to guess if anyone realized then just how important the taxi was to be. We will begin to understand in Chapter 5.

A COUPÉ FOR AUSTIN . . .

Austin had targeted the USA as a major export market. The little A40 Devon and

Dorset had sold in a modest way in America, but its big brother, the A70 Hampshire, did not sell well at all. Its replacement, the A70 Hereford, was to be introduced at the 1950 Motor Show, and Austin asked Carbodies to make a coupé version, to be announced at the same time. This, Austin hoped, would boost all overseas sales. As in the Hillman, the B-pillars were moved back, the rear doors discarded and two new front doors made specially, this time featuring Carbodies' own design of internal capping. It was a slightly easier job to adapt the coupé design for the Austin. All models in the new range had separate chassis, so the amount of stiffening in the adapted body was not so critical to the car's integral strength.

...LANCHESTER...

Lanchester was the first independent British car maker. Once renowned for its innovation, it had been bought by BSA in 1931 to become a second string to Daimler, which BSA had owned since 1910. The first all-new, post-war model to carry the Lanchester name was the 14hp, subsequently known as the Leda. This four-cylinder 2-litre saloon went into production in 1950, and Carbodies produced a drophead version, using Jack Orr's patent three-position head, and the same construction method as on the Hillman and Austin. Scheduled for release in 1952, the coupé appeared on Carbodies' stands at both the 1951 and 1952 Motor Shows. Works engineer Alf Robinson, along with personnel from Carrier Engineers of London, had installed at Carbodies a low-temperature paint plant that year, and the Leda coupé had the honour of being the first car to be put through it. Perhaps no more than the Motor Show cars were made, but the Leda coupé was Carbodies' first formal job for Daimler.

...AND FORD

At the 1950 Motor Show, Ford announced their revolutionary new Consul and Zephyr Six saloons to an astonished public. Designed in Ford's American styling studios at Dearborn, Michigan, the new car's unit-construction body, advanced technical specification and above all its fiercely competitive price stunned an austerity-wearied Britain. The following year Ford had another surprise up its sleeve: an American-style convertible (but we will of course say 'coupé'!). There had been open-top versions of the 10hp cars before the war, but soft-top versions of their big models were only made outside the UK.

Ford's new chairman, Pat Hennessey, approached Carbodies and asked them to build a Consul and a Zephyr, and made two specific demands: that the Zephyr hood should be powered, and that both cars should be ready for the 1951 Motor Show. This second proviso meant that Carbodies had only six weeks to do the job! Ford had provided no drawings from which to work, so Jack Orr, along with Jake Donaldson who

The first prototype MkI Ford Zephyr coupé, prior to exhibition at Earl's Court in 1951. Note the Everflex covering on the top of the windscreen frame. The boot hinges were moved to the outside of the body to make room for the hood mechanism. The original line of the bottom of the door sills was changed on the production model.

The hydraulic operating mechanism for the Zephyr coupé, driven by a Lucas starter motor.

had returned to Carbodies after his spell at Daimler, and Ben Johnson had to use all their experience and skill. As with the Hillman and Austin, the hand-made prototypes featured two, larger front doors. New rear wings covered the old rear door-shuts, and chrome-framed windows and drop quarter-lights were fitted. Jack Orr thought long about how to power the hydraulic top to make it work for the Zephyr; he could fit up the hydraulic rams and pipework, but could not figure out how to power it. Freddie Smith, the welder in the toolroom, then asked for an ordinary Lucas 12-volt car starter-motor: he simply attached the square boss on the end to the hydraulic pump, and the show car's top was made to work!

Ford displayed the coupés on their stand at the Motor Show, but Carbodies did not get the opportunity to do so that year. In its show review of 1951, *The Autocar* described the cars as prototypes, which is what they

were, because Carbodies had simply not had enough time to engineer the body fully or the top to an acceptable production standard. Not surprisingly, no one was allowed to drive the cars, and they were returned to Coventry where the job was done to a proper standard; this delay meant that the cars were not generally available for either the export market or the car-starved UK until the end of the following year. In the range, only Consul and Zephyr Six models were built, but a de Luxe Zephyr Six coupé with two-tone paint was introduced in 1953, at the same time as the Zephyr Zodiac saloon.

Ford in their wisdom decided to query Carbodies' expertise in the building of drop-head coupés: after some months of production, they asked why the gap at the top of the door-shut was wider than at the bottom. Certainly it is noticeable, but this widening gap was necessary, because no matter how much strengthening is put

Ford Consul and Zephyr coupés in the finishing shop. This shop was called the Motor Packing, after the previous owners of this section of the factory. The hood-sticks can be seen strapped up under the front of the hood. These unfolded and located into the windscreen header, and the white plastic knob screwed tight to lock the sticks rigid. The push-button door handles of the saloon were changed for the lever type, which were compatible with the double door latches.

into an open car's floor, its body, when loaded, will sag very slightly because it does not have the support of the roof to prevent it from doing so. Nevertheless Ford wanted it changed, and would stand for no counter arguments from Carbodies. To satisfy Dagenham's orders, a Ford coupé was built with the door-shuts set as they wanted. Four rather large gentlemen then came to test the car, and took it for a drive. Things seemed fine until they tried to get out, and couldn't – neither of the doors would open! Ford had to concede that Carbodies was right on this point, but then demanded that extra strengthening be fitted to prevent the body sagging at all, thus obviating the need for the widening gap. Jake Donaldson accepted that additional strengthening *could* be fitted, but pointed out that the extra weight would hamper performance, and also raise the price. Carbodies had therefore proved that they knew what they were talking about, and the Ford coupé remained in production until 1956 as originally engineered.

A NEW AUSTIN, BUT HILLMAN DEPARTS

The four-cylinder Austin Hereford coupé was a slow seller, too expensive, and with already dated styling. In 1952 the saloon was joined by a new baby brother, the A40 Somerset, which replaced the extremely successful Devon. The Hereford coupé was then dropped, and from late 1952 a coupé version of the Somerset, similar in every respect except size, replaced it on Carbodies' tracks until 1954.

Carbodies continued to make the Minx coupé until 1952, but then Rootes decided that they should build more of their bodies in-house and the car was moved to Thrupp and Maberly. Such is the perilous nature of subcontract work – it could be lost as quickly as it was won. Thrupp and Maberly then began producing an additional model, the new Hillman Californian, a two-door hard-top coupé version of the Minx using door pressings similar to those used on the drop-head.

An export Model Ford coupé body-shell. Note the double door latch, used to prevent the door opening as the body flexes, and Carbodies' own design of door capping.

Early 1954, and Peter Dawson, in white coat, checks out a second load of MkI Ford coupé body-shells before delivery to Dagenham, whilst driver Paddy Corrigan looks on.

CRISIS POINT

Bobby's frustration with Ernest's dependence on Jack Orr grew. Bill Lucas, superintendent of the toolroom, and Joan Swaine (née Harper – she had married production line foreman Stan Swaine) remembers how difficult it was working in this atmosphere. In particular Joan recalls how her husband's work was made difficult by the feud between father and son:

Stan would be seeing the vehicles off the end of the track, and Ernie would ask him how many he thought he'd get off that day. Stan would give a figure and Ernie would say 'OK', but told him that if the old man [Bobby] wanted any

The seating buck for the Austin A40 Somerset coupé. The chassis was actually that of the Devon, although the boot is clearly from the Somerset. As well as laying out the seating position, the buck was also used to work out the design of the hood mechanism.

The tryout press. The toolmaker is machining out the cutter paths left by the Keller die machine. As part of the job he will ensure that the clearance between the top tool, above his head, and the bottom tool, which he is machining, is adequate for the thickness of the metal.

more, to say that he couldn't get any more off. So then Bobby would come up and ask the same question, and Stan would tell him, and sure enough Bobby would say, 'Well, see if you can get a few more off.' Bobby and Ernie had this little thing going between them, and they used to fall out something awful.

Bill Lucas remembers something more disturbing:

Bobby telephoned me and said, 'Can you come over to the office, young Bill? – he always called me young Bill. It was a long office, and Bobby had got his desk and Ernie had got his. Bobby stood there at one end and he said, 'Right,

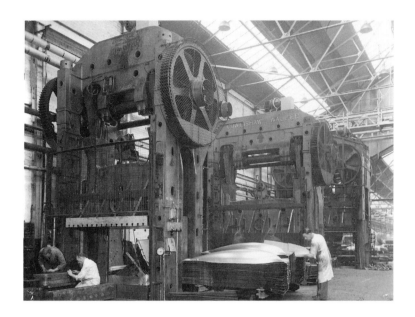

The press shop. Cowlishaw Walker presses turn out the separate halves of aircraft drop-tanks. Carbodies was the only company in Coventry able not only to turn out the pressed halves, but to weld them together successfully without distortion.

Bill, I want you to stand there,' and he said to Ernie, 'Now come and hit me in front of a witness. My own son has just hit me!'

Ernie took a long draw on his pipe, blew the smoke in Bobby's face and said, 'You silly old sod!' Ernie used to embarrass employees. You didn't know which camp to fall into.

Snowy Beebe, working in dispatch, recalls an incident that revealed all too clearly the strained relations between Bobby and Ernie:

Old Bobby sacked Jack Thompson in personnel, but when he came back from lunch, Jack was still at his desk. So Bobby said, 'What are you doing still here?' And Thompson said, 'Jack Orr said to carry on, to take no notice!' So Bobby went to Jack Orr, and asked who had given him the authority to countermand his orders. Jack Orr said, 'Ernest.' 'Did he?' said Bobby, and went to see Ernie. Ernie confirmed that he'd

said that, and also that he considered his father would forget about it after he'd had his dinner. 'Oh,' said Bobby, 'well I haven't, and the three of you can clear off!' Ernie came back after a week.

BSA TAKES OVER

By 1954, Bobby was in his eighty-first year, and the rows between him and Ernest were getting steadily worse; but no one could have predicted what was to come. Steve Stevens, who had left the company in 1940 but returned in 1947, recalls the decision Bobby made one day in the spring of that year:

Bobby came to my desk and said, 'I'm going to sack Orr, and I'm going to sack Thompson. Will you make out cheques to take to them?' A week or so later, Jack Orr went to Daimler (a part of the giant BSA empire), taken on by Richard Smith.

Bobby had begun talking to BSA in the early part of 1954, although it is not clear as to who made the first approach. Steve Stevens remembered John Rowe of BSA visiting Carbodies to see if the company was worth the asking price, but otherwise Bobby kept the business a close secret until he had made up his mind. Then one day he called Bill Lucas and Ben Johnson into the office; Lucas describes the meeting:

I'd become the apple of Bobby's eye, and Ben was a very great friend of his

through his knowledge of sheet-metal work. Bobby said, 'I've got you two in because I'm telling you that I'm going to sell the company to BSA. I'm selling for a million pounds, and you two are the first to know on the shop floor'.

They were not only the first to know on the shop floor because Bobby had not even told his own son of his intentions to sell; Ernest did not find out until very shortly before the formal agreement. One can only speculate that Bobby had seen that Ernest was not

Working Practices

The demands of the motor industry, and the skills available on the shop floor, resulted in a mixed bag of work within the factory. Bobby still kept his old wood mill, because in the early post-war years commercial vehicle bodies were wood-framed. Although the presses and the Kirksite foundry meant that hand work was no longer the main means of shaping body metal, there was still a demand for the sheet-metalworkers' skills, especially so in experimental, where Ben Johnson and his team would make a prototype body by hand. Apprenticed under Johnson in 1949, Brian Evans remembers the sort of very simple tools in use after the war, tools with which a skilled panel beater could not only cover the wood frames on production car bodies, but make a one-off body:

In the old days we didn't have hardly any machines in experimental, only a little treadle guillotine, a little old bender, a bending machine and a box folder, but we had a lot of hand tools – Bert Heath's and Dickie Bruce's toolbox was really an Aladdin's cave for hand tools. What we went on to do on a machine, they had tools they'd made themselves that they could use to make it by hand. You could turn or joddle [*form a stepped edge on a sheet of metal to so as to form an overlap to join it to a second sheet*] with them, and they were brought up that way, when it was all done with the hammer and skill on the wheel.

There was no limit on the wages a man could earn at Carbodies. A price for each job was set by the rate fixer with Bobby or Ernest, and it was not changed unless the nature of the job changed. If the price was set it didn't bother Bobby if a man was doing five pieces an hour or twenty, because he knew what it was costing. A supervisor wouldn't stand over a man. They'd time the first ten, but the next took less than half the time. However, if the rate fixer had set the price too low, no one could persuade Bobby to put it up!

As an example of what could be earned, one man was employed to tack-weld the corners of the door-skins of the taxis to secure them. He had the largest welding nozzle and the thickest welding rod he could use. He was on a rate of 2s (10p) a door, but he could do up to twenty doors an hour. On a forty hour week, that amounted to £80 per week in 1954. At the end of his shift he'd change out of his overalls and into a suit, and drive home in a Jaguar! He was doing the work of four men, but if anybody said anything to him about this earnings, he'd say, 'Here's the torch, *you* have a go.'

Work for Austin

A much-used and loved Austin J40 pedal car.

Part of the extensive toolroom. These Keller die machines are used for finishing steel press tools after casting. The original wooden pattern is traced by the machine, guiding the cutting heads which machine the tool to the exact size. The panel on the wall at the right of the picture is for an Austin A40 Devon Countryman, part of a number of body panels made for Austin.

The managing director of Austin, Leonard Lord, had a pet project. He wanted to build a factory to provide employment for disabled miners in South Wales: it was to produce children's pedal cars. Austin's hand-made prototype was called Joy One, and was styled like the immediately pre-war Austin models. The production models were different; one was the Pathfinder, a replica of the pre-war Austin 7 Ulster single-seat racing car; and the other was the J40, or Junior 40, a miniature replica of the all-new A40 Devon. Joe Edwards asked Carbodies to produce Kirksite dies for the production models.

As well as making the FX3 taxi and the A70 Hereford and A40 Somerset coupés, tools and panels were produced for the other Austin cars, including the body of the utility version of the A40 Devon, called the Countryman. The die for the side panel can be seen on the wall on the right of the picture. When Donald Healey entered negotiations with Leonard Lord to make his show-stopping Healey 100 Sports car in 1952, Carbodies was asked by Austin to provide patterns for the car's early bodies.

taking control of the company as he had urged; instead, his dependence on Jack Orr had eventually become too much for 'the Old Man'.

At a specially convened board meeting on 24 June 1954, Carbodies became a part of BSA. Present for Carbodies were Bobby, Ernest and company secretary Steve Stevens, along with representatives from their accountants and solicitors. On BSA's side were Richard Smith of Daimler, John Rowe and Frederick Ellinghouse. John Rowe passed the cheque to Stevens, quipping as he did so: 'Here you are, Mr Stevens, I don't suppose you will handle a cheque for a million pounds again!' But whilst Stevens was holding it, Bobby, to everyone's stunned amazement, offered BSA one million, one hundred thousand pounds to buy Carbodies back! Why? Perhaps, seeing his empire vanish before his very eyes, in the end Bobby couldn't bear to see it go. Or maybe he had planned this final move, hoping at last to convince Ernest that he, Bobby, his father, really *did* want him to be the boss,

but not to be so dependent on Jack Orr. Ernest, however, sat there and never said a word, making no attempt to back his father up, or to retrieve his inheritance. For Ernest, the sale was a bitter blow: he had lost his family firm, and on Bobby's ultimate death, the opportunity to take control – which in Bobby's eyes he should have done already.

Legal and professional fees aside, not all of the million pounds would go to Bobby: Ernest was paid his share, based on his ten per cent shareholding, and at the time of the sale, the low-temperature paint plant installed by Carrier Engineers was not fully paid for – there was still a large sum of money to be paid.

For Carbodies as a whole, the changes brought about by the new régime were to prove very unsettling, certainly in the short term. However, before we find out about all this, it is important to go back a few years to 1945, to look at the story of a vehicle that would set the course of Carbodies' fortunes: the Austin FX3 taxi.

5   The FX3

'Without Mann and Overton there would not now be the London taxi, nor a London cab trade as we know it.'

Jack Everitt, retired senior
inspecting officer, Public Carriage
Office, London

Mann and Overton, London's largest and longest-running taxi dealership, began selling Austin taxis, based on the old 12/4 car chassis, in 1930, and by 1934 Austin cabs were outselling rivals Beardmore and Morris by almost three to one. In 1936 Austin brought out a new 12hp private car with a lighter, lower chassis, and the old lot, dubbed in retrospect the 'Heavy 12/4', remained to be made exclusively for the taxi. However, with the outbreak of World War II, Austin ceased delivery of the Heavy 12/4 chassis, which by then had been made for almost twenty years, to Mann and Overton.

In 1940 Austin's old rivals Nuffield, makers of the Morris cab, introduced the new prototype Oxford taxi and ran it throughout the war. The London dealer for Morris cabs, Bobby Jones' old employer William Watson, retired after the war and the dealership was passed to Beardmore's in Hendon, North London, who had no new cab of their own. With a sustained effort from Nuffield, the Oxford was passed for use in London in late 1946. It was put into production in 1947, enabling Beardmore to sell the new cab to a trade whose fleet had been decimated by

The FX chassis. Cab drivers L. W. Cuthbertson and L. W. Harvey examine the new chassis at Mann and Overton, 28 December 1945. Note the crocodile bonnet and vertical slats in the grille.

Mann and Overton

The story of London taxicab dealers Mann and Overton is as old as London's motor-cab trade. The Overtons were a farming family from the Sutton area of Surrey, and in 1896 young Tom Overton went to Paris to study as a motor engineer, believing that this new and exciting industry was where his fortune lay. There he met the flamboyant J. J. Mann, an Englishman living in the French capital, and they set up a business to import continental motor cars, including Hotchkiss and Mercedes, into England. Mann stayed in continental Europe, and when each individual car ordered was complete, sent it over to their London showroom in Lower Grosvenor Place.

Overton in London and Mann in Paris were in a position to see how quickly the cab trade was turning to motors – by 1904 something like 6,000 motor cabs had been put on the streets of London, when almost every other form of transport still relied on the horse. They both recognized that this was a boom industry: the motor car was still for the very rich, but if it could earn its keep in the taxi business, there would be far larger orders to be had. The car dealership continued for some time after, but the taxi business became far more important when in 1907 Mann and Overtons began importing the French Unic cab, modified to comply with the new Metropolitan Police Conditions of Fitness for motor cabs which came into force in 1906; this included altering the steering to meet the requirement for a 25ft (7.6m) turning circle. The Unic was more powerful than the two-cylinder Renault run by the newly formed London General Cab Company, and far more reliable and serviceable than many of its other competitors. Tom Overton worked to expand the new business; but in 1907, J. J. Mann retired from the company due to ill health and sadly died in 1908.

In 1910 Mann and Overtons moved to new premises in what is now Ebury Street, Pimlico (then called Commercial Road), and from then on concentrated solely on the taxi market. After the Great War the firm moved to Battersea Bridge Road, and Tom Overton put his interests into property development; however, his brother William joined the taxi business in 1916 along with Herbert Nicholls.

Mann and Overtons continued to sell Unics until the late 1920s when import duties made this already ancient cab too expensive. Will Overton had seen how the Austin Heavy 12/4 had given good service in provincial taxi work, and with the help of Mr Harfield, a friend who was a senior engineer with the Austin Motor Company, modified the chassis to be able to meet the Conditions of Fitness. Will Overton then went to see Herbert Austin with a firm business proposal, but Austin refused to see him. Will, however, was determined and sat outside Austin's office until close of business. Austin came out, saw him sitting there and exclaimed 'Are you still here?' 'Yes,' said Will, 'and I'm staying here until tomorrow and the next day until you see me. I've got an order for you for 500 chassis!' Herbert Austin agreed to supply the modified chassis, and Mann and Overton put the Austin cab on sale in 1930. By the end of 1931 its keen price, reliability and serviceability made it the best-selling cab on the London market, with sales reaching nearly 1,200 cabs in 1935.

Owner-drivers in London are called 'mushes', a name given to them by the French mechanics who had come over to service the London General's Renaults. The term is a very old French one, referring to anyone who is constantly on the move; it had also been given by nineteenth-century French settlers in North America to fur trappers driving dog sleds. An important part of Mann and Overton's service to the cab trade (the plural 's' was dropped from their name at this time) was the formation of a subsidiary company, Mechanical Investments Ltd, which provided finance for drivers who wanted to buy their own cabs. In 1938 Mann and Overton moved to new premises in Wandsworth Bridge Road, Fulham, where they remained until 1983.

wartime bombing and a dearth of spare parts. This put Mann and Overton in a desperate situation: they had been market leaders, and now they had to come from behind if they were to stay in the game at all.

THE FX AND THE FX2

With peace in Europe, Austin offered Mann and Overton a modified version of their current 12hp chassis (itself then ten years old) with a 14hp, 1792cc sidevalve engine, and the steering adapted to cope with the mandatory 25ft (7.6m) turning circle. The first special cab chassis was delivered to Mann and Overton's premises in late 1945, and specifications were published in *The Steering Wheel*, the London cab-trade's journal, in December. Austin at the time identified all their models with a one-, two- or three- letter code such as B, BS or BSQ, and thus the new taxi was given the code FX. Mann and Overton began testing this chassis with a body adapted in their own workshops from an old cab, but soon found that the engine was not powerful enough for modern traffic, and shortcomings were also found in the chassis.

Austin clearly valued the taxi market, for in January 1947, J. W. R. Penrose of Austin's sales department sent drawings of a new

chassis to the Public Carriage Office, apologizing for the delay in producing them. In his covering letter he wrote:

> . . . we had to cancel the whole of our previous design and introduce a new model with a special frame and a new engine as now included, which has caused some considerable amount of work for our drawing office over and above new models the Company is introducing at the moment. It is hoped we shall also be able to have a prototype vehicle for inspection in early February.

The new chassis, named FX2, was stronger and had a slightly longer wheelbase, but it was as conventional in design as its predecessors, having semi-elliptical springs, a beam front axle and rod-operated brakes, plus the luxury of a Jackall hydraulic jacking system. The design of the new engine, also thoroughly conventional by standards of the day, took Austin in a different direction. Before the war they had made only sidevalve engines, but when Sir Herbert Austin appointed Leonard Lord as works director in 1938, Lord put into effect a new design of six-cylinder, 3½-litre overhead-valve lorry engine, from which they planned to develop four-cylinder engines for 14hp and 18hp cars. The 1,800cc 14hp engine, the same size as

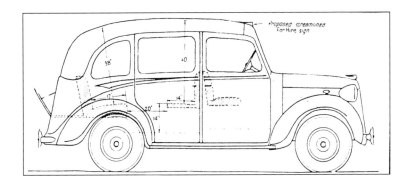

'The cab you will operate in the future' said Mann and Overton of this outline drawing in their advertisement in The Steering Wheel *in January 1946. The Austin 14, as the FX was known, bears some resemblance to the final version, but the 'crocodile' bonnet was rejected by the PCO on safety grounds.*

the Oxford's, was installed in the FX2. Submitted to the PCO, it received type approval on the 9 March 1947.

A BUILDER FOR THE BODY

Whilst Austin were redesigning the chassis, Mann and Overton still had to find someone to build a body for the new cab. Pre-war cabs had been coachbuilt, but the cost of this method, if the labour could be found for the job, would be far too expensive. The Oxford had a pressed-steel, panelled body and the FX2 would also have to have one. However, despite their obvious willingness to provide the chassis, Austin were simply not able to produce a steel body; they were having enough trouble finding production space for their new models, without having to do a specialist job at around fifteen a week. But where would Mann and Overton find someone with the resources to take on the job?

Austin's Joe Edwards was able to help. Some short time after Austin had begun work on the FX2 chassis, he invited Robert Overton, who had entered his family's busi-

ness in the 1930s, to attend a meeting at the Ministry of Supply. Here he was introduced to Ernest Jones and Jack Orr. Austin of course had made use of Carbodies' skill with Kirksite tools during the war and with the Three-Way van. Talking to Overton, Orr and Jones saw they could build an all-steel body for the new taxi in the small numbers required; it would fit in well with Carbodies' policy of taking on small contracts that the big companies couldn't handle. Most importantly, with Kirksite tools it could be done at a realistic price. A deal was struck to develop the cab, where Austin would supply the chassis to Carbodies, who would build the body, mount it, paint and trim it and arrange for delivery of the complete cab to Mann and Overton in London. Sales outside the capital would be handled by Austin themselves through their Redditch, Worcestershire, department. A hire-car version, code-named FL1, was to be made too. The initial development costs, and all future alterations, would be financed on a three-way basis. Mann and Overton would provide 50per cent of the money, whilst Carbodies and Austin would pay 25per cent each of the balance. This gave Mann and

Jack Orr with the FX2 prototype in Carbodies' canteen, prior to its examination by officers from the PCO. The large 'for hire' sign was one of the features to be changed.

Overton the major share and an exclusive right to London sales, two factors which would have important consequences for our story later on.

Mann and Overton delivered the FX2 chassis to Holyhead Road late in 1946, and Austin's first general layout drawings were delivered to Carbodies' chief draughtsman Don Cobb. Jack Orr set his team in the experimental department, under foreman Ben Johnson, to building a prototype body. Finance was slow in coming from Mann and Overton who were dependent on income from re-selling and servicing pre-war cabs, and the first prototype was coachbuilt, clad in aluminium panels. On 1 May 1947, Ernest sent drawings of the body to the PCO, prior to their inspectors coming to Carbodies on the 20 May to look at the cab.

At the visit, the design of the body was discussed between Robert Overton and Herbert Nicholls of Mann and Overton, the PCO vehicle inspectors and Ernest Jones and Jack Orr. A report submitted to the Commissioner of Police by Mr H. Gould, the chief examining officer at the PCO, outlined its general style; it also mentioned that, although the Commissioner's requirements did not specify any particular design of body . . .

. . . Mr Overton stated that many sources of the cab trade preferred to operate the three-quarter limousine type of body, as this gives more privacy to passengers. He agreed that in the main the drivers who sought this type of body were night drivers, and it

Ernest Jones' photograph of the FX3 prototype at his favourite location, Charlecote Park.

therefore suggested that there was some other underlying reason for their preference.

Mock panels were made to partially cover the window, but it resulted in . . .

. . . the whole outline of the body being changed from an up-to-date, modern and pleasing appearance to that of a drab, old-fashioned vehicle resembling somewhat a funeral hearse, and it was decided to continue with the three-window saloon.

For passenger privacy, darkened glass was to be used in the back window, and no interior driving mirror would be allowed.

Among the number of detail changes to be made, the size of the FX2's hire sign had to be reduced to meet with approval. However, the PCO couldn't decide which shade of yellow should be used for the glass: Ernest Jones would go to Pilkington's in Lancashire to get a new sample and take it down to London; that same evening he would telephone Carbodies and say, 'No, it's no good, they won't have it!' and he would have to return to Coventry and repeat the process again. Eventually a colour was chosen, but only after *three weeks*!

Type approval for the FX2 was given by the PCO in June 1947, but in October of that year Austin's plans for their new private cars meant that Mann and Overton had to accept a larger engine for the cab. Austin's proposed 14hp and 18hp cars would not appear; the new medium-sized cars would be the A70 Hampshire and the A40 Devon, with completely new bodies and chassis. The Devon's brand-new 1200cc ohv engine would be too small for the cab, but the A70 had a four-cylinder engine developed from a larger version of the big six, the 2.2 litre unit fitted in the stop-gap 16hp car. As with the supply

of a body, Austin decided it would be uneconomical to produce the 14hp engine in such small numbers for the taxi alone. The 2.2 litre engine was fitted to the FX2 by early 1948, and preliminary tests showed only a slight increase in fuel consumption. By October, with the new engine, hire sign and detail changes, the cab gained a new model number: FX3. By now, sufficient money had come through from Mann and Overton, and Carbodies was able to tool up for production of the full steel body. Although most of the main structure of the body was to be steel, wood was to be used for the cant rails, windscreen header and wheel arches, and to give structural strength to the lower part of the B-pillars; this gave the cab a satisfying 'coachbuilt' feel when the doors were closed. Now, two-and-a-half years since the first chassis went to Mann and Overton, it was time to get the cab on the road for evaluation by the trade.

ROAD TESTING, AND INTO PRODUCTION

The FX3 was announced to the cab trade from Mann and Overton's premises in Wandsworth Bridge Road on 11 June 1948, and in that summer two London fleet garages took a working prototype each: Central Autos of Chelsea took the original coachbuilt cab, registered as JXN 842, and W. H. Cook of West London took the second cab to be built, the steel-bodied JXN 841.

The FX3 was shown at the Commercial Motor Transport Exhibition in early October, and eight more cabs went into fleet service in London between December 1948 and January 1949. Included in these was the Commercial Motor Exhibition model. Like the Oxford, it was offered in a standard colour, black cellulose, but other colours could be had at extra cost. Contrary to

Ready for delivery: Mann and Overton's press release shot of the FX3, taken round the corner from M&O's premises outside the gates of South Park.

popular belief, there has never been a law that says London cabs have to be black, but as most buyers of cabs were fleet owners, ('cab masters' in the London parlance) they opted for the cheaper standard colour. From this time we can find the origins of the London 'black cab': before the war, fleets would paint their coachbuilt cabs in their own colours, but in the early 1950s the pre-war cabs still in service were painted black to blend in with the new models. The FL1 hire car was introduced at the same time as the FX3, and as we have seen in the previous chapter, it was shown at the Earl's Court Motor Show in the same year.

Sales were slow in the first few years of the FX3's life. With the burden of double purchase tax, its on-the-road price of £940 was more than double that of the old 12/4. London, along with the rest of the country, was still struggling to recover from five years of war and greatly increased living costs. People had little spare money. To add to the burden faced by cab masters and drivers alike, fares did not increase from pre-war

levels until 1951, and fuel costs had almost doubled since the late 1930s; moreover the Austin's big engine returned 18mpg (15.7L/100km) compared to a pre-war cab's 25mpg (11.3L/100km). An attempt to improve fuel consumption was made by fitting a smaller carburetter, but three changes were to come about which would improve the lot of Mann and Overton and the London cab trade as a whole.

DIESEL POWER AND A BETTER DEAL FOR BUYERS

In 1952, Mann and Overton and Austin found themselves, by default, in a monopoly situation. Austin and the Nuffield Organization had merged to form the British Motor Corporation, and the Oxford cab was the first casualty; Leonard Lord, now boss of BMC and an 'Austin man', was not going to make two vehicles for the same limited market. The FX3 was the newer design and so the Oxford went. The following year, after strong lobbying from Robert Overton and other prominent cab-trade people, the Runciman Committee recommended that both purchase tax and hire purchase restrictions were removed from the sale of cabs. This certainly helped sales of the FX3, but something else was to change things financially for the better, and along with the black paint finish, it set the character of the London cab for more than half a century: the diesel engine. As a refinery by-product, diesel oil – Derv – was at that time subject to very little fuel tax and was therefore about half the price of petrol. In 1953, the Hackney Transport and Engineering Company adapted the German Borgward Hansa diesel engine to fit the FX3. This 1.8 litre engine made the cab extremely slow, but it returned a much better fuel consumption. Later the same year, Birch brothers of Kentish Town, in North London, experimented with the Standard Motor Company's new diesel engine that had been developed for the Ferguson tractor, and by the end of the year Perkins were offering the fitting of the P4C diesel in both the FX3 and Oxford for £280.

The London General Cab Company in Brixton was the longest-serving and biggest fleet in the capital. Former managing director Geoff Trotter joined 'The General' in 1952 as fleet manager, and he remembers well the investigation into diesel power:

> When I joined the company we were experimenting. We had the Ferguson, a Mercedes-Benz and a Borgward. I think the Mercedes was too big, and we had difficulty locating the Borgward in the chassis. The obvious one was the Ferguson, and we converted the entire fleet – we couldn't do it fast enough: as far as we were concerned, it was an economic necessity. Mann and Overton and Austin didn't like it, of course, and

> it wasn't good for the image of the trade. After all, it's an Austin taxi, and we took out their engine and put in a Ferguson.

Austin responded in December 1953 by announcing that they were going to make a light diesel engine, and by mid 1954 a diesel FX3 with the new engine, developed from the 2.2 litre petrol unit, gained type approval, and a small number went for a six-month trial. In 1954 the FX3 was shown at the Commercial Motor Exhibition with the new engine. In tests the diesel cabs had returned 30mpg (9.4L/100km) from the cheap fuel – an enormous improvement in running costs. The trials went well; a few instances of excessive oil consumption and cracked valve seats were the only complaints. However, Geoff Trotter's recollections of the Austin diesel in fleet service were not good:

> I remember the Austin was a very poor engine to deal with. We used to get split blocks and core plugs blowing out. There was one particular fault called reverse running. If the timing wasn't spot on, it would fire before the top of the stroke and send the engine into reverse with clouds of smoke blowing everywhere. When drivers had that happen it frightened the life out of them! It was cured eventually, of course, but the Austin was never a very good engine.

Nevertheless the die had been cast. Austin soon sorted out the teething troubles of the new engine, including fitting a 'freewheel' device to the fuel pump to prevent reverse running, and by 1955, 90per cent of new FX3s sold were diesels. In addition, owners began to have their petrol-engined cabs converted to Austin diesel power, as did a number whose cabs had previously been

The Public Carriage Office and the Metropolitan Police Conditions of Fitness

Two sets of standards ensure that the London cab trade is the envy of the world. One is known as 'The Knowledge', and describes the arduous, world-famous test given to every aspiring London cab driver of his knowledge of the streets and places of interest throughout London; a test that he or she must pass in order to be granted the famous 'green badge'. The other is the Conditions of Fitness, the regulations that govern the design and construction of London cabs; these are formulated to guarantee that the public is served by a cab that is safe, secure and reasonably comfortable.

The Conditions of Fitness

Although records of control go back to Oliver Cromwell's time, the London cab trade has been continuously licensed since 1694, and Conditions of Fitness for horse cabs were laid down even in those times. The electric Bersey 'Humming Bird' (an example of which is in the National Motor Museum in Beaulieu) which came into use briefly in 1897, was the first horseless cab to work in the capital, but motor cabs were first seen in London in 1903; new Conditions of Fitness were laid down for them in 1906. The rapid developments in the motor trade at that time soon left these regulations far behind, however, and they were updated significantly in 1929; they continue to be altered from time to time. As was found in the late 1920s, they still present something of a challenge to a newcomer to the taxi-making business.

The Conditions of Fitness cover such aspects of design as seating and door dimensions, floor height, the materials which may be used in the construction of the cab, passenger headroom, and of course the famous 25ft (7.6m) turning circle. A brief glance at the regulations governing interior dimensions would lead one to believe that it must be a simple matter for a manufacturer to follow them and produce a taxi; however, the turning circle requirement, especially with the adoption of front-wheel drive on the great majority of cars, may be seen as a barrier to new manufacturers wishing to enter the London cab market. Nevertheless, very few cab drivers in London, or any other city using London-type cabs, would be without it. But the floor height, the partition, the door aperture and seating dimensions too, have meant that in practice almost all motor manufacturers have found it uneconomical to adapt their existing vehicles, or to produce a specialist vehicle for such a relatively small market unless those requirements are taken into account in the initial stages of designing a new vehicle.

There has never been a monopoly given to any manufacturer to build a cab for London; the market is open to anyone. However, it is essential for any aspiring designer of a new model of cab to work in conjunction with the Public Carriage Office, and they in turn are happy to work alongside any serious applicant. Any new type of vehicle is closely checked from the drawing board (or today, the computer printout) stage to ensure that it meets the standards laid down. Simply because of the limited market only Beardmore, Winchester and Asquith models, and Metro-Cammell's Metrocab, have been type approved as competitors for the Austin/Carbodies cabs since 1948. Of these, the Metrocab has been the most successful.

The Public Carriage Office

London's Public Carriage Office is responsible for the licensing of London's taxis, their drivers and proprietors. Its colloquial name of 'The Yard' comes from Victorian times when it was based in Great Scotland Yard, off Whitehall, then the headquarters of the Metropolitan Police. In December 1926 the headquarters were moved to Lambeth Road, initially controlling twelve passing stations, which had the responsibility for licensing cabs in their area and undertaking spot checks on the road.

In 1966 the Public Carriage Office came under one roof at Penton Street, North London. It is at

'The Yard', in the passing station, that cabs undergo a rigorous annual examination which they must pass before being given their white licence plate; this authorizes them as fit to be worked. Cabs are still subject to quarterly examinations and spot roadside checks, and any that are found unfit are given a 'stop notice'; the proprietor must then rectify the faults, and subsequently present the cab at the passing station for re-examination before it is allowed back into service. This must be done within seven days unless the proprietor notifies the PCO that the job will take longer.

Here too at Penton Street new designs of cab must be presented for 'type approval'. Every single cab licensed in London is issued with a type approval certificate when first passed for use, and subsequently no cab will be examined for passing unless the certificate is presented with it. Before being assessed for the Conditions of Fitness, all cabs must comply with national and European regulations governing the construction and use of motor vehicles. Modifications to basic design within the laid-down regulations are permissible. Carbodies and Austin have improved and upgraded the FX4 series throughout its life, but any modification made to an existing cab must also be submitted for approval. The PCO's attitude is that if a modification to a cab's design is sensible, safe and enhances – or at least doesn't compromise – passenger safety or privacy, then it will be considered. And if a modification is considered suitable, and complies with all relevant regulations – those governing safety and standards of construction as laid down by statute law or defined in British Standards Institute or passed by the Motor Industry Research Association, where appropriate – then it will be approved. Brand-new cabs have to undergo the same examination before being licensed for the first time, and it is not unknown for a cab straight from the dealers to be rejected!

The Conditions of Fitness are written by the Public Carriage Office, and ratified by Act of Parliament. Likewise, any changes to the conditions have to be made by the PCO. Some are specific, such as the turning circle, and the door and seating dimensions, and some are open to expert interpretation. For instance, one regulation states that the '. . . controls must be properly protected from contact with luggage.' Thus if carriage officers inspecting a new or modified cab feel that say a gear or handbrake lever might be moved or damaged by a suitcase, then they have the authority (and the duty) to reject that design as unsuitable, and changes would have to be made to it.

NOTE: It is a fallacy that the London motor cab driver has to carry a bale of hay for his horse and no such regulation has ever existed for motor-cab drivers! Former PCO senior vehicle examiner Jack Everitt did find a regulation demanding that a horse-cab driver carry sufficient fodder for his horse during a day's work, and this has surely been turned around by some members of the general public to bait a favourite target: the cab driver!

The Birch cab of 1953: it was built by North London taxi fleet proprietors of that name on a modified Standard Vanguard chassis and powered by a Standard ('Ferguson') diesel engine, and shows that the Conditions of Fitness of the time did not insist on an archaic design, nor on a requirement to have just three doors. The design bears a strong resemblance to the Standard 10 Companion estate car, and was imaginative, with the luggage compartment at the rear. However, the fourth passenger seat was sited alongside the driver and faced rearwards and, separated by a partition, must have created practical problems. Licensed in London, it did operate for a number of years, but never went into production.

installed with Ferguson and Perkins engines. The Suez crisis of 1956, and the resultant fuel rationing, was timely confirmation that Austin had made the right decision.

ROOF-MOUNTED INDICATORS, AND EXPERIMENTS WITH DOORS AND GEARBOXES

In 1954 the FX3's bodywork and fittings were updated. Steel wheel arches and B posts replaced the wood, and the semaphore trafficators, which were giving trouble in service, were replaced by roof-mounted Lucas Limpet flashing indicators. The modifications, which also included redesigned tail lights to comply with forthcoming changes in the law, were fitted to a cab and presented to the PCO for approval in May 1954; the cab chosen was UXP 136, from Levy's fleet in King's Cross – and it was uniquely different for another reason. A year before, Robert Drake, an American serviceman, had been fined £80 plus costs at Marylebone Magistrates' Court for the damage he caused by opening a cab door before it had stopped. Although the American was held responsible, some need was felt to avoid any further occurrences, so this particular cab was fitted with forward-hinged rear doors. The Conditions of Fitness demanded that rear doors were hinged on the rear pillar, because the PCO felt that a potential bilker (someone who runs off without paying a cab fare) might escape too readily from forward-hinging ones; but they were prepared to consider changes in the light of concerns over safety. The cab was put into service, and whilst no adverse comments were made officially, it was the only one of its kind. David Southwell, the new managing director of Mann and Overton, decided to wait and see what further reaction there

FX3/FL1 production line: putting an FX3 body together: the foundation of the chassis jig . . .

. . . The scuttle sub-assembly is made up from steel windshield pillars, wooden cant rail and steel scuttle . . .

would be before deciding whether to build all new cabs with this type of door. His reasons for staying with the old design are not recorded, but one can surmise that he was not prepared to spend money on something that was not required by law.

For the purpose of evaluating an automatic transmission in London taxi work, Austin adapted an FX3 chassis to take the Borg-Warner DG150M unit, and in March 1957

. . . And is mounted on the chassis jig . . .

. . . along with the front sub-assembly. The B-posts and cant rails are fitted, joining the rear and front sub-assembly. Derek Fairbrother checks for alignment of the B-post . . .

. . . The rear panel assembly is welded to the wheel arches and rear window panels on a sub-frame. (Only one man could weld the three pieces of the rear panel together. Thankfully he was never off sick!) . . .

. . . The Spider jigs are pushed into place to square up the body shell. In the prototype stage, a body was assembled and trued up, and a spider jig made up to fit it – there was not the money available to make the jig first! . . .

The roof is welded on, and the rear seat pressings, partition and the B-pillars are welded into place.

. . . Lead loaders fill in the joins in the panels . . .

. . . After washing and painting the body is trimmed out, ready for mounting and delivery.

submitted an automatic FX3 to the PCO. Type approval was given for twenty FX3s to be adapted. Overall, favourable reports came back via the PCO's passing stations from the drivers and operators chosen to test the eighteen that were built. The only consistent complaints were of oil leaks and a drop in fuel consumption of 3–4mpg (94–71l/100km). Austin never offered automatic gearboxes in production FX3s. The Hobbs Mecha-matic Transmission, made by a constituent company of the BSA group, was also tested in the FX3, but PCO records do not show a cab so converted on test in London.

COMPETITION IN LONDON, AND SALES IN THE PROVINCES AND ABROAD

In early 1954, two years after the deletion of the Oxford, Beardmore introduced their new MkVII cab. It had only a modest effect on the sales of the FX3, however. With the backing of a company the size of Austin, Mann and Overton's service and Carbodies' supply of replacement pressed-steel body panels, the FX3 was a better cab all round to maintain. It was popular with the cab masters, and its lead as No 1 in the London market place was consolidated. However, outside the capital and other major cities, where the option was open to the trade of either a purpose-built cab or a saloon car, the situation was not so clear cut.

Mann and Overton had the sole concession for sales of the FX3 in London. After all, it was 'their' cab: they had commissioned it and paid for half of it and they took the largest share of the profits. Operators in large provincial cities such as Manchester and Glasgow had been using London-type cabs for decades. Besides buying ten-year-old examples from London they could also buy new FX3s directly from Austin in Redditch.

Attempts to sell the FX3 to smaller provincial towns varied considerably. Although cabs with limousine configuration were the norm throughout the country until the 1920s, most provincial licensing authorities began to allow their cab operators to use saloon cars, and cabmen had got used to increased levels of comfort and performance. In the FX3 they were isolated from their passengers in what they saw as a cold, impersonal vehicle, and they were not prepared to put up with its slow performance. Besides, their saloon cars were much more sociable vehicles for off-duty use. To have the same benefit they would have to buy a private car in addition to a more expensive purpose-built taxi; so where the use of London-type cabs was not mandatory, the FX3 was the exception rather than the rule.

Austin envisaged the FX3 operating much further afield. In 1950, a number of left-hand drive FL1s were tried in New York. The riding public in the 'Big Apple' loved them, but the New York 'hack' drivers did not: they liked their big, lazy Hudsons and De Sotos. The FL1's turning circle was no advantage in New York's grid of wide avenues, and the cramped and underpowered Limey cab got a

'Bronx cheer'. The FL1 might have sold better in New York if an automatic gearbox had been offered at the time. Later, some 500 cabs were exported to Spain. With most of them painted white to reflect the heat of the Spanish sun, the majority went to Madrid, and they were certainly more successful there than in New York.

THE FL1

The FL1 hire car was made from the outset in order to maximize sales and profitability for both Austin and Carbodies. With four doors and no roof-mounted 'For hire' sign, it was easy to distinguish from its taxi sibling. Although the FL1 had the same leather trim and, after the first year or so, rubber floor mats, two forward-facing seats were fitted in place of the taxi's rear-facing tip-up ones, and a full-width front bench seat accommodated both the driver and a fifth passenger. An umbrella-type handbrake replaced the lever mounted on the FX3's transmission tunnel, but the floor gear change was retained, despite a virtually universal move by the industry to column gear changes.

The FL1 had forward-facing, tip-up seats.

When the FX3 received an Austin diesel engine, this too was offered as an option for the FL1.

The FL1 sold in smaller numbers than the FX3; about four taxis were built for every hire car. In its early years much was working against it. Purchase tax had been removed from the FX3, but a four-door version was never type-approved by the PCO, despite there being no regulation to prevent it; as such it could not be considered as a taxi or a commercial vehicle in the eyes of the Exchequer, and the FL1 incurred purchase tax throughout its life. At its introduction the tax set the price of an FL1 at a hefty £971 17s 3d. Despite the dire shortage of cars on the home market, the hire-car trade could buy expensive-to-run pre-war Rolls-Royces, Daimlers and British-assembled American cars for a lot less money. As the home market improved and spares, already sparse, became more expensive or virtually unobtainable for some of these older cars, the FL1 became much more viable.

Some provincial licensing authorities allowed four-door FX3s to be used, and with

The FX3/FL1 chassis made a good basis for the Evening Standard *delivery van. The* Standard's *rival, the* London Evening News, *used similar vans, but theirs were fitted with rubber wings. Because of the tight turning circle, most delivery drivers considered they were the best vans for the job.*

Many celebrities chose the FX3 as their personal transport. This example, an ex-London General cab, belonged to Her Serene Highness Princess Grace of Monaco. Another famous customer was Liberace.

The Enclosed-drive Taxi

When the FX3 went on general sale in 1949 it was advertised as the 'enclosed-drive taxicab'. It may seem odd to describe it as such when there was no nearside front door, but in fact it was the first London cab ever to be presented with full weather protection for the driver; in all previous models this side was exposed to the elements, and in fact driver's door windows were unknown until 1937! Patents for two designs of partition were applied for in 1948 in the joint names of Carbodies and John Hewitt Orr. One had two glasses that slid back and forth, and in the other the glass rose up and down. Both patents were granted in June 1949, but the sideways sliding one was approved by the Public Carriage Office. The rising partition fouled the meter drive, and its bulk was thought to take up too much luggage space. Besides, it was considered too difficult to remove in an emergency were the cab rolled onto its offside in an accident.

Nuffield were quick to adopt the patent sliding partition for the Oxford Cab.

the weather protection and the extra seat beside the driver they found some favour. The FL1 did find an ideal market as a passenger ambulance for day-care patients. This was long before the advent of the Ford Transit minibus, and the only other choice was a coach body on a 3-ton lorry chassis. Designed for commercial use, the FL1 was a durable vehicle, and even with purchase tax it was cheaper to buy and more economical to run than its competition.

Both Mann and Overton and Austin had envisaged a ten-year life for the FX3, and by the late fifties the cab, with its rod brakes and three-door configuration, was past its best; even in 1948 it had looked antiquated alongside the new Hillman Minx coupé at Carbodies. It ended production in late 1958. Altogether 7,267 had been made, an average of about fifteen per week. But let us now return to our main story, and the changes at Holyhead Road under new ownership.

6 BSA – The Daimler Years, 1954–59

'Carbodies will be the brightest jewel in the BSA crown'

Clinton John (Jack) Hellberg,
Carbodies' first general manager
under BSA's ownership

Daimler was a prestige name in car manufacture, enjoying royal patronage, and even in the 1940s the emphasis of its production was on expensive, coachbuilt cars. In 1940 Sir Bernard Docker became chairman of the BSA Group, and in 1944, managing director. In 1949 he became the third millionaire husband of Norah Collins, a miner's daughter from Nottingham; with her ostentatious lifestyle the new Lady Docker was soon making front page headlines. She had Daimler build some of the most flamboyant cars made in post-war Britain, proclaiming with justification that they represented the best of British craftsmanship. She loved the prestige of owning and being seen in these cars; but she was also reputed to have commented to Bernard that the public had probably never heard of Daimler since all their customers were emperors and potentates. She decided that they could not live on prestige alone, and told her husband that there must be a Daimler for the people. Whatever this car would be, and wherever it was to be built, Daimler needed to expand their manufacturing capacity – and there was a company which had exactly what was needed just a couple of miles from their giant Radford Plant: Carbodies.

In about 1953 a new Lanchester project, the Sprite, had begun at Daimler, and as part of this, aluminium body components and the possibilities of an all-aluminium saloon were being examined; in fact Jake Donaldson left Carbodies for a short time in about 1950, and went to work for Daimler on such research. A French-built Panhard, which itself had an all-aluminium body-shell, was brought in to study. The prototype Sprite was built in Carbodies' experimental department, and the people at Daimler, including Richard Smith, the managing director and brother-in-law of Lady Docker, believed that Carbodies could build an all-aluminium car. One can surmise that Smith might have arrived at this conclusion during Daimler's dealings with Jack Orr on the Lanchester Leda coupé.

However, building an aluminium body wasn't the straightforward job that Daimler thought. Bill Lucas, then superintendent of the toolroom, explained to Dick Smith that the technology was still in its infancy, and although they had the know-how to make such a body, they did not have the expensive spot-welding heads that the job required. Besides, the painting of aluminium then was an elaborate, six-coat process. But Carbodies had expertise in a great variety of work, it had an extensive press shop and toolroom, and it looked to be just the kind of acquisition that would fit in with Daimler's plans for the future. As we have seen in Chapter 4, in June 1954, with the formalities completed, Carbodies became part of BSA.

BSA

There is much genius in Warwickshire'

Richard Newdegate, MP for Warwickshire, responding to King William III's appeal for a
domestic small arms industry

The BSA Group's history goes back more than three centuries to the time when William of Orange decided that Britain should make her own small arms, instead of relying on imports from Holland. In 1692, acting on a petition by Richard Newdegate, he contracted for '200 muskets at 17 shillings per week ready money' from five Birmingham gunsmiths.

In 1861 fourteen of those gunsmiths formed the Birmingham Small Arms Trade, buying twenty-five acres of ground in Small Heath. But warfare is a fickle mistress, and such a group needed to find a more stable product with which to continue business during periods of peace. The bicycle boom provided the answer, and in entering this industry, the company found that manufacture of both complete cycles and bicycle parts provided them with steady growth.

Motorcycles, the product with which most people associate the name of BSA, were not made until as late as 1910, at the same time as cars. However, the cars the company made were not entirely to the directors' liking, and in that year they took over the Daimler company, one of the greatest and oldest names in the industry. The Great War of course provided a great increase in the arms trade, and it became necessary in 1919 to restructure the company into divisions. Then in 1931 they bought Lanchester, the first native British motor manufacturer and one of the most innovative, and it became the name for medium-sized, middle-class cars which fell neatly between the stately Daimlers and the BSA's own three- and four-wheel light cars.

World War II gave the group another great impetus, not only for arms, but for motorcycles which were bought in great numbers for military use, as were Daimler's excellent armoured cars. During and after the war many more companies, including the coachbuilders Hooper and Barker, Idoson castings, Hobbs Transmissions Ltd and their old rival firms Triumph and Ariel Motorcycles were acquired. In the 1920s and 1930s the BSA Group was one of the largest industrial conglomerates in Britain. Besides its armaments industry it was the world's biggest motorcycle manufacturer.

NEW FACES IN, AND AN OLD FACE COMES BACK

Takeovers rarely run smoothly. Differences in management style, policy changes, clashes of personality and often raw power struggles are part of the whole business, and this one certainly upset a few of Carbodies' key people. Bill Lucas's days at Carbodies seemed to be numbered. He recalls an interview with the top man at Daimler, Richard Smith, Norah Docker's brother-in-law, whom Sir Bernard had put in charge of Carbodies:

Bobby had thought about making some more directors besides him and Ernest, and I was in line until BSA took over out of the blue. I had to go and see Dick Smith at Brown's Lane. Jack Hellberg, who'd been sent down as our general manager, sat there. Jack was quite a character, but his knowledge of Carbodies was virtually nil. Dick Smith said to me, 'I hear things were going to look very bright for you.' I said, 'That goes for one or two of us.' He said, 'As far as I'm concerned you've got to prove yourself.' 'Oh, have I?' I said, 'I'll give

Lady Docker

Norah Docker was, it seemed, something of a complex character. Some described her as having the common touch, whilst certain other Carbodies employees, having met her on one of her visits, applied the word 'common' to her in less than flattering terms. Whilst she often derided Sir Bernard about the source of their wealth, she nevertheless spent the money with alacrity. Fascinated by a company that made London's taxis, she paid a visit to Carbodies; Bill Lucas remembers her visit:

Jack Hellberg said to me, 'We've got the Dockers coming, and she wants to see this Keller die machine.' So I got her a nice white overall, and I got one for myself. Then Lady Docker came in, and I had the shock of my life. She'd got this beautiful mink coat on. I led her into the toolroom and we came to this big Keller. There was Alf Norman sitting on a seat, working the machine. He'd got a big die on there, with oil splashing over the place. She said she wanted to go and sit up on the machine and watch him working it, so I offered her the white overall. She said 'I'm not putting any white overall on!' and she went up and sat on this dirty seat in this beautiful mink coat. I thought if oil got on the coat she'd go mad. Well, Alf's eyes popped out. I stood there like an idiot, watching the oil splashing out, and Alf was having to explain what the buttons were. Thankfully she didn't get any oil on her coat, but well, she was a character.

Lady Docker had several flamboyant Daimlers built to advertise the name and to promote British craftsmanship worldwide. In 1951 she had a straight-eight chassis fitted with touring limousine coachwork, and all the brightwork was dipped in real gold; not surprisingly the car was named the 'Gold Car'. Then in 1956 the last, and possibly the most extravagant car was built for Lady Docker, called the 'Golden Zebra', a DK400 with ivory sports saloon coachwork by Hooper, and zebra-skin upholstery. This had gold-plated fittings too, a feature which Stan Swaine, the production line superintendent had to organize.

you a month's notice then.' I'd already got a job lined up for myself at Airflow Streamline at Northampton when the takeover took place, and I left in May.

Very shortly after the formal takeover, Jack Orr returned as works manager, possibly by agreement with Smith prior to, or immediately following the hand-over. With BSA, the insidious trait of nepotism was strong because not only was Smith a relative of the Dockers, but so was Jack Hellberg. His dapper figure was soon to become a familiar sight in the factory, with his shooting stick and a fresh flower in his buttonhole every day. He announced that 'Carbodies would be the brightest jewel in the BSA crown'. As general manager Hellberg would be accountable to Dick Smith, but he was never made a director, and both he and Jack Orr remained on Daimler's payroll. When the takeover was finalized, the only board members appointed were Sir Bernard Docker as chairman, and Dick Smith. At a further board meeting a week later, Smith was appointed managing director, and Frederick Ellinghouse as joint company secretary, along with Steve Stevens.

Ernest Jones, Jack Orr and Bridge Clock Motors

Christmas 1961: a 'firm's do' for Bridge Clock Motors at the Chesford Grange Hotel, Kenilworth. Jack Orr, standing at the microphone, raises a laugh from Ernest Jones. Ernest, looking remarkably well, was heavily drugged against the pain of his cancer and had only three months to live.

At the bottom of Carbodies' drive, by the entrance to Holyhead Road, was a garage, a dilapidated place with four pumps, a corrugated iron shed and a black ash forecourt. In 1953 the owner retired, and Ernest bought it; later he developed it, in two stages, into Bridge Clock Motors. Jack Orr and Ernest were very close personal friends, and although Orr returned to Carbodies after BSA's buyout, from 1954 he began working for Ernest at Bridge Clock.

Facing Holyhead Road, on the other side of Carbodies' drive to Bridge Clock, was a piece of land, part of which belonged to Wardle's metal foundry. It came up for sale, and 'Steve' Stevens, who had stayed on under Daimler as joint company secretary, advised the company that they should move quickly to buy it if they wanted to keep the drive onto Holyhead Road open, particularly as Ernest had also wanted it for some time. In fact Ernest moved first, and this gave him two lots of frontage, with Carbodies' driveway coming down between the two on his land. Now, Jack Hellberg, Carbodies' commercial manager, loved fast cars. He owned one of the first Daimler SP250 sports cars, and he used to race this car up and down the drive, much too quickly in Ernest's opinion, whose temper became increasingly inflamed – until one day he said, 'I'll stop the so-and-so! So he built a brick wall across the drive, making not only Hellberg, but all Carbodies' traffic use an alternative entrance further along Holyhead Road.

A 'DAIMLER FOR THE MASSES', AND MORE

In 1953 the Lanchester Leda was fitted with a 2.5 litre six-cylinder engine and a Daimler grille and badges, and was relaunched as the Daimler Conquest, the body provided by the Pressed Steel Company in Cowley, Oxfordshire. Here was Lady Docker's ambition in the metal: a 'Daimler for the masses' – and Daimler had more plans for the Conquest family up their sleeve. A more powerful version, the Conquest Century, was introduced in 1954 and Daimler had

Trimming the Daimler Conquest Century coupé. Completed, trimmed shells were sent back to Daimler to be fitted on the chassis.

Carbodies build a drophead coupé version at the same time. The coupé was a logical step because the development had already been done on the Leda. Just like the Ford convertibles, the saloon bodies in white (bare metal) were shipped from Pressed Steel to Carbodies and modified in the same way: painted, trimmed and fitted with a de Ville head, they were returned to Daimler for mounting on the chassis. Like the Ford, the power-head was operated from the de Ville position, and the seat back could be moved forwards on an hydraulic ram to allow it to be stowed neatly behind.

A sports version, the Conquest Roadster, came out in 1953, and the 1954 Motor Show saw a very special version, a fixed-head coupé. This most elegant car, finished in pale grey over red, won Carbodies a gold medal in the coachbuilders' awards, although sadly the model never found more than three buyers. The following year, Carbodies was commissioned to make a three-seat drophead version where the third passenger was seated sideways – 'thwartship' was the word used in Carbodies' description in the 1955

Motor Show catalogue – in the back. This model did sell, giving of course all the fine weather advantages of the Roadster, and the complete protection of a fully enclosing, power-operated head.

Whilst Daimler were moving into what was, for them, volume car production, they did not forget the market for large limousines. The DK400 was to be the newest in a long line of cars for heads of state. Barkers and Hoopers, part of the BSA Group, were able to supply special coachwork on the chassis, including sports bodies for wealthy eastern royalty. Carbodies was asked to design a standard limousine for the new car, and under Jake Donaldson they produced a six-light body that followed closely the style Daimler designer Jim Rogers had produced for the Regency and Conquest. It was put on Carbodies' stand at Earls Court in 1955. Lady Docker is reputed to have taken a dislike to it, and Rivers Fletcher at Hooper produced an Empress Line version which was to become the basic model – if 'basic' is an appropriate word for such a vehicle.

Artwork for Jake Donaldson's Daimler DK400 seven-seater limousine, described in the press release as 'one of the world's largest cars', follows the contemporary practice of falsely accentuating the lines.

The DK400 itself, looking somewhat less sleek, follows Jim Rogers' style for mainstream Daimler models.

The DK400 interior; simply trimmed, but spacious and airy.

THE THREE GRACES: FORD'S NEW CONSUL, ZEPHYR AND ZODIAC

Ford's MkI Consul and Zephyr Six coupés had gained a reputation as glamorous cars. In December 1954 Ford began engineering a MkII range, and within a year saloon prototypes were ready for extensive road testing in Europe. Both convertible and estate versions of the cars were planned from the beginning, and Carbodies had much more than six weeks' notice to develop the convertible! This time there was to be a Zodiac coupé with leather seats and a power-operated top as standard. The power-top was to be standard on the Zephyr Six too, but optional on the Consul along with hide trim. Although the new cars were all designed at Dagenham, they bore a very close family resemblance to their American cousins, and in Carbodies' drawing office, Jake Donaldson was sent working drawings of a 1954 convertible version of Ford's medium-priced car, the Mercury, to help him maintain the family likeness.

Much more time could be given to the body engineering of the new car, which included strengthening the underside with the addition of substantial flitch plates. This time the shell was strong enough to allow door locks, with just one catch per door to be fitted. Jack Orr's patents had been transferred to BSA's name, and the 'one touch' electro-hydraulic operating system for the power-top covered by them was adapted for the new cars. As with the MkI Fords, Carbodies was to bring in complete body-shells, then remove the roof and the doors, and press new doors and rear wings. They would paint and trim

The first MkII Ford coupé, a Consul, in the experimental shop. Push-button door handles were fitted to the MkII because the floor was made rigid enough to obviate the need for the double door locks. The boot hinges still had to be mounted outside the body to allow enough room for the head to fold down flat. The wheel in the bottom left-hand corner of the picture belongs to the prototype FX4 taxi chassis.

The reason why the new Ford's shell was so much stiffer than the MkI: large flitch plates reinforce the sills and the transmission tunnel.

The internal quarter-light mechanism of the MkII Ford. The internal body cross-brace can be seen – and yes, you can see the factory floor through the door panel!

the bodies and ship them back to Dagenham for wiring and the fitting of the mechanical components.

The saloons were revealed to the public as the 'Three Graces' at a ceremony in London's Harringay Arena in March 1956. The convertibles came out at Earl's Court in October of that year, and as in previous years, Carbodies featured the cars on their stand, too. The new Ford was every inch an American car in a smaller size, and the convertible was Britain's version of the Hollywood film star's favourite kind of automobile. Even the colours – five

The Ford finishing line in 1959. A number of the face-lifted 'Lo-Line' Zephyrs can be seen on the tracks.

This Ford body is held on a rotating paint jig being cleaned in preparation for paint.

choices of two-tone paint, including Pembroke coral pink or Conway yellow with white – were a bright contrast to the greys and greens of the Humbers and Bentleys on neighbouring stands. Their impact at Earl's Court was remarkable.

THE DOCKERS DEPART

Judging only by the cars being produced it might have appeared that everything at BSA and Carbodies was going well; but this was far from the truth. At Carbodies, a £72,000

Changes in Industrial Relations

Although Bobby Jones had been a very hard man to work for, he was straight and he was blunt, and in the old days if he wanted to sack a man he would do it in person. In the early BSA days there was what was called on the shop floor 'the 4 o'clock parade': if a man was washing his hands after his day's work and a visitor told him to come to the office, he knew he wouldn't be at work on the Monday. Such practices were not unusual in a large company, but in a smaller place like Carbodies, where older hands had got to know each other over the years, it would create a very bad atmosphere.

In the late 1950s, union relations on the shop floor began to change. As more modern production techniques took over throughout the motor industry, long-established unions such as the sheet-metal workers were superseded – and in fact had been losing their grasp on power since before World War II. The old school of union officials believed and practised the principles of fair pay and working conditions, principles from which the whole trade union movement grew; these older members were retiring, or being ousted by this new breed of more militant Communists, or by those who sympathized with that cause. This destructive trend had begun in the 1930s, and looked like continuing. What seemed to be a saving move for the Sheet-Metal Workers' declining membership came from an unexpected source. A quiet revolution had been taking place in the plumbing industry: the old lead pipes in buildings were being replaced by copper, and plumbers were finding themselves out of a job. Trade unions would only take on members who had served a full apprenticeship in their particular craft. The plumbers had been apprenticed in their own trade, and the Sheet-Metal Workers' Union made a concessionary move and took them on as auxiliary members, where their talents proved very useful as lead loaders on the tracks. Irregularities could appear where body pressings were welded together, and in the past these had been beaten out on the tracks by panel beaters. This job was to be taken over by the plumbers, who filled the low spots in the bodies with lead, very quickly and expertly.

Unbeknown to this long-established union, Communist influences were at work. The World Federation of Trade Unions in Prague controlled Communist trade unionists directly, right across

profit at the time of the takeover tumbled to a net loss of £22,932 in 1956. At some time in 1955 (there is no precise record of this) Jack Hellberg instructed Steve Stevens to sack Jack Orr, an instruction which no doubt came from Dick Smith. No direct reason was given, but Smith, at a Christmas function, made an analagous reference to 'removing cancerous growth'. One must remember that Jack Orr was still good friends with Ernest Jones, and Orr's removal might have seemed by Smith to be expedient. Only one board meeting had been minuted at Carbodies between October 1954 and November 1955, profits were falling fast, and in troublesome circumstances such as these, scapegoats are readily sought. In Orr's place Smith appointed Percy McNally to works manager, and it is worth noting that McNally, who had joined Carbodies in the war years, had been sacked by Jack Orr in 1951.

Jack Hellberg himself was not proving satisfactory as general manager, in spite of the fact that he put in a great deal of effort. He was 'moved sideways' and given the post of sales, or commercial manager, and over a period of less than six months Dick Smith tried at least two more men in his place, eventually deciding to appoint a true Carbodies man. Steve Stevens was called in by BSA's board and invited to take over as 'acting general manager'. He was to hold this the whole of British industry, bypassing even the British branch of the Communist party. It was a simple matter to plant a man into a factory to cause disruption.

The concession offered to the plumbers by the Sheet-Metal Workers was a gift to the infiltrators, and in 1956 a strike was called in Carbodies, which lasted for several weeks. About three weeks later Carbodies were on strike again. After six weeks, *The Coventry Evening Telegraph* stepped in and rang Carbodies, and asked why they wouldn't negotiate with the union. Carbodies' spokesman told the *Telegraph* that they'd been waiting for the phone to ring! From that, the story of how the strike was orchestrated came out. A meeting of all the factory work-force was called, and voted to return to work.

An excess of zeal can backfire on the zealot, causing some embarrassment, as recalled vividly by one of Ben Johnson's apprentices, Brian Evans, when he returned to Carbodies after his National Service:

When I went in the army, Joe Donoghue was the shop steward. When I came out two years later he'd lost all that and these Northampton blokes were running things. I thought, there's something wrong here. A bloke came up to me in the experimental, a bombastic so-and-so, and wanted to know why I hadn't been to a union meeting for the last two years. He hadn't asked me where I'd been. Joe had kept my name on the books because he knew I was National Service and you were guaranteed to come back to wherever you worked for six months after. This bloke had never bothered to ask Joe that, so they 'branched' me for not attending union meetings. Bert Heath, whom I worked with in experimental, was an old union bloke, real Labour; he remembered the Depression. He asked me if I was going to tell them, and I said I wasn't. This fella didn't ask me, so why should I tell them? Let him make a fool of himself. When we got there, they took me in and they stood me there, and they asked me why I hadn't been, and I told them I'd been in Germany. They said, 'Why didn't you tell us?' I said, 'Why didn't he ask me?' When I came out they asked me if I wanted to go on the committee!

position for six months, in the course of which he had to ask on more than one occasion for management backing to prevent Hellberg trying to reassert some sort of presence for himself.

At the top level Lady Docker's extravagance, and Sir Bernard's indulgence of her in it, was doing the concern no good; moreover losses incurred by BSA had not been reported at the 1955 annual general meeting. Jack Sangster, who had joined BSA when his Ariel motorcycle company was taken over, was sickened by this wasteful treatment of such a proud industrial heritage, and he began, with the help of Stanley Aston, to plan the removal of the

Dockers. At an extraordinary general meeting on 19 November 1956, Sangster removed Sir Bernard Docker from the chair of Carbodies and was elected in his place, and Dick Smith was removed from the managing directorship.

To bring some degree of profitability and stability to Carbodies and to BSA as a whole, Sangster engaged Alistair McKay for several months, to help locate and resolve specific problems. As a result, the whole BSA group was restructured, with separate divisions set up to encompass the varied interests. Carbodies came into the Automotive Group, under Triumph, and Edward Turner was appointed to the board. Turner had joined

BSA when they had taken over Triumph Motorcycles; he had been chief engineer there, and had designed the highly successful Triumph Speed Twin. Fred Ellinghouse and Steve Stevens were to stay on at Carbodies as joint secretaries. With the removal of the Dockers, things began to improve. Carbodies' balance sheet produced in July 1957 showed a profit after tax in excess of £68,000, and in 1958, following another healthy balance sheet, the board recommended that a dividend of £50,000 be paid to shareholders.

A NEW DAIMLER MODEL

The Regency and Empress saloons of 1952 and the One-0-Four of 1954 were part of Daimler's move into all-steel saloons. They had farmed out the tooling design and construction of the Regency to Motor Panels Ltd, up in Foleshill, adjacent to Jaguar's old plant. For the 1958 model year Daimler developed the One-0-Four into a new model, the Majestic: whilst retaining the One-0-

Four's front end and roof design, the Majestic was to have new rear wings, doors and boot. But Daimler were very short of money, and the new model would have to be produced on something of a shoestring budget; it fell to works manager Percy McNally to find a solution. McNally's talents lay in management, however, and he did not understand the engineering involved in the manufacture of press tools, nor the behaviour of sheet metal when subjected to pressing. He decided that, instead of making complete new tools in either Kirksite or steel for the Majestic, he could adapt those of the One-0-Four. This was a disaster, and Peter James, who then worked under Jake Donaldson in the drawing office but was to go on to become chief engineer, described the resultant equipment as 'the most primitive form of tooling he had ever seen'.

Some explanation of the differences in the techniques of casting steel and Kirksite in the making of press tools is needed in order to appreciate fully just how much of a botched job it was. Steel has a high melting point, and when cast in a closed mould keeps its heat for long enough to stay liquid and flow into the cavities. Kirksite on the other hand has a low melting point and must be cast in an open mould, so that a flame can be played on it to keep it in a liquid state in order for it to fill the entire mould. McNally drilled and tapped holes in the faces of the steel One-0-Four tools, and screwed in ¾in (19mm) bolts. He then inverted them over new open moulds made to the shape of the Majestic's panels, and poured Kirksite into the mould; the bolts acted as anchors for the Kirksite, as it would not adhere on its own to the steel. What resulted were in effect cast steel tools with lumps of Kirksite stuck to them, and the body panels pressed from these tools were appalling. They were what

is known as 'first draw condition': rough, uneven and inconsistent, and each panel had to be hand finished before being ready for assembly on the car. It was fortunate that Carbodies had such a large force of lead loaders to call upon, because they were needed to fill in the imperfections in the panels when they were fitted on the body; eventually during production a trench had to be dug alongside the tracks, so that the lead loaders could stand at a more convenient height in order to fill the imperfections of the lower parts of the Majestic's body! The bodies were then sent on to Daimler for painting, trimming and mounting on the chassis.

The extra labour involved in finishing the poor quality panels made the cheapness of

The first Daimler Majestic saloon, introduced in 1958.

the tooling alterations a false economy, and in the long run it would assuredly have been better to have invested in completely new Kirksite tools, for the low production run of around ten cars per week. Carbodies were to produce less than 2,000, between 1958 and 1962, of the 2,670 Majestics and Majestic Majors built.

Undoubtedly this was a sad episode in what had been an excellent record of body-making by Carbodies, particularly as the standard of the Majestic's body belied the engineering advancements of the car, which boasted all-round disc brakes and full automatic transmission.

A DAIMLER DRAWING OFFICE AT CARBODIES

By 1959 Daimler were in a very difficult financial situation. Hooper's coachbuilding premises in London were effectively closed down, leaving just a maintenance depot, and a small section of the drawing office was moved from Radford to Carbodies. The design work for two projects was undertaken here, both ultimately unsuccessful. One was the DN250 saloon, a proposed replacement for the Conquest. It was based around the P-type Vauxhall body-shell, and was to use the superb new 2.5 litre V8 engine already lined up for the SP250 sports car. A mock-up was built at Radford using a complete set of Vauxhall body panels screwed together with self-tapping screws, but the project was never followed through. It was scrapped following Jaguar's takeover of Daimler, and the excellent MkII Jaguar-based V8 250 saloon was built instead.

The second project was a limousine version of the six-cylinder Majestic. Radford sent a lengthened chassis to Carbodies, who literally cut a Majestic body in half, mounted each end on the chassis and proceeded to fill in the gap. They did this by making an internal running board-cum-step, concave in shape, and a cant rail following the same profile. The huge roof was joined with a panel and lead loaded for a smooth line. The proto-

---

Sad Farewells to Bobby and Ernest

Bobby Jones enjoyed good health for another four years, following the same routine that he had done all his life. But on the morning of 21 December 1958, Lillie heard an unusual noise from the down-stairs lavatory; unable to open the door, she called their gardener for help, and they found that Bobby had collapsed. He was taken to a Leamington nursing home where he died later the same day. He was buried at Stoneleigh Parish Church on the 5 January 1959. Reporting on his memorial service, the *Coventry Evening Telegraph* recounted that the vicar of Stoneleigh, the Rev. G. H. Parks, called Bobby, 'A man of great purpose and great character. He was one of those who have served and given to the community by . . . industrial achievement. He was a man with a great sense of humour and the virtue of very real and unassuming generosity.' Carbodies was represented at his funeral, among others, by Jack Hellberg, Percy McNally, Bill Bailey and Ben Johnson. Freddy Connolly, of Connolly leather, a long-time family friend, was also there to pay his respects.

Ernest ran Bridge Clock Motors successfully, but in 1960 he developed the first signs of cancer. The disease was found to be inoperable, and finally he died at the same place as his father, River Park nursing home, Leamington Spa, in March 1962. Jack Orr went on to run a number of businesses, both on his own or with his son Bernard, and died in his eighties.

The body on this Alvis 12/50 'ducks back' (a retrospectively applied name – and a polite variation on the usual one!) is a replica of the Carbodies original, by Wilkinson/Selway.

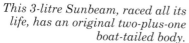
This 3-litre Sunbeam, raced all its life, has an original two-plus-one boat-tailed body.

This MG 14/40 tourer dates from 1928, and has one of the first bodies to be built at Holyhead Road.

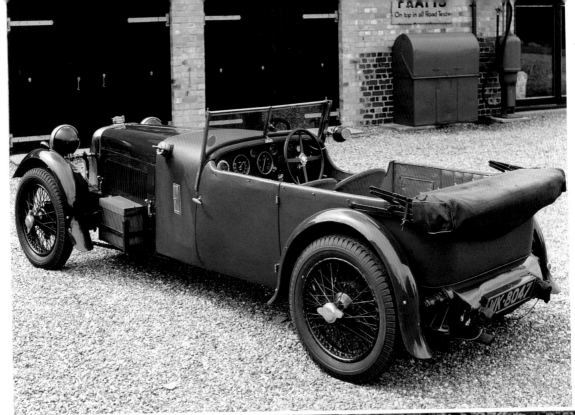

Front-wheel drive allowed Alvis to produce a very low slung chassis for the 12/75. The Carbodies light tourer body sits well on it.

The Sportsman's Saloon body on this 1926 Alvis 12/50 was a popular choice, light in weight yet offering full weather protection. Variations of this body were also seen on early MGs, and called the Salonette.

This MkI MG 18/80 two-seater is the one featured on Carbodies' first Motor Exhibition stand, in 1929. Since renovation the wings, originally ivory to match the bodywork, have been painted green.

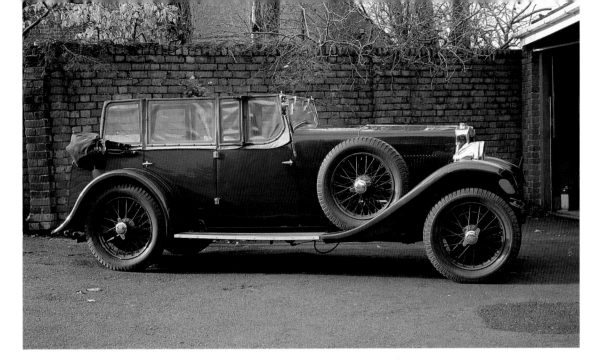

A 1930 MkII MG 18/80 with a four-seat tourer body, regularly used in club events and driven the length and breadth of the country by its owner.

A unique, original two-seater body on a 1931 low chassis S-Type Invicta.

An Alvis 12/60 sports. This body, dubbed retrospectively the 'beetle back', was one of the last to be built by Carbodies on a pre-war four-cylinder Alvis chassis.

A 1932 J2 MG Midget. This standard Carbodies-made body shows the cutaway doors and slab fuel tank that was to become the distinguishing style of the English sports car for more than two decades.

A 1935 MG N-type Magnette with an Allingham Airline coupé body. The authentic-looking MG 'Cream Cracker' colours on this car are actually from modern manufacturers' stocks.

A smartly restored Alvis TA14 drophead coupé, showing the head struck in the de Ville position.

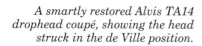

Believed to be the oldest surviving FX3, this 1949 petrol-engined example was built before the Public Carriage Office would allow wheel trims. It still has the maroon overspray it received in 1953 to commemorate the Coronation of Queen Elizabeth II.

A 1954 Ford Consul MkI coupé, in totally original condition, with a wonderful 1950s patina. Its history is a car salesman's dream: it really is a low mileage car, owned from new by two old ladies!

A fully restored Austin A40 Somerset coupé.

A Daimler Conquest Century drophead coupé in original condition, with its power head still in full working order.

One of only three made, this Daimler Conquest Roadster fixed-head coupé is the actual car shown on Carbodies' 1954 Earl's Court stand. The car is in entirely original condition, including its French grey over red paint.

A Daimler Conquest Century Roadster Drophead Coupé in original condition.

A 1959 Daimler Majestic in original condition. In almost forty years this car has covered just 55,000 miles.

Non-standard wire wheels set off this MkII Ford Zodiac coupé, one of around a dozen still remaining in the UK.

One of the oldest FX4s still in existence, this 1961 example has had some alterations during its hard life.

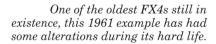

The unique 1971 Ford Capri
MkI 3000E coupé.

*A 1977 Triumph 2.5S
estate, one of the last to
be built, fully restored
in Pimento Red.*

*This Cortina
Coupé is an
example of the
last private car to
be made by
Carbodies before
concentrating
their efforts
entirely on taxi
production.*

type was taken out early one morning for test along the fast A45, a favourite route for, amongst others, Jaguar and BSA and Triumph motorcycles. Peter Ludford, a Daimler draughtsman working on the limousine, was one of seven passengers in the car, and recalls not only exceeding 100mph (160km/h) down this road, but also the monumental dressing-down they received when their boss found out about it! The Majestic limousine was shown on Carbodies' Earl's Court stand in 1959, but a different version was chosen for production, built on the V8 Majestic Major chassis, and adapted from Carbodies' saloon by Motor Panels.

It would take a couple of years and another false start before the much desired stability and profitability at Carbodies was achieved. Before we go on with that part of the story, however, we must go back to 1956, to the beginnings of what was to be the most important vehicle in the whole of Carbodies' history: the Austin FX4 taxi.

7   The FX4

The world-famous London 'Black Cab'

When Mann and Overton's managing director David Southwell began talks with Jack Hellberg and Austin's design department in 1956 to discuss the replacement of the FX3, they were thinking of producing a vehicle that might have, perhaps, a ten-year life. They could not possibly have known that they were about to build one of the longest-running and most widely recognized British motor vehicles of all time. It would be a vehicle that some would love and others detest, but Londoners and visitors from all over the world alike would come to identify the familiar shape as an essential part of the capital's scene.

The new cab started life in Austin's Longbridge drawing office as ADO6. From the foundation of BMC this system, the letters of which stood for 'Austin Drawing Office', was used for all new designs. Albert Moore's team of engineers and Charles Benlow's draughtsmen began to plan out the chassis, but the design of the body was undertaken not by Dick Burzi's team in the styling studio, but by Eric Bailey of Austin's body design department.

Retrospectively the cab was given the designation FX4 after Austin's old system, and there would be a new hire car version, the FL2. Although the Conditions of Fitness do not specify that a London cab should have a separate chassis, it made economic sense to update the old FX3 frame with modern running gear from BMC's parts bin. The

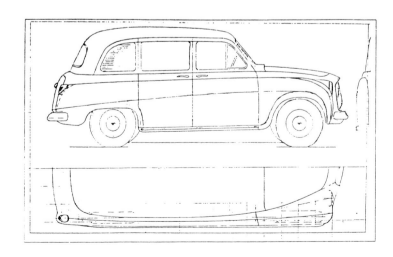

Eric Bailey's first outline drawing of ADO6, soon to become the FX4.

Sankey-built independent front suspension from the Austin Westminster was scheduled, along with the rear axle from the same car, and dual circuit, parallel master cylinders were specified for the Girling drum brakes. From the outset a Borg-Warner DG150M automatic gearbox was to be fitted as standard with the diesel engine, but neither a manual gearbox nor a petrol engine were to be offered.

Austin sent a chassis and general drawings' layout for the body over to Carbodies, and Percy McNally produced a (very) rough mock-up of the cab. David Southwell and the PCO's Mr Gould were invited to examine it, along with Jack Hellberg and works manager Percy McNally, on the 4 June 1956. It was a very different animal to what we would currently recognize and Mr Gould's report seems almost to be talking about a totally different vehicle from our now familiar cab. It had only three doors; although the idea of a fourth was suggested – there had never been anything in the Conditions of Fitness to disallow one, and Birch Brothers of North London had produced a single four-door prototype on a Standard Vanguard chassis in 1953, and it would be acceptable to the PCO so long as luggage space was not restricted. Whilst Mr Gould thought an upward-hinging bonnet could be blown open at speed, blinding the driver, McNally's idea of hinging it on the front of the chassis found favour. Gould was less than happy about the fitting of a fixed windscreen, maintaining that an opening one was an asset in dense fog, a regular occurrence in London before the clean air acts; he did concede, however, that it would be preferable in the light of modern motor vehicle manufacturing practice. The head-rests fitted to the rear seats were thought to be unhygienic, and were dropped.

Eventually the design was finalized, and under Percy McNally, senior draughtsman

Jake Donaldson's team produced working drawings for the pattern-makers and tool-makers. Jake had worked under Don Cobb on the FX3, and had gained an understanding of the demands made on the design of cabs by the Conditions of Fitness. The FX4 is rightly called a purpose-built cab, but to say that it is merely designed for town traffic and the carrying of fare-paying passengers in safety and privacy is to tell only half the story: it was also designed with ease of maintenance in mind, and was therefore purpose-built in every sense – after all, a cab off the road is a cab that doesn't earn money, and one that costs a lot to repair eats into profit.

Although the new cab would look very different from its predecessor, the method of constructing the body was essentially the same: two rigid structures, a boot assembly and scuttle were to be held together by the framework of the sides and the roof, and the inner sills were welded to the side frames. The outer sills were bolted to these to make them easily replaceable in the event of an accident. The floor had removable panels, steel at the front and plywood at the rear, so that the PCO could remove them to examine the chassis for corrosion. The partition contributed greatly to the body's overall strength, but the torsional rigidity of the vehicle was very much dependent on the chassis. The entire front wing assembly was designed so as to be unbolted from the main body-shell, simplifying the repair of any front end damage, and the rear wings also bolted on. For durability and ease of cleaning, each of the interior trim panels were one-piece plastic mouldings.

The responsibility for the tooling and production engineering of the FX4 fell on Percy McNally's shoulders, and although most of the toolroom and pattern shop personnel were still at Carbodies, after the BSA takeover the skills of Jack Orr and Bill Lucas would be very much missed. McNally

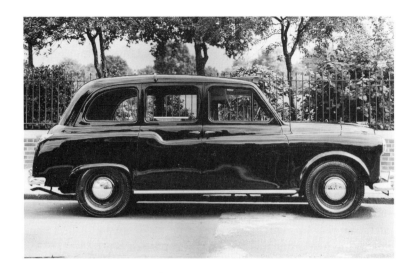

The factory demonstration model FX4 VLW 431. The picture was commissioned by Mann and Overton and is at the same venue as their picture of the FX3 in Chapter 5, outside the gates of the South Park in Fulham. The cab went into service with York Way Motors in King's Cross.

began developing his own Kirksite press tools, patenting a good many in his own name. He designed the doors so that the structure and strength was in the inside pressing, with the outer skin flanged, fitted over and spot welded around the inside seam; like this, the removal and replacement of a damaged skin would be a quick, rela-

tively low cost operation. He planned the complex curves of the roof to be formed in one piece, and the even more complex bonnet to be pressed twice – once to bend it in half, and the second time to add the details.

The first the London cab trade saw of the new cab was when they were asked to go to Coventry early in 1958 to evaluate the

This rear view shows the original boot pressing with the number-plate light below the plate. The requirement for a darkened rear window was carried over to the new cab. The original door handles, tail-lights and indicators are clearly seen, and the circular partition opening is just visible.

The luggage platform partition and driver's compartment from VLW 431, very different from later production versions.

prototype. Their reaction was not good, as the London General Cab Company's then managing director Geoff Trotter recalls:

> When we saw the prototype, we thought it was too big and too heavy, also the doors opened the wrong way and the bonnet was diabolical. It was a recipe for disaster. I remember the comment made by Barney Davis, who was the managing director of Felday Cabs in the East End. Barney was a little man behind a big cigar. Carbodies asked him what he thought. A man of few words, he took a long puff on his cigar and said, 'Well, it's just a bloody awful vehicle, that's all I can say!'

It seems that, despite the court case with the American serviceman in 1953, rearward-opening doors were not thought an important enough advancement!

The original application for approval for the FX4 chassis was submitted to the PCO on 10 January 1958, and the first complete prototype was seen at the 'Yard' on the 27 June that year. This prototype, VLW 431, was passed by the PCO on 14 July. It went to work in the fleet of York Way Motors of King's Cross for evaluation purposes, and was used that year for promotional photographs and films.

The FX4 was formally announced to the trade in September 1958, the FL2 hire car being shown at the Earl's Court Motor Show and the FX4 at the Commercial Motor Show. It was described in a press release as '. . . considerably lower and more streamlined than its predecessor', although it was actually less than 2in (50mm) lower, and as its style was somewhat traditional rather than advanced, we must view the epithet 'streamlined' in relative terms. In the same press release a projected London sales figure of fifty a week was to prove optimistic. General type approval was granted on 25 November 1958, and the cab went on sale.

As soon as production started, the severe inadequacies in Percy McNally's tooling began to show themselves. Neither the complex curves of the roof nor the bonnet could be pressed without great difficulty, if at all. The main board of BSA's Automotive Division asked former toolroom supervisor Bill Lucas to return to sort out the tooling for this troublesome panel. He recalls just what he had to do:

> When I walked into his office McNally welcomed me with open arms, saying 'You and I, Bill, will be a great team!' Where McNally went wrong with the roof panel was that he tried to press it

Ever the showman, commercial manager Jack Hellberg escorts film star Jayne Mansfield to the 1958 Motor Show to introduce the brand-new London taxi (albeit due to the rules of the Society of Motor Manufacturers and Traders it had to be the FL2 hire car version!). Miss Mansfield was a great fan of the London taxi, and had one for her own personal transportation. The FL2 on display had a list price of £1,250 plus purchase tax, almost £300 more than the FL1.

Percy McNally's attempt at pressing the large FX4 roof panel in one. The dent in the roof (lower item) is plain. Puckering around the rear pillar can also be seen. The upper item is the Kirksite press tool.

in one action, including where it came down around the back window. That meant the press would have to draw to a depth of 19in [480mm], but it could only draw 12in [305mm]. They'd only done thirty panels out of about a hundred sheets, but they eventually ran off fifty-nine. The steel had puckered, and those panels had to go to Abbey Panels to be ironed out on a crimping machine.

McNally had patented over twenty different type of crash tool, and the first thing I did was to revoke the patents because it was just a waste of money. I started delving among the tooling and I took the biggest gamble ever in my life – I'd have been kicked out if it hadn't have worked. I realized that the cast-iron die-line of the roof was wrong. With Joe James, the foreman of the pattern shop, I got the tooling altered. The roof

was success, but if it hadn't been, production of the cab would have stopped because there'd have been no roof panels.

A simple but effective way to press out the shape of that 'diabolical' bonnet came from the shop floor, as Lucas recalls:

The FX4 bonnet was a hell of a shape; we just couldn't get it right. George Dodson, the foreman of the toolroom, came into my office and said he'd got an idea to cut out a vee on the bend and re-weld it. I agreed to it, George got it cut and welded it up, and they pressed it like that. We never had a bad bonnet after.

These production difficulties seriously held up delivery of the new cab. In June 1959 David Southwell had to write to Mr Gould at

In this picture from 1982 the weld which stiches together the two halves of the V-cut, as suggested by George Dodson, and which made the bonnet easier to press, is clearly visible. The ability of Carbodies to press such a complex shape enhanced their reputation amongst the 'body bashers' in the motor industry.

the PCO, apologizing for the delay. At that time, London's cabs were expected to be licensed for a period of ten years, but if any proprietor wanted to run a cab for longer, it had to be granted a special extension. Because of the delay in delivery of new vehicles, Gould had to extend the working life of quite a number of old FX3s, and Southwell requested the names of the proprietors who had been waiting the longest, so that they would receive their cabs first.

But not all was well when those cabs *were* delivered. By comparison with its predecessor, the FX4 was a more sophisticated cab, and things went wrong. It must be said that

no matter what tests are carried out by a manufacturer, a far tougher test of a motor vehicle and its components is taxi work on the streets of London. The General took the keys of their first FX4 from Mann and Overton's David Southwell in front of the cameras of the cab trade press, and Geoff Trotter recalls the early days of operating the cab:

When we were evaluating it we gave it to reliable men, but we also gave it to a pair of real cowboy drivers who would do a thousand miles a week in it. The first problem we found was with

The end of an era. Photographed on Victoria Embankment in 1968, the FX3 on the left is heading for Waterloo Station, taking its passengers to catch a boat train. Not only was the FX3 on its last plate, but the last steam-hauled boat train ran two years previously, and travel by ocean liner was rapidly being superseded by air travel.

The interior of VLW 431. See the puckering on the interior rear side window. Even this pressing had to be re-tooled.

the bonnet. When the front suspension bounced, the bonnet came up on the safety catch. David Southwell said, 'That can't happen. The first time that happens, I'll eat my hat.' But in the first couple of weeks we had a cab going to the airport and the bonnet flew back and smashed the 'For hire' sign, blinding the driver and causing an accident.

Interior fittings were sourced from other Austin models, but considering their experience with the FX3, Longbridge surprisingly underestimated just how hostile the environment was in which a taxi had to work. For instance, interior door handles were breaking within two weeks; they were Austin Westminster items and were fine in light use in a saloon car, but in a cab these handles are used twenty or thirty times a day. Also the cable fitted to the front door to enable the driver to pull it closed would break too easily. A stouter cable couldn't be had for another year or so, because parts have to be ordered in bulk to

get a cheaper price, and on small productions it takes a long time to clear old stock.

Austin soon decided that much of McNally's tooling couldn't be used. The FX4 was losing Carbodies money, and Bill Lucas, along with David Southwell and production supervisor Stan Swaine, told Austin's Arthur Burton so. Initially Burton didn't want to lay out any more capital expenditure, but

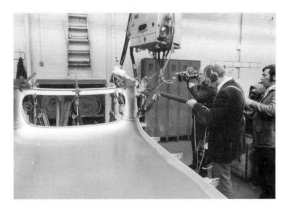

The revised roof assembly, consisting of two separate C-posts and a lower panel.

FX4 chassis delivered from Austin's factory at Drews Lane, Birmingham, line up in the mounting shop awaiting the fitting of bodies.

FX4 production gets underway. The main body assembly is lowered onto the chassis. The steering wheel and fuel filler pipe await fitting. The front wings and bonnet are bolted on separately, and this was the way the cab was built until its end in 1997. This is a manual transmission cab, photographed in 1966.

eventually agreed, and from then onwards provided a subsidy of £100 on each cab. In early 1960 Billy Betford and Geoff Salmons of Austin retooled the roof for Carbodies as a four-piece assembly, and also retooled the outside of the boot lid. The cost, split three ways between Austin, Carbodies and Mann

and Overton as on the original contract, amounted to over £180,000.

The original design of the door assembly was a disaster. As an idea it seemed good, but in practice it was difficult to make and finish. By mid-1961 Mann and Overton were again asked for tooling money; the door was changed to a clinch type, and by 1962 the old outside door handles inherited from the FX3 changed to larger, more sturdy ones with greater leverage.

Fitting the (DG) Detroit Gear automatic gearbox as the only option for the diesel engine raised a great many problems unforeseen by either Austin or Borg-Warner. Today, almost all of London's cabs have an automatic gearbox, and the choice of it in London traffic seems obvious. Trials with the small number of FX3s had brought positive results in the hands of selected drivers, but in 1959 it was very difficult to sell even the idea of automatics to most cabmen. Geoff Trotter remembers:

To the older cab drivers, the automatic was a very unnatural means of driving, and we had a lot of trouble persuading the drivers to drive the automatic box. We carried out a conversion from automatic to a manual because they were troublesome, but when the automatic box became more reliable we converted back. I remember going to the factory along with Ronnie Samuels and some others from the Proprietors' Association to meet some Borg-Warner reps as a result of our complaining about the gearbox. A chap from Borg-Warner opened his case, threw some components on the desk and said 'Look at those! We've got millions of these gearboxes in use all over the world and we never had any trouble with them until we put them in London taxis. Talk about abuse!' It was down to drivers putting the gearbox into neutral at traffic lights, revving the engine and slamming it into drive. Perhaps they hadn't been taught properly or whatever. Borg-Warner were very disenchanted with the cab trade and so were we with the gearbox.

The problems with the automatic gearbox were not only due to abuse. There were other technical problems, and the whole process was an expensive one for all concerned. With a cast iron casing, the DG 150M transmission was a rugged 3-speed unit. Fitted to Jaguar and Studebaker engines, it could handle the 200-plus bhp that these units could put out, and in the USA the 'box regularly lasted for 100,000 miles. However there were unforeseen characteristics of the Austin diesel, as former Borg-Warner engineer and sales Director Peter Whybrow remembers:

We engineers at Borg-Warner were not aware of the enormous torsional vibrations created by this diesel engine. These put much higher stresses on the gear train components than had been believed. Secondly, to try and improve fuel consumption the speed at which top gear was engaged at light throttle was reduced to the range of 14–16mph. The DG was unusual at that time in that top gear by-passed the torque converter, and was direct drive, through a single plate clutch. One of the advantages of a torque converter is that it tends to dampen out torsional vibrations and here we were throwing this advantage away! There were also a lot of problems with the damper springs in the direct drive clutch breaking up due to these torsionals.

There certainly was abuse on the part of the drivers; we tried to give instruction on how best to drive an automatic transmission vehicle, the main thing being to leave it in 'drive' when stopped at traffic lights. This they did not take to at all, probably due to having to keep the pressure on the brake pedal. [A diesel engine ticks over at a higher speed than a petrol one] It was a sad introduction of automatic transmission to the London cab trade, which cost all concerned a lot of money.

By September 1961 type approval had been gained from the PCO for the four-speed synchromesh gearbox from the Austin Gypsy gearbox to be fitted in the FX4 as an option alongside the automatic. Austin then had to re-print all its FX4 and FL2 brochures, altering the artwork. The early brochures for the manual model show a cab with a gear change lever for a manual gearbox, but no clutch pedal! Although Borg-Warner's new Model 35 auto gearbox replaced the DG in 1964, the real time of the automatic gearbox for cabs was twelve years into the future. In 1962, now that all the fittings for a manual gearbox were available on the chassis, the 2.2 litre A70 petrol engine, which had been the original powerplant of the FX3, was introduced as an option. Provincial operators would appreciate the extra speed of the petrol vehicle, but there must have been pressure from buyers of hire cars and hearses. The FL2 chassis was an economical base for a hearse as was the FL1 before it, but although the diesel engine's fuel consump-

A familiar face at the Motor Show. Sid James, star of Carry On Cabby, *visits in the early 1960s and tries out a white FL2. Sid also starred in his own BBC comedy-drama series* Taxi, *written by Jack Rosenthal and Harry Driver, in which he played a cabman. Note the wing-mounted indicators – the detested limpet items had already been replaced on the FL2!*

tion was much better, the noise did detract somewhat from a solemn occasion. No automatic gearbox was offered in the UK market with the petrol engine, either for the FL2 or FX4.

Having four full doors, the FX4 offered far greater weather protection than the FX3. Still, its shortcomings for the driver were revealed as it piled up the mileage. The PCO would not allow soundproofing on the grounds that it was a fire risk, and the noise of the diesel engine became tiring. It also made communication with the passengers through the small circular partition window very difficult. Tall drivers found the driving compartment cramped and uncomfortable, and they had to bend to look through the windscreen; they would have to wait another ten years for their needs to be accommodated. However, in 1960 the circular opening in the partition was changed for a centrally placed vertical sliding one.

With the tooling problems solved and the mechanical specification sorted out, the FX4 and FL2 settled in for an anticipated ten-year production run. Now we must return to our main story, for changes were once again in the offing for Carbodies.

8 BSA Years, 1959–73

'. . . Whatever you name, they can make it'
Claim made on behalf of Carbodies'
development engineers, in a 1961
brochure

A NEW MAN AT THE TOP

Bill Lucas had signed a new contract a month after returning to Carbodies to sort out the mess that Percy McNally had made of the taxi, but rather than appoint Lucas as general manager, Jack Sangster said that

there would be 'A. N. Other' above him. He would not tell him who, but it was in fact an outsider – Fred Habbits, from Motor Panels, a part of the Owen Organization. On 1 June 1959 Habbits was appointed director and general manager, the highest title BSA had for a constituent company under Jack Sangster's regime.

STEEL TROUBLE

Triumph had developed two new scooters, the BSA Sunbeam and the Triumph Tigress. Carbodies was to make the pressed-steel body panels, and Fred Habbits was told to

BSA's first serious attempt to break into the scooter market came too late with this model. Sold as either the Triumph Tigress or the BSA Sunbeam, the complex pressings were made at Carbodies. Experimental resin tooling was tried for the cowling over the handlebars, but its technology was not fully understood at the time and the material was not used by Carbodies again for many years.

In 1961 Carbodies published a brochure telling not only the motor industry of the company's versatility and talent, but claiming to the rest of industry that they could cope with any problem relating to sheet metalwork and press tooling. The sixteen-page brochure made this claim for the development engineers: '. . . Whatever you name, they can make it'. As a result the shop floor began to see a whole range of non-motor work, such as washing-machine casings for Colston washing machines, radiators and under-floor air ducting for BSA heating, and sink tops for English Rose.

A great variety of non-automotive press work kept Carbodies busy in the early 1960s. Here, washing-machine casings are being made.

obtain sufficient steel for a big production run. At the time it was difficult to get steel of any quality, let alone in the quantities required. Eventually a supplier was found in Belgium, and Habbits ordered a huge amount from them, not only for the scooter but for everything else Carbodies was making. Unfortunately the steel was of poor quality with a lot of surface pitting; moreover there was much more than could be held in Carbodies' stores, and the stocks had to be held outside the factory. The scooters were just too late on the market and sold poorly, and thousands of tons of this steel, for which Carbodies had no use, was sold off at below its true market value. That year it was Steve Stevens' unenviable task to present the audi-

tors with figures showing a loss for the year ending July 1959, after tax, of £91,580. After two years of profit, Carbodies' financial future was looking grim. Changes had to be made, and fast.

TOP MANAGEMENT CHANGES

In May of 1960 Jack Sangster reached sixty-five years of age, and he retired as chairman of both BSA and Carbodies. That year BSA reported that for 1959 it had recorded its best-ever performance, as a group – but from over thirty companies, Carbodies was one of just two group members whose figures were poor. Sangster was replaced on BSA's main

Bespectacled Fred Habbits at the annual presentation of prizes to the Carbodies Social Club angling section.

board by deputy chairman Eric Turner, an accountant by training who had come to BSA from the Blackburn Aircraft company. That same year Arthur Burton left Austin to be made managing director of BSA's engineering division, and by August he was appointed to Carbodies' board. In November he was followed to Carbodies by his fellow ex-BMC colleague, Jim Munday, who was initially made production director. The new management was able to start a turnaround, and the balance sheet for the end of July showed a profit of nearly £12,000. It was too late for the unpopular Habbits, and by the end of July 1961, his resignation was on Eric Turner's desk. In November 1961 the main

A commercial vehicle project that came to fruition: complete sets of panels for this AEC lorry cab were supplied for assembly by AEC themselves.

And one that didn't. Jake Donaldson's scheme for a unitized box-body for Vauxhall-Bedford was not taken up by the Luton concern who were fearful that they would jeopardize the business of the independent commercial body-builders.

board authorized a significant subvention payment, a subsidy, to enable Carbodies to continue trading.

Eric Turner promptly appointed Jim Munday as the new general manager. The likeable Munday had spent many years in the motor industry in Australia, but his talents were in administration – he had little or no hands-on experience of the nuts and bolts of car building, vital knowledge for a small company like Carbodies. But Munday recognized this in himself, and began to assemble a close team of Carbodies' people around him, people who knew the company intimately, and held strong loyalty to it. He made Bill Lucas technical and sales director, Jake Donaldson was retained in charge of the drawing office, and Steve Stevens, who had been promoted to financial controller by Alistair McKay, kept his usual diligent eye on the money. Bernard Bevin was appointed works manager in place of the dismissed McNally, and Peter Dawson works supervisor (Dawson, who had followed his father Mick and grandfather Bill into Carbodies in 1948, had moved to Bristol Siddeley to super-

vise the production of Sunbeam Alpine sports cars for Rootes, but had returned in that year, 1961).

There was no room in the new team for Jack Hellberg. Despite a great deal of effort and his very useful liaison work with Ford, he had not achieved much in the way of results, and he left the company. His prediction of Carbodies becoming 'the brightest jewel in BSA's crown' did not materialize under his stewardship; the simile was somewhat pretentious, after all, and it might be better to think of the firm as becoming more of a solid rock in a turbulent sea. The combination of talents Jim Munday had gathered around him looked to be ideal to turn Carbodies' fortunes around, and would enable them to weather the changes that were to sweep through not only BSA but the whole of the motor industry.

DAIMLER DEPART...

In 1959 a new version of the Daimler Majestic, the Major, was announced.

The Ladybird

The Ladybird light car was a classic example of how BSA, during the post-war period, managed to do everything 'too little, too late'. The bubble car boom had received a boost in Britain during the Suez crisis, and this had encouraged Leonard Lord of Austin to start development of the BMC Mini. By 1960 the bubble car was all but a spent force in the market place, superseded by the Mini. However, in 1961 Edward Turner decided that he could build a light car with a motorcycle engine, and a commercial version, that would sell. The car was to be an open two-seater, with three wheels and a 250cc twin-cylinder engine. It was anticipated to sell at around £250, and that perhaps 200 vehicles a week might be made. In one form the commercial version was envisaged as a milk float, and it was thought it would sell for about £300.

Ben Johnson had the task of building the car body by hand, but when it came to designing the press tools for it, Bill Lucas considered that, in the form it was, it simply could not be made in pressed steel. But by the end of 1961 no firm decision had been made as to what to do about the project, and it was eventually abandoned. To start such a car in the early 1950s would have seemed reasonable – Berkely, Peel, Bond and Frisky were British companies who built competitors to the German BMW, Heinkel and Messerschmidt – but in 1960 it was madness. A second prototype was built with a body design that was somewhat easier to make, but in 1962 the whole project was dropped.

The BSA Ladybird.

Powered by Edward Turner's superb 220bhp aluminium-headed 4.5 litre V8, it had a 120mph (193km/h) top speed that was to surprise many a sports car owner. The body was modified by enlarging the boot, and adding air-intake grilles inboard of the head-lamps on the slightly reshaped front end. The option of two-tone paint, and a flying 'D' to the bonnet, set the car apart from its predecessor.

Jaguar boss Sir William Lyons was desperately in need of more factory space, and in early 1960 BSA sold the Daimler factories at Radford and Brown's Lane to Jaguar; along with them went the oldest name in British motoring history. Gradually, Daimlers were to become badge-engineered Jaguars, although for the next eight years, production of the Majestic series would continue. The build quality of the big car was never good, however, due largely to the poor tooling; it had come in for criticism from Lyons after the takeover, and Fred Habbits had been obliged to improve it. At a production run of

Jack Hellberg, with the shooting stick, watches the loading of Ford Consul 375 coupé body-shells, trimmed and painted, before they are shipped back to Ford at Dagenham for completion.

ten bodies a week with a lot of labour-intensive lead loading, the big Daimler did not make Carbodies much money, and by late 1961 its total production was taken over by Jaguar.

ROOTES RETURN . . .

In 1961 Rootes introduced two new models, the Hillman Super Minx and the Singer Vogue. Planned originally to replace the

The Daimler Majestic Major, introduced at the 1959 Motor Show. This pre-production car has minor detail differences from the production model, such as the circular air intakes and flying 'D' mascot.

Minx and Gazelle, they were to be built alongside the existing cars and Rootes would be struggling for space to make them. The Humber Hawk and Super Snipe estates were being assembled at the Singer plant in Birmingham from part-assembled body-shells shipped up from the Rootes-owned British Light Steel Pressings plant in Acton, West London. The prototypes had been made at Airflow Streamline in Northampton when Bill Lucas was there, and Rootes approached Lucas to see if they could take production of the Humber estate from Singer's plant and give them more room.

Holyhead Road was bursting at the seams with all kinds of work, ranging from the Ford coupé and the FX4 to motorcycle mud-guards and washing-machine casings; so Bill Lucas had to find new premises. Baginton airport was about to be converted into an industrial estate, and he arranged to move into the old Lancaster bomber repair hangars there. This was long before the terms of the lease were settled; the

conditions eventually imposed were not favourable, but Carbodies themselves had to have the space.

The press tools and jigs for the estate panels were moved into Holyhead Road, and the body-shells assembled and painted; from there they were shipped to Baginton where works engineer Eric Blackburn had laid down a track for the shells to be finished. They were then delivered to Rootes at Humber Road, Coventry, where they were fitted with mechanical components. Production of these big Humbers averaged some twenty per week over the six-year period.

Estate versions of the Singer Vogue and Hillman Super Minx were planned, and Rootes, still trying to find space, asked Carbodies to assemble the Vogue estate in a similar fashion to the Humber. With the big Ford now obsolete, there was room to spare at Holyhead Road, but the Vogue was never a money-spinner; its main advantage to Carbodies was to keep a number of skilled

A superb start for the new director and general manager Jim Munday, who proudly displays the IBCAM gold medal won at Earl's Court in 1961 for the Humber Super Snipe estate. This was the first time Carbodies had exhibited the Humber.

men employed in the factory, and not to lose them elsewhere.

Painting the bodies caused problems. Rootes specified the option of two-tone paint, and the masking of the first colour was time-consuming. Moreover when metallic paint was introduced on the model, difficulties were encountered in getting a good, even finish on each car: on one panel the paint would be even and shiny, whilst on another it would be patchy and dull and would have to be flatted and re-sprayed. Both the Singer and Humber estates continued in production until 1967, when Rootes deleted both models.

. . . AND FORD MOVE OUT

Ford were happy with the standard of finish that Carbodies had put into the prestige model coupés; they had won a silver medal at the 1960 Motor Show. However, falling orders meant that at the end of that year production had to be cut back, and so 250 men faced redundancy. Following a four-week-long strike, the management agreed to cut the layoffs to 121 and re-deploy the rest throughout the factory, but this meant a three-day week all round.

A MkIII Zephyr and Zodiac range was under development at Dagenham, and the design of the floor-pan was significantly different from the MkII. In September 1960 Carbodies had quoted a price of £285 per body plus £300,000 for tooling a MkIII coupé, but by February 1961 Arthur Burton had to report to Carbodies' board that Ford were not interested in making one. Two years further on the big MkII Ford coupé, one of the most glamorous British cars of the period, ceased production.

The history of the motor industry is full of vehicles that never made it to production, like the MkIII Ford Coupé. Lea-Francis were

FX4 and Singer Vogue body-shells being cleaned prior to painting. Note how the taxi-body components – the bonnet and the front wings – are separate from the main body assembly.

struggling to survive in the post-war climate, and developed a new chassis using a Ford Zephyr engine. Abbey Panels built them three prototype bodies for the sports version, the Lynx. Carbodies was approached to quote for the building of the body, but with no orders resulting from the 1960 Motor Show for the Lynx, there seemed very little hope for the car and Carbodies declined to continue. In the words of Carbodies' minute book at the time: 'It was agreed that it was not advisable to proceed further in this matter.'

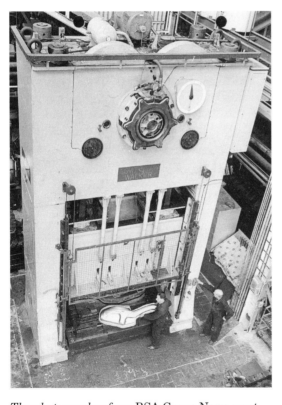

The photographer from BSA Group News *went up in the rafters for this shot of BSA Beagle light motorcycle frames being pressed on a 1,000 ton Cowlishaw Walker press. The 70cc Beagle was an unsuccessful attempt in 1964 to take on the mighty Honda 50 Step-Thru.*

STANDARD-TRIUMPH

By 1964, both the Ford coupé and the Daimler Majestic had gone. Production of the BSA scooters had dwindled to nothing, and only the Humber and the loss-making Singer Vogue estates kept the FX4 regular company on the tracks. Taxi production had settled down to about twenty per week (a far cry from Jack Hellberg's prediction of fifty!). Some non-automotive work for companies such as BSA Heating and Rolls washing machines kept the company in profit, but the loss of the Ford left a gap in car production.

Bill Lucas had known his fellow SMMT council member George Turnbull a long time. Turnbull was made managing director of Standard-Triumph shortly after truck manufacturers Leyland had taken over and one of his tasks was to try and make a job of the Standard Atlas van which had been launched in the late 1950s. An ungainly vehicle and very much underpowered, it was relaunched as the Atlas Major with a 1.7 litre engine, and eventually renamed the Leyland 15. The van was being made at Speke, in Liverpool. Labour relations there left a lot to be desired, and besides, Turnbull needed the space it was occupying to expand production of the forthcoming TR4 sports car and 1300 saloon.

George Turnbull asked Bill Lucas if Carbodies was interested in taking on the van, which was to include a new, larger capacity version, the 20. Lucas agreed, and the whole of the production line machinery was transferred complete from Liverpool so that Carbodies could begin making the body-shell of the new model, in both pickup and van version. Assembled bodies were painted and sent to Standard Triumph's factory at Canley for trimming and fitting on the chassis. As coachbuilders, Carbodies displayed the Leyland on their stand at the Commercial Motor Show in 1964, and

Leyland 20 vans in the finishing shop. From here they were shipped to Canley and mounted on the chassis.

The 1964 Commercial Motor Show, and BSA Carbodies shows off its latest product, the Leyland 20 van. Bill Lucas is in the driving seat, and beside him is Bob Broughton, who ran all of Carbodies' Motor Show stands at the time. In the back is Keith Stansfield, apprenticed to the company in the early 1960s, and who worked as Bob's assistant at the shows.

production averaged a useful twenty a week. The Leyland 20 was eventually moved to Stampro-Leyland's subsidiary in India where it was sold as the Standard 20, promoted by the delightful catchphrase, 'Standard 20 can do plenty!'

THE TRIUMPH 2000 ESTATE

For Carbodies, a much bigger job for Standard-Triumph was on its way. The Triumph 2000 saloon was an instant success when it was launched in late 1963; mock-ups

Straight from Canley, the Triumph 2000 body-shell, minus roof, boot-lid and back doors, on the holding jig.

of both an estate car and a five-door fastback had been built, but no decision had been made about which to make. Pressed Steel at Swindon, who produced the body-shell for the saloon, had quoted nearly half a million pounds to tool up for the estate. George Turnbull thought this too much for his envisaged production run of no more than twenty cars a week, so he and Arthur Ballard, Triumph's chief body engineer,

looked to Carbodies for a better deal, telling Bill Lucas that the tooling costs had to reflect the low production run. Lucas said he was interested, but told them that to keep the price down the body would have to have a lot of lead loading. He quoted £75,000 for the tooling, and Standard-Triumph agreed.

Standard-Triumph wanted a smooth, unbroken roof line, so the roof panel would have to be a one-piece pressing. At Bill Lucas'

The 2000 shell with spider jigs fitted, and new cant rails welded in place. Removing the roof and the panel behind the rear window takes away the integral strength of the saloon shell. The jigs will hold the body rigid whilst the new components are tack-welded in place.

request a saloon body-shell was sent up from Swindon, minus the roof. At this particular stage Triumph wanted the estate, but couldn't decide if they wanted a fastback, so the mock-up of it was sent to Carbodies as well. The 2000 estate car was the first major project undertaken by Jake Donaldson's assistant, Peter James; Jake simply gave him a pile of saloon drawings and he said, 'Here you are, get on with it!' The fastback was a rush job for James because he was going on holiday, and he worked to within about two hours of leaving in order to get the outline on the drawing board for the team in experimental to make the back end. The one-piece rear door was an incoming feature on estate cars at that time, and needed an especially strong rear cant rail to take its weight. Both estate and fastback were presented to Triumph, and the estate was approved. Like the estate, Triumph wanted the support mechanism of the fastback's tail-gate to be enclosed within the body. The much larger assembly, including its unique window, was too heavy for the torsion bars that worked so well on the estate, or for the MGB GT-style coil springs that were also tried. This factor, along with Triumph's other doubts about its marketability signalled the end of the fastback project.

PREPARING FOR PRODUCTION

With the estate car design signed off, hard tools were made up for the roof, the tailgate, the rear doors, the floor panel with a space for the spare wheel, and the folding rear seat. The assembly of the body was done on a spider jig, a frame of steel tubes that holds the body in place while the new panels are tacked on. The welds were completed, and the bodies went onto the tracks and the joints were filled in with nearly 120lbs(54kg) of lead. The new Triumph 2000 estate was released at the 1965 Earl's Court Motor Show on Carbodies' stand, and it was a huge success. Carbodies have two gold medals for two of the years when the finished vehicle was displayed by them as exhibitors in the estate car class of the coachbuilding section.

At this time lead prices were fluctuating wildly, so an agreement was made with Arthur Heinz, Triumph's purchasing director, to adjust the body price up or down every three months according to the cost of lead. During the production run, Triumph had an inspector permanently at Carbodies, and he began criticising work on the front of the car. Carbodies' work was all done on the rear of the car, so to counter this Bill Lucas

The outstanding features of the Triumph 2000 estate were a one-piece flat floor, a large tailgate and a huge load-space. Bill Lucas disagreed with Standard-Triumph's chief body engineer Arthur Ballard about where the draught welt for the tailgate should be fitted. Lucas said it should be on the body, to make an easier job of finishing; Ballard won this particular argument, however.

bought a Triumph 2000 saloon, and if there was anything the inspector marked up on the front end of the estate, Lucas would take him outside and show him the faults already existing on the saloon. The inspector was soon more selective about his criticisms!

THE FX4: IMPROVING COMMUNICATIONS WITH THE CAB TRADE

As time wore on, Mann and Overton were getting a poor reputation for not passing on complaints about the FX4. The cab proprietors had the impression that although Mann and Overton knew of all these faults, they weren't necessarily passing them back to the factory. Very much later Mann and Overton were to say that as agents they felt it was up to them to filter the complaints that were coming back and only to pass the really serious ones to the manufacturers. However, Carbodies wanted to respond to all criticism, so Jake Donaldson and Bill Lucas began to

visit garages such as the London General, where they could talk to both proprietors and drivers alike.

At the Public Carriage Office, Jack Everitt had been promoted to senior vehicle examiner. In a further attempt to understand fully the operational problems of the FX4, Bill Lucas set up regular informal meetings with Jack Everitt. With the rapport established between the two men, what had seemed like a barrier misguidedly created by Mann and Overton between manufacturer and those on the 'front line', was circumvented. However, when it came to making any alterations, the finance was not always forthcoming from Mann and Overton, and the FX4 continued fundamentally unaltered until 1968.

AN FX5?

In 1968, London's last FX3 was retired and although a relatively small number of Winchesters and Beardmores were worked, the FX4 reigned supreme on the streets of

1965 Motor Show, with the FL1 hire car, plus a full line-up of estate-cars: the Humber Super Snipe in 'police special' trim, the Singer Vogue and the Triumph 2000. In the utility coachwork class for that year the Singer won an IBCAM silver medal for Carbodies, and the Triumph a bronze for Standard-Triumph.

London. In 1968 BMH had introduced a new light van, the Austin-Morris JU250. Following the formation of BLMC, Alec Issigonis, the genius who created the Mini, started a project at Longbridge along with Rover's top designer David Bache, to build a new cab. This was based on a proposed replacement of the JU250, and on paper the idea, code-numbered LM11, was sound. Although the use of the JU250's beam axle was a retrograde step in terms of vehicle development, its use meant that no difficulty would be encountered in achieving the

25ft(7.6m) turning circle. But when Bache and Issigonis took the full-size mock-up to Carbodies, it got a very definite thumbs down; in the opinion of Bill Lucas and Jake Donaldson, it was the most appalling thing they'd ever seen. Donaldson and Peter James immediately produced a new mock-up design which Issigonis and Bache preferred to theirs, and gave it the go-ahead, and a prototype body-shell was made in Carbodies' experimental department. At BLMC, however, the new chairman, Donald Stokes, was dismayed at the financial mess he encountered, and the project went no further when his cost-cutting axe fell upon it. However, Bill Lucas was tired of having to depend on Mann and Overton to approve, and very often reject, any improvements to the FX4, and began to form the idea of building a cab independently of the London dealers.

FX4 FACELIFT

An FX5 was not to see the light of day at this time, however. Instead, in 1968 the cab trade received what might be called a MkII version of the FX4, which answered some of the trade's criticisms. BLMC's best-selling 1100 range had been face-lifted, and on Peter James' suggestion the FX4's rear end was adapted to take the car's new tail-light units, and the hated limpet indicators were banished. Under the bonnet, the two large six-volt batteries were moved from against the bulkhead to a position over each wheel arch. Previously, rainwater had collected under them, and in the space of three or four years, the metal had rotted through, allowing the water to pour onto the poor driver's right foot!

The FX4's driver's compartment dimensions had been taken from the FX3, but a new generation of cabmen were coming along

1967: Ben Johnson (foreground, with his back to the camera) and Bill Bailey (far right) retire, and their work colleagues gather for a presentation. Among those in the picture are Eric Blackburn, George Fletcher, Percy Lloyd, Fred Shufflebotham, Frank Troughton and Doug Blackshaw. Both Johnson and Bailey were with the company from the very early years.

A short-term contract for the Rootes Group in 1968 were a number of crew-cab conversions on the Commer lorry cab, to be fitted to dustcarts.

who had been raised under the Welfare State, and they were on average much taller and needed more leg-room. After a long fight, Austin and Carbodies persuaded Mann and Overton to agree to pay to have the whole partition angled back, allowing a tilting seat and thus 4in(10cm) more leg-room. The sideways-sliding partition from the FL2 was installed, the upholstery colour was changed to black (vinyl had replaced leather for the trim material in 1967) and at long last sound-proofing was approved. What was not thought important at the time was the fact that repositioning the partition prevented a wheelchair from being pushed into the cab. The general feeling was that the cab trade never saw any passengers in wheelchairs, so why worry? Whilst this attitude had prevailed for many years and would continue to do so, the effects of these alterations were

The Triumph 1300 estate bears a strong family resemblance to its big brother, the 2000, including its one-piece tailgate.

to have an impact on the vehicle's development nearly twenty years later.

NEW TRIUMPHS: A MKII 2000 AND A 1300 ESTATE

The first Triumph with front-wheel drive, the 1300, was introduced in 1965. By 1969, Standard-Triumph, as part of BLMC, were considering their future models, including what might be done with the 1300 bodyshell as an eventual replacement for the Herald range. Carbodies was invited to convert a 1300 saloon into an estate, and a prototype was built up and delivered to Canley by the end of the year. The decision was taken to restyle the whole 1300 range, with a longer boot on more expensive models, and the existing short boot retained on the new lower price Toledo variant. These complications meant that it would be unrealistic to put a proposed estate car into production. Triumph did, however, extensively restyle the 2000 saloon in 1969, and the popular estate version continued in production, retaining the original MkI style at the rear.

A NEW DIRECTOR AND GENERAL MANAGER

Jim Munday used to boast to Eric Turner that there wasn't enough work at Carbodies for both him and Bill Lucas. Although both men would joke about this, a surprise phone call disturbed Bill Lucas' lunch one day in 1969:

Jim Munday came in and told me he'd got to go to BSA to see Eric Turner at 1.15. I was in the dining-room when the phone rang for me – would I get over to BSA immediately. Jim Munday was there and Turner said to me, 'Munday's always said that there isn't enough work for both of you at Carbodies. One of you has got to go.' I thought 'Oh, no,' and said, 'Which one of us?' Turner said 'Munday. I'm sending him to Meriden to try and sort it out there. As from now you are director and general manager of Carbodies.' A photographer for the paper was waiting, and Jim and I had our pictures taken side by side. That's how I became director and general manager!

Jaguar

Jaguar boss Bill Lyons went up to Carbodies in 1961, complaining that he was being charged too much by Abbey Panels for virtually hand-making the bonnet for his new E-Type. The costings and the price of the car demanded that the bonnet, like the rest of the bodywork, should be pressed and at a sensible price.

Bill Lucas studied the wooden buck of the bonnet and established how he could press it in as few operations as possible – the more times the panel has to be pressed, the higher the labour cost. He quoted for a Kirksite tool, and Lyons agreed, subject to Abbey Panels agreeing too, as they had the contract; at over twenty tons, the tool was one of the largest to be made of Kirksite – only that for the roof of a Commer Superpoise van was larger. With the corners of the sheet-metal blank radiussed off to prevent it tearing, it was successfully pressed in one go.

Some 18,000 E-Type bonnets were made at Carbodies. The press used for the job was sold to Abbey Panels very shortly after, they also bought Carbodies' Kirksite foundry at about the same time, and used the material to make racing bodies for Ford and Jaguar. Carbodies also made doors and floor pan for the E-Type body. Other components for Jaguar included solid brass grilles for the MkX and early XJ6 variants.

E-Type Jaguar bonnet successfully pressed over a Kirksite die.

Bill Lucas took over the helm at a difficult time for the British motor industry. Industrial relations throughout the industry were at a very low ebb: strikes, known world-wide as the 'British disease', were creating havoc in production, and the manufacturers were undergoing major changes. Ford's Product Plan would not find a place for a coupé. BLMC would see its profits fall dramatically, and they would not be looking to outsiders to make any more specialist models. Rootes were making all their own

bodies at Linwood in Scotland, but they were heading for deep trouble and by 1970 Chrysler would take them over completely. Despite this, Bill Lucas would have the strength of the same loyal management team around him, and a workforce that enjoyed good wages and were comparatively dispute free.

After his first year as director and general manager, Lucas promoted Steve Stevens to the post of financial director. Jake Donaldson was also given a seat on the board, as

*Derek 'Mac' McLaughlin,
who succeeded Ben
Johnson in the
experimental shop, with the
first Ford MkI Capri coupé.*

engineering director. On the work front the building of spare body panels and press work for many manufacturers' current models were earning good money for Carbodies. Lucas would be grateful for the success and continued production of the Triumph 2000 estate, but it was the steady captive taxi market which was to become much more important for the company's economic future.

A SPECIAL FORD COUPÉ

A top executive in the Ford Motor Company, Sir Leonard Crossland, had been number one at Briggs Bodies. Briggs had been taken over by Ford, and Sir Leonard remembered the coupés of the 1950s and 1960s. Ford's latest model was the Capri. Advertised as 'The car you always promised yourself', it came in one body style – a two-door fastback with seating for four adults – and with an extensive range of engine and trim options. Sir Leonard decided that although Ford no longer wanted a production coupé *he* wanted a one-off Capri convertible, and he approached Bill Lucas, whom he knew from past years, to build it.

Being a two-door design the car was a simpler job in one way than the old Zephyrs and Consuls. The roof was removed, and Jake Donaldson designed a head with drop quarter-lights, just like Jack Orr's cars in Bobby Jones' day. Bill Lucas delivered the car, trimmed as a top-of-the-range 3000E, and powered by a 3-litre V6 engine. He recalls the number of motorists who slowed down on the M1 to stare at the ermine-white car as he drove it to Dagenham. Imagine – the highly desirable Capri had been on the market for only two years. The old MkII Zephyrs and Consuls were still around, and the sight of a soft-top Capri must have had plenty of people telephoning their Ford dealers asking to buy one!

A few days later, Sir Leonard telephoned Carbodies and very apologetically asked if a second car could be produced. At first Bill Lucas thought that perhaps that someone had asked for another car for themselves, but in fact the first one had been written off in an accident. Fords sent another Capri up to Holyhead Road, and a second model was built; it was registered in the spring of 1971 in the Ford Motor Company's name. In an identical colour, it differed in appearance in

With no Daimler limousines to call on any more, BSA needed a distinctive vehicle with which to meet visiting dignitaries from Birmingham New Street Station. What better, then, than this gold-painted FX4 with the BSA 'piled arms' symbol on the door? The 'new shape' tail-lights, the Leyland symbol and the stainless-steel sill cappings put the date of this picture at around 1971.

two ways: the hood was black instead of white, and the bonnet was white instead of black!

A RIVAL FOR THE FX4

In the early 1970s the cab trade and its press were still clamouring for a new cab. They had seen how much the private car had improved, and how little they seemed to be getting in the FX4 for their £1,500 in comparison with, say, a Ford Zodiac for the same money. However, BSA were in financial difficulties, and so was BLMC's Austin-Morris division. With the LM11 a non-starter, all the London cab trade had in the way of anything new was the disappointing Winchester.

In the late 1960s, the London General Cab Company, by then a part of the Associated Newspapers Group, had made attempts to introduce its own model, the Metrocab. Designed in conjunction with the bus, train and ship-building concern Metro Cammell Weymann, it too used a GRP body like the Winchester, and the same running gear. Two prototypes were built and one ran satisfactorily out of the General from 1969 to 1971. The managing director of Cammell

Laird, the MCW division that was to build the cab, visited Carbodies, and Bill Lucas showed him the production process of the FX4, telling him that whatever price he put on his cab when he put it on the market, Carbodies would undercut it by £100, and they could produce sixty units a week (!). A fortnight later Cammell Laird's man called back and said that he wouldn't be producing a cab; the taxi was to be a standby line, manned when there were no bus chassis in the works. The unions had insisted that a taxi line should be fully manned or they would go on strike. The General would not place a firm order, so Metro Cammell were obliged to bow to union pressure and cancel the Metrocab. However, this would not be the only time the name Metrocab would be heard.

GAS CABS

When the diesel engine was introduced in the FX3, the main concern about fuel was its price, but from 1970 exhaust cleanliness began to become an issue. Taxi fleet owners W. H. Cook and Sons, of West London, invested a considerable mount of money in a

Possibilities in New York

An opportunity once more presented itself for sales of a London taxi to the New York market. Mayor Lindsay, 6ft 4in (1.9m) and 240lbs(110kg) found difficulty in squeezing his substantial frame into the city's cabs, so he wanted something that he could get into comfortably, and also that would take up less space on the streets of 'The Big Apple'. He therefore visited Bill Lucas at the Carbodies' stand at the 1967 Commercial Motor Show and inquired about a left-hand-drive London cab for New York. Bill Lucas explained apologetically that the firm did not provide such a model, and that it would be expensive to produce. Although the original pressings on the scuttle had allowed for it – a small number had been tried in New York in 1959 – the scuttle had in fact been reshaped in the 1967 face-lift. But Lindsay insisted that the cost didn't matter: he wanted one.

Austin assisted in the engineering of a prototype, with a petrol engine and automatic gearbox and double bumpers to comply with new Federal safety regulations. Painted in the standard yellow, it was shipped out to New York and presented to Mayor Lindsay by Graham Whitehead, the president of British Motor Holdings (USA) Inc.

The Austin was not the only cab on trial. Peugeot had been invited to submit a 404, a model which had been in use in Paris since its introduction in 1960, so the FX4 was up against a major European rival. The FX4 ran on the tough New York streets for twelve months as part of the Columbia Garage fleet, and reactions from passengers were mixed. Some loved it, others hated its harsh ride, but it had one real advantage: when winter snows hit New York, its flat floor allowed the melt water off the passengers' shoes to run out, unlike the American sedan cabs, where it would collect in the footwells. A disadvantage was that because the door locks still complied with PCO Conditions of Fitness, the rear doors could not be locked from the inside, and this was essential to prevent the 'hit-and-run' robbery of passengers in some quarters of the city.

From the operator's point of view it was more expensive to buy, but its economics were geared to a far longer life than the two years that New York cabs, many of which were ex-police or ex-rental cars, were expected to last. Surprisingly it was also heavier on fuel than an American cab, returning about 12mpg (US gallons, approximately 15mpg Imperial 20l/100km) although its performance was well short of what the New York 'hack' driver was used to. These factors undoubtedly went against the choice of the FX4 in the eyes of the New York taxi business, and no more cabs were ordered.

fleet of petrol-engined cabs, converted to run on liquid propane gas. Because there was no fuel duty on LPG, the cost of a gallon was significantly less than diesel or petrol, so that even at 18mpg(15L/100km) the running costs were much lower. Early in 1971 the government had announced that it intended to put duty on LPG. Cook's managing director, Vernon Cook, wrote to Parliament outlining his objections to the duty, citing that this move would destroy the commercial advantages of the lower-priced fuel. Stating that the exhaust emissions of propane contained approximately ½per cent of carbon deposits compared to 6 per cent from petrol, Cook concluded his letter by saying, 'We regret that any excessive excise duty would kill off the project and with it, the end of hopes for a cleaner city.'

Ironically it was vehicle exhaust emission legislation taking effect on 1 January 1974 that finished W. H. Cook's project off for good. The FX4 and FL2 were by now the only vehicles using this engine. It did not meet the standard required by the new laws, and as sales of these versions were insignificant, BLMC scrapped the engine rather than modify it.

The first cab to be built entirely at Carbodies, in May 1971. This picture shows most of the senior staff at the time. From the left they are: Stan Beale, finishing shop foreman; Bill Lucas, director and general manager; Peter Dawson, works manager; George Fletcher, chief inspector; Jake Donaldson, engineering director; Percy Lloyd, trim shop foreman; Stan Swaine, foreman inspector; 'Ack' Johnson, mounting shop foreman; and George Taylor, chief storeman.

COMPLETE VEHICLE PRODUCERS

Carbodies were to benefit in one important way from the financial troubles that beset Austin-Morris. Donald Stokes had put George Turnbull, the former managing director of Standard-Triumph International, in charge of it. As part of his efforts to streamline this unwieldy mess of diverse factories and obsolete models, Turnbull decided that the Morris Commercial plant at Adderley Park, Birmingham, where the FX4's chassis was being made, had to close. He met up with Bill Lucas, who was a good friend and a fellow SMMT council member,

on the Carbodies' stand at the 1970 Commercial Motor Show. In an informal discussion, held in the privacy of the back of the show model FX4, Turnbull offered Carbodies the chassis manufacturing plant, on the understanding that Austin-Morris would still be responsible for making any design alterations.

Purchasing the plant would provide several advantages, but Lucas said he would only accept it if he did not have to make any redundancies. The unions had been making threatening noises about industrial action if any BLMC plant were to close, and the last thing Lucas wanted was any damaging union activity. The removal and reinstalla-

A decisive moment. Austin-Morris general manager George Turnbull, right, offers Bill Lucas the taxi manufacturing plant at the 1970 Commercial Motor Show.

At the 1971 Motor Show, Bill Lucas was approached by Sir Laurence Olivier, who asked to buy a special FL2. Sir Laurence needed a cab fitted out with a tape recorder as a mobile office; he said he was always performing one play, rehearsing a second and learning a third, and a cab was the best and most private place to concentrate on his lines! He ordered a cab, the first of three, trimmed in Bedford Cord.

Industrial Relations

In the 1960s and 1970s, industrial relations were a blight on the motor industry, but Bill Lucas was able to keep his ship running smoothly, and he could boast that during his tenure he never had a major strike. This was due to three main things. Firstly, Carbodies was a relatively small organization; even during the heights of BSA's ownership the workforce was only around 1,000, and Bill Lucas knew every aspect of its operations. Secondly, the measured day rate had become standardized throughout the industry. In this, a price was fixed for a job by the union concerned. It sounded fine, as cost controllers knew the price of each task, but in practice it allowed production workers to knock off early if their work for that day was finished, and shop floors all around the industry could be idle half the day. Also, if the procedure of any operation was altered, the stewards would argue they wanted four men instead of three men to do it. Where a job was turned down by the inspection because of poor quality, extra people might be brought in to correct the bad work. With a labour shortage in the West Midlands, the unions held the whip hand.

In Carbodies' case where there was a great deal of hand-work, Bill Lucas continued with the old industry practice of piecework, pricing an individual job and allowing each worker to produce, and thereby earn, as much as he or she was able and willing to do. Day-work money was only allowed if inspection rejected something. The works manager, either Bernard Bevin or, later, Peter Dawson, would have to approve payment for the rework, subject to who was responsible. If it was the line-worker's own bad work, then he had to put it right for no extra; but if the fault was in some way due to production techniques, then Bevin or Dawson would authorize extra payment for the job to be redone. As a guide to the level of quality control, this practice cost Carbodies an average of less than £5 per taxi in the late 1960s.

One negotiating point Bill Lucas would use in the case of a dispute – and Carbodies was by no means entirely trouble free – was to tell the men on the shop floor, 'I'm not just employing *you*: I'm paying the wages of your families, of your kids and paying your mortgage. Think about that first.' Industrial relations on the shop floor are, in the final analysis, totally dependent on the people involved. Bill Lucas freely admits that one very important factor in his strike-free tenure was his relationship with his convenor, Harry Carroll. Bill praised Harry for possessing a high degree of plain old-fashioned common sense and an understanding of the workings of the factory, his own men and the unions. In Lucas' own words: 'Harry Carroll was the finest convenor in the motor car factories in Coventry. Whatever problem I had, we always managed to ease it out.'

tion of the chassis plant would be no small matter. The tracks, jigs, overhead cranes and all the other equipment would have to be moved from Adderley Park in their entirety, and with as little upset to taxi production as possible. BSA's main board approved the money, and in just two-and-a-half weeks in the spring of 1971 the whole chassis manufacturing plant was moved into the bay at Carbodies which had once been used for the production of Ford coupés. This was achieved without a single redundancy, as promised – in fact the six men and a foreman that were transferred were to earn higher rates at Carbodies than they had been at Austin! In a report in *BSA Group News* of April 1971, Bill Lucas gave credit to works engineer Eric Blackburn and recently appointed works manager, Peter Dawson, in these words: '. . . they have put in a great deal of time and effort, but they have taken this extra responsibility in their stride.'

BSA HEAD FOR TROUBLE

For the first time in its history, Carbodies was a complete vehicle manufacturer; but even so, the outlook was looking bleak as the 1960s came to a close, for BSA was heading for serious trouble. From a high of over thirty companies in 1957, the group was down to a mere handful. The motorcycle division was the biggest, and it was quickly going broke. The management felt that they could not successfully achieve the design and production of quality small bikes, and they did not believe that the Japanese would ever produce big bikes to meet the challenge in that sphere. All the models BSA offered were ill-equipped, poorly made and unreliable, and sales were down both at home and in the all-important American market. Disaster loomed, and Carbodies was an innocent victim about to be caught in the middle.

9 Manganese Bronze Holdings to the Rescue

When you get in a cab in London don't, whatever you do, tell the driver you own the company that makes the cab – you'll never hear the last of it!

Advice from Bill Lucas to Dennis
Poore, chairman of Manganese
Bronze Holdings, plc

ON THE EDGE OF DISASTER

BSA was once the largest maker of motorcycles in the world. Then in 1966, Lionel Jofeh was appointed as the Motorcycle Division's managing director. Jofeh has been described as arrogant, distant and without any understanding of the motorcycle industry, and under his tenure, poor build quality and unreliability resulted, adversely affecting all models. No new ranges were introduced to meet the challenge of the Japanese, and between 1969 and 1970 the entire BSA group returned profits of only £1½m, a dismal figure for such a large conglomerate.

In June 1971 Jofeh offered his resignation and BSA's board accepted it; this was before a disastrous £3m loss was revealed on 30 July. Eric Turner also resigned, and the board offered the chair to Lord Shawcross.

Barclays Bank approved the appointment and granted a £10m loan, and under Shawcross the Motorcycle Division's fortunes looked as if they would recover. However, even though sales showed improvement, losses of over £1.1m were recorded in the first half of 1972, due to disruption by the workforce at Meriden, a rise in bank interest charges and a drop in US sales as a result of the devaluation of the dollar. The once-mighty BSA was on the edge of disaster, and the future of Carbodies, along with the other companies in the BSA Group, was in jeopardy.

ENTER MANGANESE BRONZE HOLDINGS

In June 1972 Lord Shawcross asked the Department of Trade and Industry, under Edward Heath's Conservative government, for financial assistance so that a new range of models could be introduced as soon as possible. The DTI responded by asking Dennis Poore to help; Poore had moved his Manganese Bronze Holdings from the manufacture of ships' propellers to the motorcycle business when he bought Villiers Engines and Norton. By November 1972 the DTI announced that they were prepared to make up to £20m available, subject to the condition that BSA and Norton Villiers should merge. According to the book *A Historical Summary* published in 1974 by Manganese Bronze Holdings, Dennis Poore was initially worried because it would dilute Norton Villiers'

Bill Lucas takes Lord Shawcross, right, on a tour of Carbodies' factory.

the remainder was to come from BSA share-holders in share-for-share exchange. MBH would sell the new motorcycle company the whole of the share capital of Norton Villiers for £1.6m. MBH would supply further funds to the new company by buying BSA's non-motorcycle companies for £3.5m; the latter were BSA Metal Components, BSA Guns, Birtley Engineering, BSA Heating, and of course Carbodies. Many within the BSA Group felt that Poore's offer of £3.5m for the non-motorcycle interests was derisory; Carbodies was valued at more than £5m on its own, and this group combined had been expected to return a profit in excess of £1m in 1973. However, the BSA board had little choice but to recommend that its share-holders accept MBH's offer. In his announcement to the House of Commons on 15 March 1973, Christopher Chataway MP, the Minister of State in the DTI, referred to the new company as Norton Villiers Triumph (NVT), a phrase used for easy reference in discussions; and thus the 'new baby' was christened.

THE TAKEOVER

At Holyhead Road the news of BSA's impending demise was causing a great deal of worry. Would they close Carbodies down? Mann and Overton were worried too, for their own future and for that of the London cab trade as a whole. By now the FX4 was the only cab available to the London market, and if the new owners discontinued it, the Conditions of Fitness might have to be abandoned, the whole industry would be thrown into a downward spiral and the unique London cab would be a thing of the past.

Bill Lucas was approached in late 1972 by Colin Chapman, the mercurial boss of Lotus Cars, with an offer of a job as managing director. Carbodies had been making

resources, but agreed, having considered that the DTI had to support the whole industry or not at all. Besides, he would not want a government-sponsored competitor.

For BSA, the choice was to agree a merger or to try and survive without financial support. They needed investment to develop new models, and Barclays were not at all keen to help BSA without the support of the DTI. Finally proposals were put forward for a new company to be formed, capitalized by £10.3m: this would include £4.8m from the government and £3.6m from MBH, and

135

stainless-steel trim for the new Lotus Elan S2, and the two men had come to understand each other very well. Lucas expressed an interest, but wanted to see what MBH had to offer; and Chapman had to temper his disappointment when Lucas was offered far better conditions by Dennis Poore than he had had under BSA, with a higher salary and greater autonomy. Moreover Poore assured Lucas that he would not interfere in the day-to-day running of Carbodies, leaving this to his group managing director John Neville, and would only visit the factory on rare occasions. He was to prove as good as his word, only sitting in on board meetings held at MBH's City of London headquarters in Love Lane, to keep in touch. Much to the relief of everyone at both Carbodies and Mann and Overton, MBH wanted to continue production of the FX4. The future was beginning to look promising for Carbodies, and might have been better were it not for a certain huge cloud on the horizon: Meriden.

TROUBLE AT MERIDEN

The plan was worked out for a two-factory scheme: BSA at Small Heath and Norton Villiers in Wolverhampton. Meriden would have to close because there was not the capital available in the plan to keep it open. The unions at Meriden objected uncompromisingly to the closure and staged a blockade of the factory, supported by Leslie Huckfield, the MP for Nuneaton, and Bill Lapworth, the Transport and General Workers Union district official for Coventry. They met Dennis Poore and proposed that NVT should sell Meriden and its main product, the Triumph Bonneville motorcycle, to a workers' co-operative. Poore was willing to sell the factory, even at a discount, but would not under any circumstances sell off the 'Bonnie'; a major dollar earner. The im-

mediate viability of NVT depended upon it. All negotiations failed, and by November the workers were issued redundancy notices; meanwhile the union blockade continued.

The general election of February 1974 ousted Edward Heath and put Harold Wilson's Labour government back in power. Anthony Wedgewood Benn, a lifelong left-wing socialist, was made Secretary of State for Industry. Benn supported the Meriden workforce, against the advice of his own civil servants and cabinet colleagues, who maintained that the occupation was illegal. The blockade continued, although the majority of Meriden's sacked workers were finding jobs elsewhere, and NVT had received offers for the factory from other industries. Also the three-day week brought about by the miners' strike hit production at Norton, spelling serious trouble for NVT. Nothing had been produced at Meriden since September 1973, and despite efforts from a Labour government intent on preserving jobs, and media pressure painting NVT as the villains of the piece, no progress was made to establish NVT's two-factory plan or to get Small Heath and Wolverhampton back to full-time work and earn some much-needed dollars. Needed they certainly were: NVT announced losses of almost £5m for the period up to the end of 1973.

Publicity in the press and on television had sided with the Meriden workers, despite support for NVT from the government and the all-important Triumph dealers in the USA. BSA's workers, who had an intense rivalry with Meriden from the days when BSA and Triumph were separate companies, were also sided with NVT, and in a mass meeting in front of Benn finally got the press to see NVT's argument. But it was all too late, and the government was not prepared to fund the cost of keeping Meriden within NVT to the tune of an estimated £12–15m. Finally a delay in the provision of some £8m of export credit guarantees to NVT forced Dennis Poore to let the Meriden Co-op have their factory and the Triumph Bonneville motorcycle. It cost the government nearly £5m, including £3.9m paid to NVT. Small compensation against the losses of 1973 and the eventual closure of Small Heath in 1975. NVT were left with Norton at Wolverhampton, and were a lot poorer than when they started. The whole story of BSA's demise, of Meriden and NVT can be found in Steve Wilson's series of books, *British Motorcycles Since 1950*; it is retold here with the kind consent of Mr Wilson.

In the long term, NVT was wound up and Wolverhampton closed, with losses estimated at between £3.5m and £5m and debts of £6m. MBH as a holding company were not technically the owners of either NVT or the former BSA companies, but shareholders in it, their role being to invest in the companies in its group, and to re-invest the profits generated in new product and plant. However, the fact that NVT suffered a considerable loss meant that money that might have been invested, never materialized. Nevertheless, production continued at Carbodies, which was still a viable concern with existing contracts to fulfil, and new work to be found.

THE FINEST CAR IN THE WORLD

Introduced in 1965, the Silver Shadow was the first unit-construction Rolls-Royce. It had been under development since the mid-1950s and Bill Lucas had worked on the prototypes when he was at Airflow Streamline. Thrupp and Maberly were producing a new, 'stretched version' of the Silver Shadow from 1969, but did not have the manpower to lead-load the extended body. Carbodies were to take the job on, lead-

loading the bodies to Rolls-Royce's exacting standards at a rate of five cars a week, until Thrupp and Maberly could engage enough skilled men to restart the job.

EUROPEAN REGULATIONS

In 1973 Britain joined the European Common Market, and all current passenger-carrying vehicles had to comply with European rules that were to come into force the following year. These rules included the fitting of anti-burst door locks and protective steering. In addition all vehicles had to be crash-tested, which involved running them on a test track into a concrete wall at 30mph (50km/h), to study whether passengers would survive such a crash. Austin, who were steadily losing interest in the FX4, had to engineer the changes to the chassis to enable the cab to pass the test, which included fitting a crash link into the steering column, and a new steering wheel with a rubberized centre bush in place of the horn button. Jake Donaldson also designed a flat fascia in Stelvatite, a PVC-covered metal, with a moulded cowl. The matter of the exterior door handles was not so simple to resolve. Wilmot Breeden, who had made all the door handles used by Carbodies, produced the disc latch lock used on most contemporary cars, but it couldn't be made to fit the taxi. The Bomero lock made by the German Happich company was adapted, along with a push-button handle to suit, and the interior handles were moved to the centre of the door to accommodate the mechanism.

Mann and Overton were told that Carbodies couldn't afford to supply a cab for the Motor Industry Research Association to test; they would have to supply one. The cab would be a write-off, but if it wasn't tested it would mean no more cabs. Jake Donaldson arranged for the test and to take the cab over. Scheduled for midday, the test was delayed until about three o'clock because MIRA were having problems that morning with a Lamborghini. Bill Lucas remembers how the event went:

When they tested the Lamborghini, the engine was right into the driver's compartment. It was terrible, one of the worst they'd ever done. When I got there they'd just finished bolting the taxi onto the railway track. They ran it down at 30mph and hit the concrete. The crash link collapsed but the steering wheel was almost where it was before, and the only thing that broke was the division glass – it was within ⅝in of where it was before the cab hit the wall. They said it was the best one they'd ever done. Of course it was because it had a chassis. It came through with flying colours.

One of the revised models marked a milestone in production of the FX4: on the 28 March 1974, the 25,000th example rolled off the production line. On being interviewed by the *Coventry Evening Telegraph*, Bill Lucas said that Carbodies expected to make 40,000 more cabs before it was replaced, after perhaps a further five years. His plans for a new model, germinated after the demise of LM11, were already under way.

Another milestone was reached in 1974, when finance director G. A. 'Steve' Stevens retired. His place on the board was taken by his deputy, Stan Troman, who had started with Carbodies after finishing his National Service in 1948. Steve had been with Carbodies for a total of twenty-nine years; he left the company shortly after the outbreak of the Second World War, but returned in 1948, to serve, in turn, three masters: Bobby Jones, BSA and Manganese Bronze. He retired to live in Coventry with his wife.

At the 1973 Commercial Motor Show, the three men with overall responsibility for producing the FX4: in the driver's seat is Robert Overton, managing director of Mann and Overton; centre, Bill Lucas; and right John Neville, managing director of Manganese Bronze Holdings.

A BRAKE ON BRAKE IMPROVEMENTS

A 2.5-litre engine, fitted from late 1971, had improved the FX4's performance, but the drum brakes had remained unchanged since 1958 and modern traffic demanded better. There were two options: either to fit disc brakes or to uprate the old ones by fitting larger drums and a servo. Disc brakes once fitted to the Austin Westminster would foul the suspension arm and restrict the turning circle, so either a new braking system or new front suspension would have to be designed. Peter James, working immediately under engineering director Jake Donaldson, produced a design for full servo braking with pendant pedals. Permission for any alterations to the FX4 still had to be obtained from Austin at Longbridge, and this they gave happily; after all, they were fast losing interest in the FX4. However, when it came to paying for the modification, Mann and Overton refused. The appalling inflation of the mid-seventies had brought their finances to a low level; fares were not keeping pace, and the price of a cab had increased from £1,500 in 1971 to almost £7,000 in 1978. Mann and Overton were going through the toughest period of their history and there was no money in the bank to pay for something that they hadn't ordered. Bill Lucas told them that if they wouldn't contribute, then neither would Carbodies, and so the whole project was put on the shelf.

But Mann and Overton knew that in truth the brakes should be improved, although they maintained that as a city vehicle the cab's brakes were adequate for the job; they had experimented with ventilated brake drums in the early 1970s, with unsatisfactory results. They specified, incredibly, that a system with a servo working on the front brakes only should be designed and fitted. In 1976 cabs went into service with the new

brakes; the results were alarming, and the cab trade was in uproar. At speeds below 10mph (15km/h) the brakes would grab and the cab would lurch to stop (one cannot help but mention the reason why the PCO had refused to allow the fitting of four wheel brakes in the 1920s: they would jolt the passengers!). Front brake drums began wearing out in 5,000 miles (8,000km), and in some cases front brake linings were lasting a mere 2,000 miles (3,000km). Despite it being common knowledge amongst motor engineers that a servo fitted to front brakes on their own would cause snatching, Mann and Overton would not officially accept that the system was unsound, and declared that drivers had to learn to drive the FX4 with the new system.

USA CALLING ONCE MORE

Bernard Bates of Austin's sales department in Redditch rang Bill Lucas and said they had received an enquiry for a taxi built to PCO specs for New York. Austin were among some twelve companies, including Peugeot and Alfa Romeo, that had been approached, so the London-type cab was on trial alongside what the rest of the world had to offer. As Austin-Morris were losing interest in the FX4, they asked if someone from Carbodies should go to New York to represent them. Bill Lucas and Jake Donaldson went, with David Southwell. One can only surmise that the FX4 was still not popular with New York operators, besides which two other factors were working against it at this time: first, its lack of power compared to the big American sedans was a distinct handicap; and second, the contract would be for 5,000 year, and they would be in CKD (completely knocked-down kit form) for assembly in the US. At that time Carbodies was making less than 2,000 cabs a year, and simply didn't have the

Ziggy Kraus admires Frank Lawton's handiwork on the specially prepared Silver Jubilee taxi which was taken to Buckingham Palace and driven in the grounds of the palace by His Royal Highness the Prince of Wales.

The Queen's Silver Jubilee, 1977. Geoff Trotter, managing director of the London General Cab Company, invited the Prince of Wales to the 'General' in Brixton. The prince suggested instead that the cab trade 'came round to his place'. Geoff Trotter, left, introduces the prince to, from left, J. R. Lewis and Bernard Bates of Leyland Cars, Bill Lucas and Jake Donaldson.

production capacity. Again the opportunity to break into the US market had to be passed over. However, had the insurmountable financial problems resulting from Meriden not happened, investment cash might have been available and the US market might have been a real money-maker for the late 1970s.

EXIT THE TRIUMPH 2000

In 1972, production of the Triumph estate peaked at 2,785. At an average fifty-five per week, this was more than the taxi; in fact at one point, because of the seasonal nature of the motor trade, some 100 estates were coming off the tracks at Carbodies. So much for George Turnbull's belief that it would sell no more than twenty per week! From then on as the model grew old, sales declined, and in 1977 the 2000 ceased production, with a mere 303 made that year. But the 2000 range was almost restarted. The Rover-Triumph division of British Leyland, as it was by then, asked Pressed Steel to produce another 12,000 shells, including 3,000 for conversion into estates. Carbodies had not yet scrapped the tools or jigs, so for them, restarting the job would be no problem; but Pressed Steel's price for the extra shells was too high for

British Leyland, and they decided not to go ahead. The Triumph estate was the last private car conversion to be built by Carbodies to a major manufacturer's specification, and their dependence on the taxi was now almost 100 per cent.

With the Triumph gone, Carbodies had to find something extra to earn money, or more staff would have to be laid off. Each major motor manufacturer makes what is known as a lifetime run of replacement body panels when a model ceases production. This run is

The Triumph 2000 estate continued in MkII form until 1977. Here, left, the bare saloon body-shells are placed on a trolley where the roof is removed . . .

. . . and right, the new estate roof welded into place.

intended to last ten years, but often the amount made is underestimated. Production cannot be interrupted to make parts for obsolete models, so outside contractors are brought in to supplement the shortfall. Jan Scott was a young man who had been apprenticed at Carbodies in the 1950s and was working as a rate fixer. Bill Lucas sent Scott around the big companies promoting Carbodies' capability in the manufacture of spare body panels, and the business he won in this respect was to make an important contribution to Carbodies' balance sheet in what was a tough time for the entire British motor industry.

CARBODIES' SALES AND SERVICE AND THE MINICAB

From its beginnings in 1961 Michael Gotla's brainchild, the minicab, had spread across the country, unregulated except for the acts of parliament that govern all road users. Abuse was rife: many vehicles were unsafe,

and the game was often in the hands of disreputable characters. Fears for public safety were widely expressed, both in London and the provinces. The first successful attempt to regulate the minicab trade was brought about within the Local Authorities (Miscellaneous Provisions) Act of 1976. Specific sections of this catch-all act gave local authorities outside London the discretion to adopt, within certain parameters, such legislation as they saw fit to suit their own patch. One paragraph stated that no vehicle that had been designed as a purpose-built taxi could be used for private hire. The first that Carbodies heard of this was the publication of the law. Bill Lucas was furious, because sales of the FL2 to the private hire trade in parts of the provinces whose taxi licensing authority did not demand compliance to London regulations were an important part of the Carbodies' income, and this was being wiped out at a stroke. The FL2 had some following in the provincial market, as it combined the advantages of the taxi or limousine without the

A Tokyo Arms Company taxi. Manganese Bronze began importing Japanese shotguns to be sold under the BSA name, and in a move designed to circumvent the tortuous Japanese import system, Tokyo Arms imported taxis for sale in Japan.

costs of a Daimler or Rolls-Royce. Lucas lobbied right up to ministerial level, but without success. The government's argument was that it was the shape of the vehicle that identified it as a taxi, and it would cause confusion in the public's mind. It was important for the public to be able to identify it as such, and the private hire trade should not be allowed to use a vehicle with which

they might be tempted to ply illegally for hire on the streets.

This sounded the death-knell of the FL2 as a hire car. Austin's Bernard Bates had travelled the country, in vain trying to persuade licensing authorities to adopt purpose-built taxis. Moreover, by now, Austin themselves had no more active interest in the FX4 and FL2. Bates admitted defeat, and so Bill Lucas took the matter of sales of both models outside London into his own hands, forming in 1976 Carbodies Sales and Service. He would be managing director, and John Neville, MD of Manganese Bronze, would be a second director. The new company's responsibility would be to take over what Austin's Redditch sales department had done for the taxi, and provide a support system to markets that did not have a local main dealer. Mann and Overton had the London market, and since the early 1970s John Paton had built a thriving and important network in Glasgow, Edinburgh and Cross Street, Manchester. Now the rest of the country would be covered directly from

Coventry, with a particular interest in the hinterland of the West Midlands. Bill Drew, works superintendent under Peter Dawson, was also given a position in the new company. Drew's special understanding of the British taxi market proved invaluable to the new company; he had an almost instinctive feel for what was wanted in the trade.

THE FX5

Tired of Mann and Overton's reluctance to spend money improving the FX4, Bill Lucas went to Dennis Poore and said he wanted to

A one-fifth scale model of the FX5. Bill Lucas took this to show Dennis Poore, who gave the go-ahead to begin development immediately.

The full-sized mock-up of the FX5, its modern appearance a complete contrast to the antiquated look of the FX4.

develop his own cab, independent of the London dealers. Poore and the board gave an initial agreement, and Lucas instructed Jake Donaldson to design what was to become the FX5. Taking into consideration the extremely high cost of engineering a car body, it made sense to see if any existing vehicle could be adapted. Jake Donaldson had some liking for the Range Rover; he felt that it might make a good basis for a cab, especially the big roof panel. A feasibility study was done over a period of nearly three years, but the body-shell was considered to be too bulky and wrongly proportioned for a taxi, and it was eventually rejected.

From that time, Bill Lucas began work on a completely new design of cab. He knew in his own mind what he wanted: one to suit the cab trade and to give the driver and operator what *they* wanted, not to give the cab trade what was the easiest and cheapest to make, regardless of the progress made by the motor industry around it. Jake Donaldson and his assistant Peter James produced an extruded steel tube chassis, and mounted the running gear from the new Rover 3500,

1979, and very much the final form of the Austin-badged cab. The cab trade was still screaming out for a new vehicle, but when the chrome over-riders were replaced by plastic ones (simply because the old tools had worn out and were far too expensive to replace) they paradoxically complained bitterly that the traditional appearance had been ruined!

which had been introduced in 1976. This included McPherson strut front suspension with disc brakes, and coil-spring rear suspension for the rigid rear axle. Both Lucas and John Neville bought Rover 3500s for themselves to test the running gear. Donaldson styled the body himself, and a quarter-scale model was made up. Bill Lucas took the model to Dennis Poore at Manganese Bronze's head office in the city of London, and as soon as Poore saw it, he exclaimed: 'That's it – go ahead!' The new

image was exactly what both Poore and Carbodies wanted.

A full-size mock-up was put together, and those representatives from the cab trade, including Jack Everitt, and Mann and Overton's David Southwell, who saw it, liked it. The new cab was modern in appearance and in specification and looked very promising, and there was a good feeling within the whole company about the project. However, Carbodies had not the where-withal to engineer the whole body; the toolroom and tool-making facilities had been run down, and the job was subcontracted out for tender. Bearing in mind that MBH was still recovering from the after-effects of the Meriden saga, and the likely cost of tooling for the new body, seeds of doubts about the FX5's viability were sown in Dennis Poore's mind.

NEW ENGINE TRIALS

After deciding not to implement the Ryder Report on the future of British Leyland, James Callaghan's Labour government put Michael Edwardes in charge of the ailing giant, and gave him the daunting task of making the unwieldy mess work profitably. Edwardes saw that rationalization was essential. The Courthouse Green engine plant in Coventry, where the 2.5 litre diesel was made, was one of many factories that had to close, and the engine plant sold off. Unlike the chassis plant, however, the engine was not destined for Carbodies, but was to be sent to India to be installed, ironically in a revamped version of the Leyland 20 that had been sold there in the late 1960s.

Austin-Morris simply did not offer an alternative engine and gearbox. Fortunately they had given Carbodies three years' notice of the change, and Bill Lucas began looking round for a replacement. A similar type of engine was being made within British Leyland, the 2.25 litre Land Rover unit. Lucas consulted his old friend Harry Webster, who had been the engineering brain behind the cars of Standard-Triumph's 'golden years' of the 1960s. Webster was unequivocal about the Land Rover unit, and told Lucas that it would be totally wrong for the taxi. Its power characteristics were all wrong, being a high-revving, relatively low-torque unit, whereas the need for low-speed power in the taxi was vital; also its valve

train and combustion chamber design were poor. Furthermore it had never been tested under the sort of conditions found in London taxi traffic.

Lucas' next port of call was Perkins, but they had stopped making their small 4/99 diesel, concentrating instead on a new, larger 3-litre unit. They could not give Carbodies the assurance of the engine lasting five years. Ford would only guarantee their 2.3 litre unit for 45,000 miles (72,405km) which would never do – a London cab would do that sort of mileage inside a year. Finally Lucas had a contact at Rootes, and through him got in touch with Peugeot. The long-established French company were delighted to be involved with such an internationally renowned vehicle, and offered their new 2.5 unit to try. Lucas and Jake Donaldson delivered a cab to Peugeot's factory in Socheux, and three months later it was ready. Bill and Jake collected it, with the old Austin engine stuffed in the boot – it took a lot of explaining to customs at Dover why the cab had a non-standard engine, whilst the log book contained the number of an engine that was in the passenger compartment!

Birmingham fleet operator Horace Faulkner, a personal friend of Bill Lucas, was given the cab to test the engine. Lucas recalls this trial period:

> The cab ran twenty-two hours a day, and in the twelve months before I retired it was only off the road once. Horace phoned me in the small hours to report that the cab had broken down. I told him to bring it over, and I phoned Peugeot. They sent someone over on the first plane, a couple of guys with a cylinder head, and they fixed it, and flew back the same day. If I had stayed there, I wouldn't have bothered about any other engine.

On the day of his retirement, Bill Lucas recalled that the factory went suddenly quiet. He was soon asked to come to the canteen, where a surprise farewell party was laid on for him. Mrs Doris Lucas is seated at the table and works manager Peter Dawson stands behind Bill. Although it appears that there are not many other people present, the photograph was taken from amongst a large gathering of employees.

A LOST OPPORTUNITY

Bill Lucas had been pressing Dennis Poore to buy Mann and Overton. He felt that, in the first instance he could increase sales of the FX4 in the provincial market by improving the cab, because he would not have Mann and Overton blocking what they felt were unnecessary modifications, and creating an artificial waiting list in London by only ordering a more or less fixed number of cabs per week. That waiting list at the time was almost two years, even though Carbodies had the production capacity virtually to eliminate it. Lucas would also have a freer hand, finance permitting, to develop the replacement that the cab trade in London and major cities so desperately needed. Poore declined. In 1978, following a dawn raid on their stock, Mann and Overton were taken over by banking concern Lloyds and Scottish plc. Mann and Overton were happy with this, although it meant that the control had been lost by the Overton family. There was the greater financial security of ownership by a larger concern, but most importantly there was a synergy with the new owners, Lloyds and Scottish obviously being keen to be involved with the provision of finance to cab drivers. For Carbodies, however, the opportunity to have greater control of their affairs had been lost.

THE DEPARTURE OF BILL LUCAS

By February 1979, ill health had caught up with Bill Lucas, and at the age of fifty-nine he took early retirement, just before the prototype FX5 was finished. He left after more than thirty years' service, only interrupted by a spell at Airflow Streamline. He brought Carbodies through some extremely difficult times, and by the time of his retirement the firm was enjoying high profits, and was the best performing company within Managnese Bronze Holdings. It might be fairly said that those who followed on owe the survival of the company to his ability to handle enginéering, management and personnel problems with equal skill.

A Sharp Lesson for Dennis Poore

Immediately following the takeover of Carbodies by Managnese Bronze, Bill Lucas had advised Dennis Poore never to tell the driver of any taxi he took that he owned the company that made it. Poore, in his own inimitable way, disregarded this advice for the first few days, but when he next saw Lucas: 'You're right!' he said, 'I got into a cab and told the driver I'd just bought the company that made his cab, and you wouldn't believe the abuse I got!' To his dying day, however, Dennis Poore was immensely proud of the fact that his company made the famous London 'black cab'.

---

10   A New Direction

'The best laid schemes of mice and men gang aft a-gley.'

Robert Burns

On Bill Lucas' retirement, the task of finding his replacement fell to MBH's Dennis Poore and John Neville. They found it in Grant Lockhart, who was then a plant director with BL cars at Cowley. A post-graduate mining engineer from Glasgow University, Lockhart went into management consultancy when the UK mining industry fell into decline. After working in a variety of British Leyland plants, he was offered his first permanent position with the corporation, at Longbridge. Disagreeing with Michael Edwardes' second wave of changes, Lockhart took a 'fairly generous settlement', and left. The first job actually offered to him, in late 1979, was that of managing director at Carbodies.

John Neville, already seriously ill, did not survive to see Grant Lockhart take up his position. With the brief not simply to replace Bill Lucas, but to steer the company towards the future, Lockhart recalls his first introduction to Carbodies:

> I couldn't believe the company when I got there – they had what I called a sub-contractor's outlook on life. Really it was very sleepy compared to the hurly-burly of the mainstream motor industry. They were terribly sheltered because of this monopoly on the London taxi cab. Dennis Poore was a typical,

very autocratic old school company chairman. He said, 'People keep telling me I've got to build a new taxi and spend millions on it, but there's nothing wrong with this one – I use it regularly. Take a fresh look at it and tell me whether I need a new one or not.

Whether or not a new cab was to be made, the FX4 was still very much in production; in fact it was the only vehicle coming off Carbodies' tracks, and was truly the company's bread-winner. Much of the production of spares had been run down, so it was important to maximize its profitability. In fact a significant change had been taking place in the nature of the London cab trade: with hire-purchase restrictions eased and the minimum deposit reduced considerably, it was far easier for cab drivers to buy a brand-new cab without building up to it step by step as before. Mann and Overton, who had long been in the business of financing both owner drivers and fleet sales, introduced a new form of finance for the individual: leasing, where for about the same amount down as a monthly payment, a mush could have a brand-new cab. Even though the FX4 was by now very long in the tooth, the lure of a 'new 'un' was very strong.

Grant Lockhart took the view, as did Bill Lucas before him, that the driver's comforts should be taken into consideration, provided the passengers' privacy and comfort were not compromised. A range of different trim levels were offered: the FL, a basic cab for the fleet owner and the HL and HLS was given added

The FL1 had been a successful passenger ambulance in the 1950s, and in 1980 an FX4 was converted to a six-seater ambulance for Nottingham Area Health Authority as an out-patient transfer vehicle. A specialist one-off vehicle, Carbodies tried to market it. There was a lot of interest, but no more were sold.

levels of equipment such as a vinyl roof and the newly allowed sunshine roof, and midnight blue and dark brown were added to the original colour options of white and carmine red. In addition, after a long period of negotiation with the PCO, personal radios were at last allowed in the front of cabs, and the take-up for these options was excellent.

We have said that if it wasn't for Mann and Overton there would be no Carbodies, and no London cab trade as we know it; but their attitude to business and to change in general was anathema to Carbodies. Grant Lockhart recalls how the board was struggling with the entrenched attitude that Mann and Overton had, even then.

The relationship between the company and Mann and Overton wasn't very healthy. Mann and Overton's waiting list was artificial because they only *wanted* to sell thirty a week. Andrew Overton would come in and say, 'We *only want this number*', and we'd say, 'We've got a factory here!' I had a battle with them to get even simple things done, like two-speed wipers: they said

they didn't need it, as the vehicle was stopped most of the time. In my environment the manufacturer made the decision and the product sold; if you made mistakes, it didn't sell. The taxi trade was quite different. Because of their dominant position, Mann and Overton could switch the market on and off and Carbodies could do nothing about it.

CR6- A NEW TAXI?

Sales outside London would have been far better with a new vehicle, and following Dennis Poore's instruction, Bill Lucas's FX5 project came under Grant Lockhart's scrutiny. He decided to scrap it, and recalls the reasons why:

They hadn't taken any of the modern idiom to try and lift the image. The chassis was absolutely massive, with no attempts to use any modern materials to get rid of any unnecessary weight

Rover asked Carbodies to prepare a clay buck for an estate version of the SD1. This was the furthest Carbodies got with it before Rover took the car over and built it to roadworthy standards for Michael Edwardes to use as his own company car.

that the FX4 had because of its design. My strong recommendation was that the FX5 as it was originally conceived was not the way to go. That alone did not answer the question of whether they needed a new one or not, but I didn't think that the FX5 was the answer.

So what was the answer? Costs for developing new vehicle bodies had risen to an even greater degree than in the late sixties. Certainly the estimates for tooling the FX5 body was considerable; that was an important factor in the decision to scrap it, and it made economic sense at least to investigate the possibilities of adapting an

The chassis from the FX5, adapted to take the Land Rover engine. The hooped cross-member above the gearbox tail-shaft is a leftover from the FX5, and would be altered for wheelchair accessiblity.

existing body. Grant Lockhart re-examined Bill Lucas's previously discarded idea of the using the Range Rover body as a base, and decided that this was 'the way to go'.

The FX5 chassis was to be the basis. Despite Lockhart's criticism, it was there, in prototype form, ready to be used. Range Rovers at this time had two doors, so Jake Donaldson and his chief body engineer Peter James began to look at the development needed to make the conversion. Artwork was prepared, a scale model built, and Donaldson and Lockhart took it to Land Rover as a proposal. Lockhart put it to Land Rover's managing director Mike Hodgkinson that the proposed new cab would give him an extra outlet for his panels, components and powertrain, and it would minimize Carbodies' tooling cost, because in making 2,000 a year they couldn't afford a new set of hard tools.

Hodgkinson and his board gave it the nod. Furthermore the four doors, with internal hinges, caught Hodgkinson's eye. Range Rover was almost at the point of ceasing production, and Rover knew from their

The CR6 artwork, submitted to Land Rover's board; at this early stage the resemblance to Range Rover is very close. The letters on the bonnet say 'City Rover'.

The scale model taxi presented to Land Rover, alongside a model of its parent vehicle.

market research that a four-door version would have a greater sales potential. Hodgkinson suggested to Lockhart that if Carbodies could put four doors on a Range Rover, why couldn't they? Here was an opportunity for Lockhart, and he offered to do the four-door conversion for the Range Rover as part of a deal that included Range Rover bodies. There would be some urgency attached to this, however, because Hodgkinson wanted first vehicles down the production line within a year. A price was given, and a deal agreed on the basis of Carbodies having the manufacturing of all the new Range Rover doors, plus Carbodies paying for the tooling of the front door, which would become part of the new cab.

From then on the project got under way.

The Land Rover engine, mated to the Rover SD1 five-speed manual gearbox, with Carbodies' own two-piece bellhousing.

Sadly Jake Donaldson died within months of the start. Jake had been with the company since the 1940s and had worked on the development and tooling design of all three previous taxi projects. In June 1980 he had a serious heart attack, which put him in hospital, and he suffered a second shortly afterwards, from which he never recovered. Following Donaldson's death, Grant Lockhart asked Peter James to take over his work; although in reality Peter had Jake's job to do plus his own, working for almost two years in the position of acting engineering director. Eventually he declined a seat on the board: it wasn't his style, and he remained as senior engineer in the drawing office. James remembers Donaldson, a native of Gloucestershire, as someone whom he admired greatly, who could 'make you feel a million dollars to work for' – an extremely significant individual. There is no doubt that the quiet, shy Donaldson was one of a handful of people whose considerable talents had made a major contribution to Carbodies' fortunes.

With the connections with Rover, a 2.25-litre Land Rover diesel engine was chosen, and the FX5 chassis, intended originally for Peugeot power, was adapted to take it. A Range Rover shell was taken into Carbodies' experimental department and extensively modified. To make the new cab recognizable from a Range Rover, the nose was redesigned so as to take headlight and indicator units from the Morris Ital. The export market, which had been so difficult to crack in a sustained way, was given due attention from the start: thus the new cab was to be built in both right- and left-hand-drive form from the outset, as were hot climate and US versions. The decision was made to announce the forthcoming cab early to the trade before even Carbodies had a running prototype. A quarter-scale model was released in June 1980 at a trade dinner

in Manchester, to a great reception. Things were beginning to look promising. At long last London, and all the rest of the UK's major cities, were looking forward to a new cab.

PROBLEMS FOR THE CR6

A requirement which was to compromise CR6's progress cropped up very early in its programme: wheelchair accessibility. In 1980, the Department of Transport had begun its preparation for the International Year of the Disabled by holding a seminar and inviting representatives from disabled persons' groups, transport providers and vehicle manufacturers. The moving force for the conference was an up-and-coming young civil servant, Ann Frye. She asked those wheelchair-bound delegates where the department should begin in trying to meet their needs and they all said, 'Start with taxis. Pavements are so bad that even if we could get on trains and buses, we can't even get to the stations and bus stops.' So their most important need was for door-to-door transport.

One of the delegates at the conference was Mann and Overton's new managing director Andrew Overton. Carbodies had already produced a one-off wheelchair-accessible cab as a private vehicle for a customer, and Andrew Overton took Ann Frye and other DoT representatives to Carbodies' factory to see it. The Ministry of Transport approached Carbodies in August of 1981, and asked Grant Lockhart if the new taxi could accommodate a wheelchair. No one at Carbodies had ever given this a thought, and the idea met with some hostility. However, Lockhart and Peter James went to a local hospital, borrowed a wheelchair, tried it in a seating buck – and it went in. The DoT asked for a vehicle to be presented at their headquarters at Marsham Street, in London's Victoria, by December. After some furious work, a prototype was put together, with the partition split so that its luggage platform side could be slid forwards to accommodate the wheelchair-bound passenger, who would turn round to face rearwards.

Just before Christmas 1981 the cab was unveiled at Marsham Street. The event was attended by several celebrities, civil servants and politicians, including Stirling

Moss, Ann Frye, her boss Sir Peter Baldwin and the Secretary of State for Health, Norman Fowler. The then junior health minister Kenneth Clarke made the presentation of the cab to the press. Cab trade representatives present initially liked the look of the light, airy, champagne-beige cab with its huge windscreen, but they were disappointed that the driving position was cramped, something they had suffered for years with the FX3 and FX4. However, the CR6 looked to be a promising vehicle: its concept was simple, its costs looked to be controllable and it was modern-looking, with an up-to-date chassis and suspension.

Later, a mock-up CR6 interior was made

Grant Lockhart with the second CR6. Morris Ital headlights were added to make it distinct from the Range Rover.

*The interior of the first
CR6 prototype.*

and displayed at Kensington town hall as part of the International Year of the Disabled. Wheelchair-bound people were, in Ann Frye's words, '. . . bowled over by it. They had never had a vehicle they could get into so easily.' More people were invited to the factory to test the facilities during development. The concept of wheelchair accessibility was sound, and had been much needed. So many disabled people had effectively been prisoners in their own home, and now they could anticipate almost as much freedom as an able-bodied person. Public reaction would take a long time to come round, however, and so would the attitude of a hard-core minority of the cab trade who were downright opposed to the idea. But Carbodies was willing to go along with the principle, and Dennis Poore was more than happy with the idea of using government money to pay for this part of the cab's development.

CR6 was sent to BL's test track at Gaydon, and Carbodies was pleased with its progress. An initial release date of 1983 was given, and the trade press and representatives were invited to drive the prototype. They were not

impressed. The CR6 was heavier and more cumbersome than the FX4, it rolled badly on its 14in wheels, and the cramped driving position was criticised.

A NEW TEAM LEADER

Although the CR6 project was not the first complete vehicle Carbodies had attempted to design from scratch, they had not got this far before. Despite having some very skilled engineers in the drawing office and on the shop floor, they did not have anyone with the experience and training to put a complete vehicle into production. Dennis Poore therefore brought in an expert, Dr Bertie Fogg, a former engineering director at Leyland and the director of MIRA, to assess what, from a management and engineering point of view, would be the best way for Carbodies to achieve its goal.

Poore also engaged a 'head-hunter' to find the right man to lead the company in the right direction: the man found Barry Widdowson, who was working for trailer-maker Freuhauf in Norfolk. In July 1982

Grant Lockhart invited Widdowson to join Carbodies, but more impending commitments meant that he declined. However, by the following January he was still in Norfolk and Lockhart made a second invitation, hinting that the job had been rethought and might be more interesting. Widdowson agreed to come and to meet Dennis Poore – although that meeting did not quite follow conventional patterns, as Barry Widdowson recalls:

> Mr Poore didn't turn up to our meeting in Pall Mall. He had not been well that day, but the head-hunter said that he would see me that night at his house if that was all right. Dennis met me in his dressing gown – he was a very imposing man, one hell of a character – and apologised for not seeing me earlier. He sat down, and then asked what I knew about Wankel engines. I was a bit puzzled, but I told him briefly and we had a discussion about them; but then the head-hunter interrupted and said, 'Hang on a minute, Mr Poore, Barry's come about the taxi project!' Poore apologised, and started straight in again about this taxi, saying 'Now what we need is a new taxi, and we need it finished quickly. When can you start?' I thought, 'I've never come across a company like this – I'll give it a go!'

Widdowson's first impressions of Carbodies were somewhat similar to Grant Lockhart's:

> To me they were a company frozen in time. Because they didn't meet the customer, they were kind of remote from the market place. Their practices were very insular, they were not in obvious competition and technically were in a monopoly. They hadn't made any changes, and I came to the con-

clusion that there was a hell of a problem.

WHEELCHAIR TRIALS FOR CR6

The Department of Transport set up a research group to investigate the transport problems of the wheelchair-bound, and put the matter in the hands of the Transport Road Research Laboratory at Crowthorne, in Berkshire. In turn the TRRL set up the Road Transport Study group at Newcastle University, and the first two CR6 prototypes, the original black cab and a second beige example, were purchased; from July 1982 they were put on test in Peterborough, Newcastle and the Potteries. These places were chosen because the CR6 was being tested for its wheelchair-carrying ability, not as a taxi, and the quieter traffic enabled the job to be done with less trouble. Also Carbodies was concerned about the commercial sensitivity of exposing the CR6 to the London trade – Grant Lockhart didn't want sales of the current model to dry up as a result of rumours that a new model might be imminent.

TYPE APPROVAL: FULL VEHICLE MANUFACTURERS AT LAST

While the FX4 still had an envisaged life of at least five years, the serious problem of national type approval and other European-inspired regulations was knocking on Carbodies' door. By 1981, Austin's interest in the FX4 existed only in that they supplied the engine, the manual gearbox and their name; they had long ceased to have an active interest in the devel-

The launch of the Peterborough wheelchair-accessibility trials. From the left are Baroness Steadman, Grant Lockhart, Ann Frye, Sir Peter Baldwin and Michael Marsh, from Rover dealers Marsh of Cambridge.

opment and manufacture of the cab, and if nothing was done to meet the new regulations, the FX4 could quite easily have been wiped out by legislation. Therefore if Carbodies was going to survive they were going to have to be a free-standing manufacturer, not a subcontractor.

With this intent, Grant Lockhart sought to take over the intellectual rights to the vehicle, and to obtain national type approval for it in Carbodies' own name, whereby both the vehicle and all its components had to meet with European standards. To comply with this, the production system was inspected by the Department of Transport to ensure consistency of manufacture, and this process was more restrictive for the cab because the PCO Conditions of Fitness also had to be accommodated; the whole process took eighteen months. As soon as it was granted, Carbodies was able to put its own name on the vehicles' licence. Previously, the Society of Motor Manufacturers and Traders had categorized Carbodies as a body-maker,

even though they had made the complete vehicle since 1971; but from spring 1982 they became listed officially as passenger vehicle manufacturers.

THE CORTINA COUPÉ

As far as Grant Lockhart was concerned, something *could* be done about Carbodies' virtually complete dependence on the taxi market. Coming from a big manufacturer which controlled its own destiny, he believed that Carbodies should re-enter the private car business. The demand for open cars had declined dramatically in the light of impending US safety regulations, and this was bad news for the British motor industry, as much of its export success had been based on the sale of open-top sports cars. By the end of the 1970s, however, the threat had subsided, and the market for open cars looked as if it might blossom again.

From small beginnings in the 1960s, the firm of Crayford, based at Westerham in

The third successful
Cortina coupé.

Kent, had made convertible versions of a wide variety of pre-registered saloon cars that had been brought to them by their owners. One of Crayford's last jobs was the MkV Cortina, which featured a T-bar top brace similar to a Triumph Stag. Then Crayford's two partners, David McMullan and Geoffrey Smith, decided to stop making convertibles because they needed all their workshop space for the production of the all-terrain Argocat vehicle. They had approached Carbodies in 1978 and offered them the rights to the Cortina, but Bill Lucas and Jake Donaldson were not impressed; they felt that the asking price was too high, and that the conversion was well below their own standard, so they rejected the offer.

In 1980 McMullan and Smith approached Grant Lockhart, and this time sold Carbodies the Cortina. It would fit in nicely with Lockhart's idea to diversify, especially as it followed the company's tradition of building open-top cars. Crayford said that the Cortina was 'a complete job', but it was anything *but* that: there were no jigs and no drawings, only some artwork, and Peter James recalls it as being 'a complete shambles'.

Grant Lockhart had intended Jake Donaldson to undertake the project, but it was at this time that he had fallen terminally ill. The engineering was therefore taken over by Peter James, and after a gap of nearly twenty-five years, Carbodies set to work on a prototype coupé intended for production. The engineers were dismayed by the workmanship of the Crayford car: edges of cut metal were unfinished, the rear seating was totally inadequate compared to what it could have been, and the fit of the hood was poor.

The correct way to undertake the job was to make a receiving jig which would hold the body-shell in its correct position, and only then to remove the roof, otherwise the shell would collapse. A jig of this kind was not supplied by Crayford, however, and the cost was too prohibitive for Carbodies to make one – and the first car did indeed start to collapse as it was cut. To replace the strength which was lost with the removal of the roof, reinforcing members were added inboard of the sill skins and around the rear suspension pick-up points; the bulkhead was reinforced to reduce scuttle shake, and the T-bar brace was fitted up to a reinforced screen cant rail. Jake Donaldson had seen the terrible job Crayford had made of the hood on the original car, and had already highlighted it. In fact there was no adequate method of attaching it, but James put a scheme together to attach the hood to the rear deck, based on experience gained with the Ford Zephyrs and Consuls. A further problem arose with the paint, the colours of which were to be from Ford's range; this included metallics, but Carbodies did not have the facility to apply it, and had to bring in equipment to do so.

Carbodies planned to sell the Cortina MkV Coupé brand-new and unregistered through Ford dealerships, and so they negotiated with Ford to bring in such two-door cars for conversion. In fact the two-door Cortina was made in Belgium and the only models type approved for the UK market were the 1.3 and 1.6-litre base and 'L' models – and the sort of customer who would buy specialist cars such as the Cortina coupé would most likely want better trim and a bigger engine. Ford's computer at Genk was re-programmed to allow the up-market two-door models to be released to Britain; Ford themselves were enthusiastic about the coupé. They gave it a full Ford warranty, and appointed three dealers to sell the car from their network: Bristol Street Motors in Birmingham, Quicks of Manchester and Perrys of North London.

The car made its debut at the 1980 Motor Show at Birmingham's National Exhibition Centre. Advertised as the Cortina drophead coupé by Carbodies of Coventry, it was offered in GL or GLS trim, with the option of 1.6 or 2.0-litre four-cylinder or 2.3 litre V6 engines, and a choice of six colours. One was built with left-hand drive and a German specification 2-litre V6 engine to special order. There was a choice of manual or automatic transmissions, although Carbodies, who targeted the car towards a more mature driver, encouraged customers to choose an automatic.

Grant Lockhart anticipated that the dealers would sell one car a week each. However, although the coupé was very attractive, and despite putting the cars in their showrooms to draw the customers in, the dealers were not so keen to sell them. The first batch had to be bought back off customers, and this was a great disappointment to the Carbodies' engineers who had struggled to make a good job of them. The faults found were rectified in succeeding cars, but with less than thirty Cortina coupés sold, the car could hardly be described as a commercial success. The Cortina saloon was almost a spent force in the market place, but the very high price was the most crucial factor in the coupé's failure. When new, a 2.3 GLS coupé cost £9,422.51, with an additional £397 for an automatic transmission and a further £42 for metallic paint. Standard Ford charges for delivery and number plates meant a bottom line in excess of £10,000, this at a time when a top-of-the-range Granada cost about £8,700 and the new Escort XR3 £5,800. At that price there were few takers – it may have been an unusual vehicle, but underneath it was still just a Cortina. When the model was deleted from the Ford range, a few remaining coupés hung around in the showrooms for months afterwards. Grant Lockhart, however, felt sure that the Cortina could have led to better things:

> Ford at top level were very supportive, but it was very difficult for a small manufacturer to deal with these powerful dealers; they didn't do half of what they promised. I was very proud of the Cortina, and we learned a lot doing it. We had intended to do other models, and we looked at the Opel Manta and the Monza. In many ways it would have been better to have put some of the resources that were going into the CR6 into developing the Ford. The taxi people hated us doing it; they said, 'What are you doing, wasting time on that? *We* need a new model!'

THE RANGE ROVER UNITRUCK

'Not a happy project', is how Peter James recalls the Unitruck. The whole thing started when a consortium of farmers based in Yeovil approached Land Rover, and asked if the four-seat Range Rover pickup they had made might be put into limited production. The Range Rover was chosen because of all its comforts. The farmers had a particular job for their conversion in mind: high-speed crop spraying. A prominent feature in a field of growing crops is what are known as tramlines. These are lines where no seed has been planted, so the wheels of a tractor will not damage a crop as it runs along them in the field. Often the job of spraying could be done at a higher speed to save time, but a tractor can only travel slowly over a ploughed field; a Range Rover, however, can drive over rough ground at a higher speed, and its track is almost identical to the tramlines. Also, it has always been a legal requirement that any toxic chemicals carried on a motor vehicle must be separated from the driver and passengers by a solid partition; so the open rear deck, which would allow the fitting of crop-spraying equipment, had a partition fitted.

As we have seen, Land Rover were going through a tough time at that point, and they were not particularly interested, but they suggested Carbodies should look at the proposed project. Grant Lockhart decided they should have a go, especially when there was promise from Land Rover that there would be concessionary prices available on all the various body components, as it was to be a conversion exercise on the three-door Range Rover. Carbodies therefore made two more prototype Unitrucks, one painted sand gold and the other blue, with GRP roofs, each with the spare wheel carried over the roof on a roll-over bar.

Lockhart felt that the price could be brought down further by having Customs and Excise classify Unitruck as an agricultural or commercial vehicle, thus

Snowy Beebe

In 1934, a young man from Nuneaton by the name of Walter Beebe joined Carbodies as an apprentice, working in the finishing shop. He remembers when he started as a young lad with almost white blond hair:

I walked into the works, and a man I'd never seen before said to me, 'Hello Snowy, my friend, I hope you'll enjoy your stay here'. And from that day on I was always known as Snowy'!

He remembers little about his early days at Carbodies, but recalls that they had no facilities for making ironwork, and other apprentices had to take what he called a 'pushy cart' over to the blacksmith they'd always used in West Orchard. At that time Coventry's motor industry provided work, but there was little in Nuneaton, and some six trains a day carried workers into the city from both Nuneaton and Bedworth. 'The Daimler', a huge concern in those days, had its own station on the railway line.

Snowy stayed at Carbodies until he finished his apprenticeship, when he was called for military service in World War II. On returning in 1945, he asked for his old job back, but as there was so little work he was given a place in dispatch, and was lucky to have that. He remembers the severe winter of 1947, the coal shortage, and the struggles to get work in the desperately difficult years following the war. He rose to become foreman of the dispatch department, and recalls dealing with Lord Rootes and David Southwell, who both knew him by his nickname.

Snowy himself was with Carbodies for a remarkable fifty years and six months. He retired in 1985, and the event was celebrated by a big party, where he was presented with a 'gold taxi', a special model of the FX4 presented to a very few select people who had given special service to the company; these included Spen King and Bill Lucas. At the party he found that his work was being done by three men, who asked him how he ever managed to cope on his own!

exempting it from Special Car Tax. The recently introduced MkIII Ford Escort van had a small quarter-light behind the B-post, and *that* was a commercial vehicle, so why couldn't Unitruck be exempt also? Customs and Excise said that in the Escort, the driver's head was actually behind the B-post and thus visibility would be impaired without the extra window, so the van was exempted on the grounds of safety. Unitruck's door glass extended behind the B-post, so they decided that it was not a commercial vehicle, and was therefore subject to the tax.

Through business contacts that had been made in Kuwait, another market for Unitruck was identified: that of the leisure owner. The Kuwaitis were known for their love of hunting in the desert and considered that the Unitruck would be an ideal platform for a rifleman to shoot game, or as mobile base for a falconer to fly his birds. The Range Rover had already proven itself as an excellent towing vehicle, and Unitruck's rear deck capacity would also suit the boat or horse owner, in that messy loads could be carried without spoiling the interior.

A presentation was staged at Stoneleigh Agricultural Centre, and the Unitruck showed itself to be the fastest crop sprayer ever! The company's stand at the 1982 motor show featured three Unitrucks, a new red

A Unitruck at Stoneleigh. The rollbar-mounted spare made accessibility difficult.

example as well as the sand gold and blue vehicles, and these produced a lot of serious enquiries – but as expected, the price was the sticking point to sales.

Changes in Land Rover's top personnel brought about a different attitude towards dealings with Carbodies. The agreement to supply Range Rovers at a concessionary price was withdrawn, and the full factory transfer price was demanded. That, combined with the Special Car Tax, put the estimated price of Unitruck way above what customers would be prepared to pay, and Carbodies was left with no alternative but to scrap it. The Kuwaiti family took delivery of two of the prototypes, and the Hot Air Balloon company bought one as a tender vehicle for the balloon they used for advertising Alka Seltzer. (Bayer, the makers of Alka Seltzer, were also the suppliers of the plastic materials that were tried on the CR6.)

11 Rover Engines, and the Birth of LTI

'It wasn't a development from free choice . . .'
Grant Lockhart, on the adoption of
the Land Rover engine for the FX4R

FINDING A NEW ENGINE

Carbodies was still faced with the need to find a suitable replacement for the Austin engine. A second attempt to fit a Peugeot engine was tried, but the cylinder-head problem persisted. There were also vibration problems, and on one occasion the propshaft actually tore loose and came through the floor. Moreover it was clear that by the time Peugeot solved these problems it would be too late for Carbodies. Three options were still available: the 3-litre Perkins, the 2.3 litre Ford and the Land Rover. There was no doubt about the performance of the Perkins, Grant Lockhart's favourite, but it was too powerful. Conversely, Ford's engine was underpowered, and they wouldn't give a release date for the new 2.5Di. The CR6 had been planned with the Land Rover engine in mind, knowing that a larger and more powerful unit was under development. Despite Harry Webster's advice, the Land Rover it had to be.

One was put into an existing cab and given to Horace Faulkner to test under working conditions, and it performed well, not displaying any temperamental traits or signs of unreliability. Grant Lockhart asked Bill Drew, Peter James and purchasing manager Derek Cripps how quickly they could have the Land Rover engine installed. Peter James took a chance and said three months. Lockhart took that as definite, and James returned to his team in the drawing office and set about engineering the conversion immediately.

From the mid-1970s the automatic transmission had become more popular than the manual gearbox, but no auto 'box had ever been mated to a Land Rover diesel engine – and as the Austin manual gearbox was also to be deleted, a replacement had to be found for that, too. Rover had the five-speed unit from the 3500, but that had never been fitted to a Land Rover engine, either. James' and Cripps' design proposals to mate both the Australian-made Borg Warner Model 40, used on the FX4 since the closure of Borg Warner's Hertfordshire plant in 1980, and the 3500 manual 'box, were accepted by Land Rover's chief engineer, transmissions engineer and purchasing director.

CR6 was put on hold, and Barry Widdowson's energies were diverted into re-engineering the Land Rover-powered FX4 for production, because if that job wasn't done properly there wouldn't be a business left to develop any new cab. As with CR6, there was no dedicated team in place for the job; bearing in mind that this was a task that a company used to such changes would find big, for Carbodies – body engineers and former subcontractors but not chassis engineers or manufacturers – it was enormous.

The factory from the air in 1981. Holyhead Road runs along the top left-hand corner, and the Coventry-Nuneaton railway line is bottom left. Top centre, the drive, diverted since the mid 1950s, dog-legs around the offices. Against the allotments at the top are, from the left, the toolroom, the pattern shop, the chassis shop and the paint shop. In the corner of the railway line and the Holyhead Road, to the left, is the finishing shop, with the trim shop above. The white metal assembly shop, where taxi bodies are put together, runs from the centre of the site to the rugby club boundary, at bottom right. The high-roofed building with the company name on the wall is the steel store, with the press shops to its left.

Widdowson began an intensive programme to set up development teams, co-ordinating the pre-production work between the designers and production people. The teams were all put into one office. Previously there had been an environment that allowed conflict between designers and production engineers; now there was simultaneous engineering between the fifty people working on the project, with production engineers advising designers as to whether any item could be made or not, as that item was taking shape on the drawing board. All this work was done outside normal production time, with all the teething troubles logged and prioritized according to whether they had to be made immediately or rectified as running changes in production. In short, everyone in

Door Locks: A Safety Issue to be Resolved

In 1961 a child fell from a moving FX4 on the M4 motorway and was run over and killed by a following car. Told to open the window, the child mistook the door handle for the non-existent window winder. In mid-1982 in Glasgow, a child was killed and a second seriously injured in a fall, both from moving FX4s. Fiercely proud of its exemplary safety record, the cab trade nationally was shocked by these events. The Public Carriage Office instigated a ruling that a sticker should be placed on the window indicating that they were opened simply by pulling the handle down, and the door handles were encased in a clear plastic shield.

By 1983 Carbodies had installed automatic locks that secured the doors, not only when the cab was in motion, but when it was stationary with the footbrake applied. Initially troublesome when fitted, the system was refined and improved. As was seen back in 1953, such actions could not only cause the forward opening doors to hit parked cars or lamp posts, but could injure pedestrians, too. Besides being effective against accidents, fitting the door locks could also prevent the likely escape of a bilker and stop passengers who are too impatient to wait until their cab stops before they open the door.

the teams knew exactly what was going on with the project. Barry Widdowson described the way in which the staff accepted the completely new working practices as 'brilliant' – but with a schedule of thirteen-hour days and seven-day weeks, these were, in Peter James's words, 'hair-raising times'.

In tests, the Land Rover-engined cab could exceed 80mph (125km/h), so it was vital that a better braking system was found to replace the previous one. Grant Lockhart asked Peter James what he would like to see fitted to the updated cab, and James's answer was simple: full servo brakes. Lockhart asked how much it would cost to engineer, and the reply was equally quick: nothing; as it had already been designed, in 1978. There was no bolt-on disc-brake option available, however, and with CR6 already under way, anything that was done on the old cab would only be a stop-gap.

The new model was christened the FX4R – R for Rover – and went into production right on schedule; it was announced to the trade in late 1982. Initial curiosity and pleasure with its silent and smooth running

turned quickly to dismay and anger at a multitude of problems. Some engines would smoke alarmingly, and the low torque of the engine when coupled to the auto 'box produced a cab with acceleration so slow as to be thought dangerous in city traffic. Fuel consumption of the automatic was as low as 20mpg (14l/100km). Clutch problems occurred on the manual model. Vibration caused the operating arm to rupture over the mounting bolt, and the plastic pipe for the hydraulics would blow itself off under pressure. The wrong clutch components were mated, and the spigot bearing in the flywheel would disintegrate and wreck the gearbox. The radiator could not handle the new engine in traffic, and auxiliary electric fans had to be fitted by many owners. And despite tests by Carbodies, Mann and Overton's engineering director Mike Ray would not sanction the extra cost of some £30 per cab to fit a larger radiator.

The intention to explore export markets resulted in one bonus: power steering, although Mann and Overton ridiculed the idea for London, even if it was vital to sales

abroad. It was offered first as an option, although the PCO would not pass cabs fitted with it for several weeks because a way could not be found to stop the box leaking fluid. In fact it robbed the engine of as much as 15per cent of its power – but even so, it was extremely popular, and within a year was standard equipment.

Every single diesel engine coming off Land Rover's production line was tested for two hours, and tuned if it did not come up to scratch. If it is considered that just one in a hundred of the old Austin engines were tested, such rigorous measures might be viewed as a tacit admission that something was seriously wrong. And after long arguments with customers, Carbodies' engineers had to agree that something was wrong, too – but they were unable to do anything about it because engine manufacture was beyond their control. The bottom line was that the new production practices had come too late to change the engine. Barry Widdowson had had originally to assume that the Land Rover engine was suitable, but the realization that it was not

was dawning painfully and rapidly on all concerned.

The engine was also available in a petrol version, and as a result of export enquiries from Australia, a few Land Rover petrol-engined cabs were offered with the option of an LPG fuel conversion. Considering all the welcomed changes in working practices, it was disappointing, to say the least, for Carbodies' staff to find that the Land Rover engine was such a poor performer. Many of these people had worked on the FX4 from the very early days, and they were all immensely proud to be the builders of the London taxi. Grant Lockhart was open about the shortcomings of the FX4R. However, he stands by his belief that at the time, the Land Rover was the only suitable engine available:

The FX4R wasn't a development from free choice. The Land Rover engine was not tolerant of any abuse, which was strange because the Land Rover had a world-wide reputation for ruggedness; but they are not high-mileage vehicles. A taxi is a slow-speed,

---

Stan Troman

In 1989 Carbodies suffered the loss of a true servant, with the death of Stan Troman. Stan joined Carbodies in 1948, and he met and subsequently married his wife, Brenda, whilst she was working for him in the wages department. Stan had been financial director since 1974, when he replaced Steve Stevens for whom he had worked loyally and conscientiously. Stan kept very much in the background, but his quiet dedication, often working very long hours and struggling with seemingly insurmountable problems during some of the company's most difficult years, cannot be underestimated: his work had been vital to Carbodies survival.

---

high-mileage vehicle with a lot of time spent ticking over. What was disappointing was that when we tried to resolve the problems, my old company (BL Cars) was in such terrible trouble they wouldn't give us any engineering help.

Land Rover's engineers, too, were appalled at how their engine was performing in taxi work. They tried to solve the problems as best they could, but any further modifications or alterations to the engine were ruled out from higher up, as a new diesel engine was under development.

The FX4R might be described as a 'curate's egg': some parts bad, some parts good. It was the quietest diesel cab Carbodies had yet produced, and after ten or more years, some could be seen still giving good performance – yet some performed poorly throughout their lives. The power steering was welcomed, and the servo brakes were the best yet offered. Still, the project provided a vehicle to establish vital new working practices.

CARBODIES SALES AND SERVICE AND THE PROVINCIAL MARKET

Over the years, many different individuals expressed an interest in the FX4, such as oil millionaire Nubar Gulbenkian with his coachbuilt taxi. There had been individual sales through BSA Guns' associations in Japan, and to the diplomatic service for users such as the Falkland Islands' governor, Rex Hunt; and there had been failed attempts, such as those in New York. Most of the customers of Carbodies Sales and Service were in the Midlands. John Paton had acquired Scottish distribution rights in the early 1970s, and had established a thriving business which had been extended to Manchester's Cross Street Garage. This was deeply unpopular with Mann and Overton, who felt that all energies should be directed to the London market. But London was saturated; Carbodies couldn't expand and prosper on its existing levels, or those of the other British cities which used London cabs, and now that they were manufacturers in their own right they could investigate other markets more fully.

It was unfortunate for provincial sales that the FX4R turned out to be such a disastrous vehicle. Where just a short journey can take a cab onto country roads, its sluggish acceleration, coupled with its 1950s handling characteristics, made it wholly unsuitable. There were many stories of its unreliability, and of poor service back-up. The high initial price, despite Carbodies' calculations showing that it was a better long-term investment, meant that provincial operators would not buy what they knew to be an inferior vehicle for their needs. Where there was an option, the 'R' was rejected, and in provincial towns a very bad feeling was engendered towards London cabs and to Carbodies in particular.

EXPORTS TO THE MIDDLE EAST

At Carbodies' stand at the 1983 Motor Show some visitors from Quatar expressed an interest in buying a number of taxis for their own use at home. When they were delivered they caused quite a stir amongst other Arab countries, especially Saudi Arabia, where a small number were ordered for Jedda airport. A Kuwaiti had come to the UK to set up in business, and ordered some vehicles for his home country. Further sales of taxis to Quatar and limousines to Dubai followed – but the problems of the FX4R were very much magnified in the hostile desert climate. The Land Rover petrol engine, mandatory in the Middle East, was not man enough to power both the cab and the vital air-conditioning unit fitted to the vehicles.

Updesh Ramnath had started at Carbodies in 1968 in the purchasing department; he was now transferred to Carbodies Sales and Service where he was responsible for parts distribution and servicing for the UK. When the Quatar cabs – yellow, in imitation of American practice – were delivered, Ramnath was put in charge of supplying spares and service to the Middle East. However, the cab was antiquated compared to other vehicles on the market, and the frequent servicing intervals were not appreciated by the Arabs. The cabs soon gave trouble in use, and no more were ordered.

CR6 PROGRESS

Peterborough drivers were generally pleased with the CR6's performance in the wheelchair trials. Wheelchair passengers

A Dubai cab. The camels proved more reliable in the desert environment.

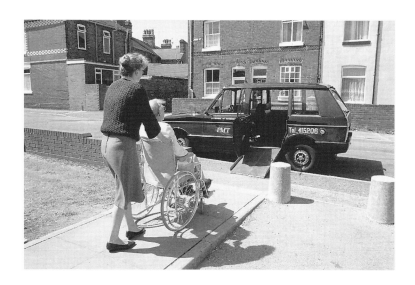

The CR6 on wheelchair accessibility proving tests in Peterborough.

however, although delighted because there was now a cab that could take them anywhere almost on demand, were not happy with the headroom; some people might risk suffering back strain if forced to travel with their head bowed, and it was obvious that the roof would have to be altered. In early 1983 a report published by Newcastle University, which was monitoring the trials in their city, agreed with the Peterborough results, including asking for wider doors.

The Department of Transport was disappointed that a larger-than-average wheelchair would not fit into the CR6. Carbodies found that they needed to extend the chassis by an estimated 4in (10cm) to allow for wider doors, and were willing to do so, but they estimated it would cost around

These experimental plastic front wings were tried, but eventually discarded. There were already two materials used in the body, aluminium and steel, and the introduction of a third would have made the process of painting, both in the factory and in repair shops, even more complicated.

£2m. The government was prepared to give some money through the Department of Trade and Industry and the Department of Transport, but there would be a shortfall of £0.7m. Fortunately for Carbodies, the Greater London Council's Labour administration had begun a policy of equal opportunities for people with disabilities, and the brief of this covered public transport; consequently the GLC was willing to give a grant to help what was seen as the taxi of the future.

A third CR6 was built, with a longer wheelbase and a higher roof pressing. This solved the accessibility problems, but unfortunately it made an already bulky cab even bigger. Further problems were occurring with the ground clearance of the steering mechanism – but much heavier black clouds were on the horizon as a result of the FX4R falling flat in the market place. Its second-hand value was considerably lower in comparison to the Austin-engined cab, and with interest rates at record levels, mushers and fleet owners held on to their older models. Carbodies couldn't spend more

money on development at the same time as their income was shrinking, and this conspired to make the CR6 more difficult to bring to fruition, with the envisaged cost of the cab rising from some 10per cent above the price of an FX4 to over 20per cent more. By this time, Mann and Overton had paid nearly £1.93m, and were due to pay a further £1.92m. Further costs of the project were estimated to be £4.5m, and another £1.4m was needed to extend the factory. In January 1984, Carbodies announced a postponement of the release date to 1985.

THE PURCHASE OF MANN AND OVERTON

Mann and Overton had been at their Wandsworth Bridge Road premises since 1938, and compared to modern motor garages these were now antiquated and cramped. Previously, they had only serviced cabs under their six-month 40,000 mile (64,500km) warranty, and this was one of the reasons why they did not, or could not,

The final version of the CR6, stretched by 4in (10cm) and with a new, domed roof. Ironically, Jake Donaldson thought the Range Rover roof would be a good panel to cover a taxi . . .

understand the long-term problems that arose with the FX4: they simply did not see these things for themselves at first hand! But now the old guard – Robert Overton, David Southwell and the works director Bill Bateman – had retired, and Peter Wildgoose and Mike Ray were rising up the echelons, and Robert Overton's son Andrew was the new managing director. For the first time Mann and Overton began managment training in a very much more professional way, changing its working practices quite radically.

In 1993 the company decided it was time to move. Market research and their own records showed that most of their customers were to the north or east of London, so why stay in the south-west of the capital? Their first choice was a site in London's East End; the second was in Acre Lane, Brixton, just two miles from the London Cab Company. But both of these sites proved unsuitable, by which time Mann and Overton were committed to selling the old place; so in November 1983 they moved to their third site choice, erecting new, purpose-built premises around the corner at a riverside location in Carnwath Road.

In 1984 Mann and Overton's owners, Lloyds Bowmaker as they had become, decided to split the dealership into finance and retail components, and to offer the retail side for sale. Bill Lucas had long asked both BSA and MBH for the money to buy Mann and Overton, but both had refused. But Grant Lockhart had experienced the firm's reluctance to make detail improvements to the cab, and under pressure, Dennis Poore raised a rights issue on the Stock Exchange to buy Mann and Overton. As a result, in 1985 London Taxis International was born. Three divisions were created within the group: LTI Carbodies, the manufacturer; LTI Mann and Overton, the dealers; and

Mann and Overton Finance. This was to become London Taxi Finance, which would supply a dedicated, experienced and, most - importantly, independent service to the dealers that Mann and Overton had served for decades. Andrew Overton moved to Holyhead Road to take up the position of sales and marketing director, and his place at Mann and Overton was taken by Peter Wildgoose. Now Grant Lockhart's plan, to have complete control of both manufacturing and sales, had come to fruition: the company made the entire vehicle, they controlled the all-important London market through the new subsidiary, and they could make all their own decisions regarding the future development of their sole product, the London taxi.

METROCAB

The opportunity to buy Mann and Overton and the setting up of LTI was timely. The FX4 had had the London market to itself for a decade and a half, but a newcomer was on the horizon: the Metrocab. The original artwork distributed to the cab-trade press in 1984 showed a modern shape, and with the backing of one of Britain's biggest producers of public transport vehicles, Metro-Cammell Laird, it looked to be the first real challenger the FX4 had ever had. Its development team would include some very experienced people; namely Geoff Chater, Derek Cripps and Jan Scott. All three had left Carbodies to join the new project, with a working knowledge of both the FX5 and the CR6, as well as the production know-how of the FX4, under their belts. In fact all the Metrocab was challenging was a vehicle fundamentally unchanged for nearly thirty years, and the promise, continually delayed, of the much more expensive CR6.

'A luxury executive limousine in a class of its own, styled to your personal taste.' So said the 1982 brochure. Prompted by the demise of the FL2 as a hire car, the London limousine could be had with leather trim and any luxury fitting the customer wanted. Power was from a choice of petrol or diesel engines.

D.F. LANDERS AND THE 'GLIDER'

In 1985 Grant Lockhart moved over to Carbodies Sales and Service to consolidate the drive to improve both provincial and

D. F. Landers, president of the London Coach Co. Inc.

export sales. The American market tempted Carbodies once again, with its sheer size, and the knowledge that there was legislation afoot to create wheelchair accessible facilities on public transport and taxis. After a protracted search, Grant Lockhart's long-standing connections with Ford in the USA established a contact with specialist motor manufacturer D. F. Landers in Mount Clemens, Michigan, an ex-serviceman who had a business manufacturing specialist vehicles for military applications. An agreement was signed with Landers, who set up the London Coach Company Inc to adapt and market the cab, both in taxi form and as a limousine, 'The London Sterling', and to sell around 500 vehicles in three years.

Because the Land Rover engine would not comply with US emission regulations, Carbodies was to supply what were known as 'gliders', without engine or transmission. The engine was to be a US-made, 2.3-litre, four-cylinder Ford. According to Grant Lockhart, Ford gave superb co-operation, approving the engine with the Federal Government's regulations. To Ford it was

In the brochure, London black replaces US yellow, but Federal specification lights (including tail-lights from a late model MGB) and impact-absorbing bumpers distinguish the export model. The grille and plastic door handles would be seen in the UK a few years on.

The London Sterling: 'timeless elegance', said the brochure, of a vehicle marketed as a more manoeuvrable alternative to the 'stretch' Cadillacs and Lincolns, with the bonus of headroom for top-hat wearers. The vinyl half-top reflects both 1930s American town car design, and its retrospective introduction on upmarket US models.

London Sterling – Timeless Elegance

superb publicity: the 'London taxi comes to America, powered by Ford'. The Ford was a powerful engine and gave the taxi the best performance ever; Grant Lockhart recalls being stopped for speeding by the Highway Patrol on the interstate freeway but he didn't get a ticket because the cops couldn't stop laughing – a London taxi doing 85mph (137km/h)!

The cab and the Sterling began to generate sales when they were exhibited, but the economic climate of the mid-1980s struck hard, the exchange rate having climbed to around

2.5 dollars to the pound, inflating the price of the cab dramatically. It became clear to Landers that he couldn't afford to sell at the $17,000 price he had originally announced, when the most popular US taxis, the Ford LTD and the Chevrolet Caprice, sold for around $11,000. The whole-life cost of the FX4 meant that a premium could be asked over the price of a domestic sedan, which had a life expectancy of some four years as a taxi, but the market would not stand a big increase. However, Landers was forced to raise the price to a level the market found

The first attempt, by Tickford, to produce a stretch version of the FX4.

unacceptable. The plan to sell 500 vehicles in three years did not therefore materialize, and by mutual assent the project was called off. About fifty vehicles had been delivered, with some 150 in the pipeline.

A NEW ENGINEERING DIRECTOR

In 1985, Barry Widdowson was promoted to managing director of LTI to replace Grant Lockhart. Since Jake Donaldson's death. Peter James had held down both the post of chief engineer, involving major design work, and of acting engineering director, which meant some degree of time spent in the board room. When offered the position of engineering director, he declined, preferring to work in a more 'hands-on' post. It was therefore vital to find a new engineering director if the plan to turn the company around was to succeed. The new man was Ed Osmond, invited to join LTI in early 1985, and who

The extra length of the Tickford conversion gave the opportunity to fix the rear-facing seats down permanently alongside the console.

came recommended by his former boss, Spen King. A graduate apprentice with the Leyland Motor Corporation, he had moved to Reliant in 1977 as engineering director where he was responsible for the SS1 sports car and the Scimitar GTC. When Osmond accepted his new appointment he had been quoting for bodies for the new Metrocab, and in working out three months notice, had to inform MCW that he could take no further part in the project.

THE FX4S

Dennis Poore had brought in Spen King, the former chief engineer at Rover and Triumph, to look at the progress of CR6 and to examine the FX4R. One of his recommendations for improving the FX4R was to fit the new 2.5 litre Land Rover engine, although installing it was not quite as straightforward as was expected. Its new fuel pump was mounted very low on the front of the block, and the engine had to be raised at the front and tilted to the left to get it in. There was neither the time nor the money to develop dedicated engine mountings, so Peter James called in Dunlop, who sent down virtually their whole range of Metalastic engine mountings. The best available were selected and installed. The Borg-Warner type 40 automatic and Rover five-speed manual gearboxes were to be carried over.

New internal plastic cappings for the door sills were designed and made, cutting down considerably the draught coming in from under the front doors. Modern switchgear, including electric screen washers, were fitted. Simple stuff in itself, but only now was the FX4 getting the sort of standard equipment that private car owners had enjoyed for the previous fifteen years!

One aspect of Osmond's task was to motivate his engineering staff, and it was an unenviable one. In the preceding five years, Unitruck had failed to reach production, the Cortina Coupé was a failure in the marketplace, the FX4R was an embarrassment, and the CR6 was looking less and less viable. It was important to make the staff realize that their work meant something, that what they did could reach production and have real worth. The new model, named the FX4S, needed to be brought to production as a quality product, not only with a better engine, but with all the performance and warranty problems encountered on the 'R' engineered out from the start. In view of the company's difficult financial situation and its almost total dependency on the taxi, future developments had to be done in what Ed Osmond described as 'bite-sized chunks'. To start a research and design programme properly integrated with marketing and manufacturing, new people were needed who were experienced in total vehicle engineering – so against a background of major redundancies across the industry, an employment policy was adopted which was in fact at odds with that favoured at the time. But as Osmond himself observed, he had:

> . . . not come to Carbodies to do nothing. I was brought here to bring professional engineering to the company, and what I do, happens. I needed trained, skilled staff so I brought them in at that level. Our philosophy then was that the best people were those who had experience in the industry, so I employed people of fifty, fifty-five and sixty years of age quite happily.

The experience brought by these skilled workers was a great asset, and they were to repay a company willing to appreciate their reliability and mellow attitude with loyalty and hard work.

The FX4S in the finishing shop; note the black bumpers. Wilmot Breeden's tooling for the old chrome bumpers had worn out. The cost of replacement was astronomical, so Peter James designed a rolled-steel type with moulded polyurethane ends in double quick time and at a fraction of the cost.

The FX4S was introduced on 4 November 1985 at Mann and Overton's Carnwath Road showroom. The press release said, 'Mann and Overton believe that with the FX4S they have a vehicle that will see them well into the twenty-first century'. The cab trade's opinion of this statement is not recorded. However, the price was only a little more than the FX4R, starting at £11,239 for the basic manual model. The badges front and rear identified the cab as a product of LTI, the first vehicle ever to do so. On the road there was some increase in engine noise, but this was a small price to pay for the return to a competent engine. The new cab received a cautious welcome from the trade. A serious short-term problem was caused by the installation of a faulty batch of timing belts; when they broke in service, they caused the same internal damage as when the old 2.25 engine's timing chain broke. The cab trade's cynical side, caused by years of unheeded nagging at Mann and Overton, obviously thought, 'Here we go again!' But the 'S' began to sell well, and LTI had clearly taken a step further down their intended path of first getting the existing product right – and slowly it was starting to be recognized that things were beginning to change, and for the better. However, the FX4S was soon to be challenged: it was still the only cab on the London market, but the Metrocab, as yet an unknown quantity, was looming on the horizon.

A six-door stretch limo, with all doors forward hinging. It was commissioned from limousine conversion experts Coleman Milne and built at the Woodhall Nicholson factory in Halifax, Yorkshire (hence the number plate) to test the market. It was used as VIP transport for the 1986 Motor Show, held at Birmingham's NEC.

CR6: THE END OF THE ROAD

Support for the CR6 project within Land Rover was eroding. Mike Hodgkinson had been happy about Carbodies producing the four-door conversion, but he had moved on.

After pressure on Land Rover's management from their body plant at Bordesley Green, the manufacturing rights for the four-door conversion were taken from Carbodies and re-engineered to be exclusive for the Range Rover. The cost of the CR6 doors, now

The interior of the Coleman Milne limousine, showing the fixed centre seating and the extra B-post.

exclusive to the cab, almost doubled. By this time virtually no Range Rover panels existed in the CR6; even the tailgate was to be a one-piece item in anticipation of an ambulance version.

To the Range Rover's creator, Spen King, the idea of a taxi look-alike did not disturb him at all; but things had moved on since the early 1970s, particularly in the attitudes of Rover's marketing people. To them, the use of a Range Rover-based taxi severely compromised what had become a prestige vehicle, and Grant Lockhart felt that certain people within Land Rover could make the contract for supply of Range Rover components difficult to operate. King felt that the CR6 prototype was no worse than any other that he'd been involved with, saying:

> There wasn't anything terribly specific wrong with it. It is very easy to underestimate what it takes to make a vehicle satisfactory all the way through. The designer was trying to do what a team of thirty people did more or less single-handed, and it just wasn't on. I think it could have been made to work all right, but the muscle wasn't in the company to develop it, so I was party to saying that it would be very much better to put their efforts into the existing vehicle.

In January 1986, LTI chief executive Chris Cook broke the bad news: the CR6 was to be killed off. The press release said:

> It has been reluctantly decided that the current body shape chosen for the CR6 does not have the commercial attraction that was envisaged at the start of the project. Indeed, we have detected an increasing preference, by many people associated with the taxi industry, for the classic lines of the FX4 body styling.

> Even at this late stage, after a considerable investment in the project, it is felt that the company will be better served by evolving a CR6 vehicle from the current styling. . . . We are also finding that the export market is keen to retain the traditional lines of our vehicle, and this has also influenced our final decision.

> Our parent company, Manganese Bronze, has made appropriate arrangements to provide the necessary resources to absorb the costs already involved in the 'Range Rover style body design', and has provided further funds to continue the CR6 evolving from the FX4 shape.

Those costs amounted to some £2.4m for wheelchair accessibility, which had been given by government and the Greater London Council. The CR6 had proved to be an unwieldy, ergonomically flawed vehicle, too costly to develop and too expensive to sell. That is not to say that all the work on the cab was wasted – far from it. The wheelchair trials had provided a lot of very valuable information to both the Department of Transport's Accessibility Unit, of which Ann Frye became head, and for Carbodies for the immediate future. Designers of wheelchair-accessible taxis were given a background of practical experience from which to draw. For the DoT and other vehicle manufacturers, an ISO standard for public transport-compatible wheelchairs has been laid down.

WHEELCHAIR ACCESSIBILITY FOR THE FX4

By now, Carbodies Sales and Service had been moved to Torrington Avenue in the south-west of Coventry. Here, towards

Roger Ponticelli's FX4W, with forward-hinging doors. The modification to the doors was not adopted at the time for production. They were not mandatory, and Carbodies' resources were wanted for more pressing jobs.

the end of 1985 and much against the initial wishes of LTI, a wheelchair-accessible conversion on an FX4Q was carried out. Body engineer Roger Ponticelli turned the doors round to hinge on the B-posts, and one of Peter James' designs was the sliding partition to accommodate the extra room that the bulk of the wheelchair needed. The conversion was offered as available for £1,700 plus VAT, on both used and newly bought cabs. Introduced in April 1986, this was a relatively economical way of solving the problem in the interim.

A NEW DESIGNER FOR A NEW INTERIOR

Metrocab's introduction in 1987 was welcomed by the ultra-conservative trade, but its early sales were slow, as teething troubles and MCW's initially slow response to warranty claims did not engender too much confidence. Nevertheless LTI's attitude – the desire to make the best London cab for its own sake – was still working its way through the factory. The next stage for them was the Alpha project, to investigate a

reshape of the cab involving the hanging of the rear doors on the B-posts and enlarging the windscreen. Working with Peter James on the Alpha was a young consultant, Jevon Thorpe, a graduate from Coventry University who, having spent his educational placement at Reliant under Ed Osmond, went on later to spend two and a half years as project manager on the Ford RS200 rally car. Despite the skilled work on Alpha, including a full-sized model in varnished mahogany by pattern shop superintendent Charlie Law, the project was considered to be the wrong way to go, and was scrapped.

In 1986 Ed Osmond asked Jevon Thorpe to see what could he do with the FX4's interior. Thorpe asked for a cab, some wood and some Styrofoam and said he would come up with something. When the cab arrived with its old 2.5 Austin engine, Bakelite steering wheel and no power steering, Thorpe thought it was years old; used to working on state-of-the art motor vehicles, he was astonished to find out that it was almost a current model! Working in his parents' garage, he carved the Styrofoam, fitting proprietary instruments into the dash and the existing door handles

Jevon Thorpe's dashboard in its later, Fairway guise. Unremarkable by contemporary saloon car or even light van standards, it was a revolution for the cab driver.

into the interior. Along with Ed Osmond, Dennis Poore came from London to look at the new interior. Impressed by what he saw, Poore told Osmond to get Thorpe on his team at Holyhead Road.

Osmond had not given Thorpe any false ideas about Carbodies. He had described the company to him as a firm not going anywhere at the present, but with tremendous opportunities. Thorpe moved in, and for the next eighteen months he built the master mouldings and models for the new interior.

The London Taxi Driver of the Year Show had evolved from its beginnings in 1973 into a major one-day trade show. Held in London's Battersea Park, it was the ideal place, in early September 1987, to launch the new model, called the FX4S Plus. Its new interior was in a modern grey vinyl, with the option of velour seats; the new moulded dashboard used the instrument panel from an Austin Mini Metro; push-button switches, face-level ventilation system and courtesy lights that opened with the doors were all fitted; and electric front windows were offered. In fact, the 'Plus' had everything that

would be found on a modern saloon car, but had long been missing from the cab's specification. Using most of the running gear from the 'S', the Plus's ride was improved by the fitting of laminated plastic rear springs and telescopic rear shock absorbers. A new range of colours, including city grey, Sherwood green and burgundy, was added to the already popular choices of midnight blue, carmine red, white and, of course, black. Whilst the Plus's interior specification was close to that of the Metrocab, it lacked a four-speed automatic gearbox, and the big windscreen and modern shape that gave the Metro an unassailable advantage in terms of driver comfort.

The new model received a fantastic welcome; Andrew Overton was quoted as being 'over the moon' with the Plus's reception. By contrast, Jevon Thorpe, certainly pleased with the welcome Plus had received, was still not indoctrinated into the cab trade, and couldn't understand what the fuss was about, even after being shocked by the lack of equipment on the old cab. But at last the customer, and in particular the owner driver, was beginning to appreciate that LTI meant

The FX4Q

An interesting project evolved out of the cab trade's dissatisfaction with the FX4R, and it was something that could not have happened when Austin were involved: the FX4Q. This was a rebuild taxi, using some new and some reclaimed and reconditioned parts. According to Department of Transport legislation at the time, this meant that all examples were given a 'Q', non year-related index number.

Carbodies took old chassis and checked them over fully, then fitted reconditioned suspension parts and rear axle, and the new brakes from the FX4R. They also fitted new diesel engines, effectively the Austin imported from India, and mated the Borg Warner 40 gearbox fitted with the floor-mounted selector from the 'R'. The chassis then went on the production line where they received brand-new bodies and trim.

They were sold directly via Carbodies Sales and Service to the trade through Rebuilt Taxis Ltd, a subsidiary of E. A. Crouch, a well established London Fleet proprietor, with the slogan, 'New or "Q"?'. At some £1,500 cheaper than the £9,800-odd asked for the FX4R automatic, it was a viable alternative. With the full servo brakes from the 'R', although not available with power steering, the FX4Q's specification was near what the old FX4 should have been some fifteen years before. It was

deeply unpopular with Mann and Overton; they were furious with Carbodies, because every FX4Q sold was one less new 'R' sold. It was an admission from Carbodies that the 'R' did suffer from the serious shortcomings that the cab trade had told them about, whilst Mann and Overton, who were adamant that many of the FX4R's problems were non-existent or over-exaggerated, were left to cope with those angry owners who had bought brand-new cabs.

A Q-cab, seen in service at Purley station, the southern-most rank of the Metropolitan Police District.

business, demonstrating that it was listening and, given the resources available, doing the best possible job.

MORE CHANGES AT THE TOP

Carbodies was to lose three key people within a year. Peter James left in 1986 to work for Land Rover. Apart from National Service and eighteen months at Stirling Metals, he had had close on forty years with the company and was a Carbodies man through and through. The CR6 was now history, and although James had gained an affection for the FX4, he felt that he could not spend ten more years of his life on what was, in effect, 'an antiquity . . . persistently trying to make a silk purse out of a sow's ear.'

The second departure was Grant Lockhart. During his tenure as managing director, three of the four projects started –

the CR6, the Cortina Coupé and the Unitruck – had foundered, and the fourth, the FX4R, did little to enhance the company's image. Still, in his time significant advances had taken place: the groundwork for the future, type approval for the taxi in Carbodies' own name, the move from sub-contractor to manufacturer, and the acquisition of Mann and Overton to take control of the marketing. Nor had the period been without its trauma, or teething troubles. In his own words:

> I perhaps was looked on as the person who had started a lot of projects that hadn't seen the light of day. It was inevitable that I left Carbodies because if you look at my career pattern I like a new challenge. I had been with them about eight or nine years, and my leaving coincided with the change at the top at MBH.

That change came as a result of the sudden death of Dennis Poore, by then well into his seventies. Very much a character respected by those who worked with him, he was sorely missed. His place at the head of Manganese Bronze was taken by his son-in-law, Jamie Borwick, a young man still under thirty, who took on the daunting task of guiding not only the largest and longest-standing maker of purpose-built taxis, but the whole of the Manganese Bronze Holdings group.

12 Beta, Gamma, Eta, Delta – A Cab for the World

'Well, it's different, but it's the same . . . '
Oliver Thorpe, aged nine, on seeing a
Delta prototype for the first time

THE BETA PROJECT

Getting the company into good shape was still important; to improve morale, to work on 'value engineering', the process of making a vehicle in the most cost-effective and efficient way possible, and to build quality in, rather than inspect it out at the end. But the main priority was to build a wheelchair-accessible cab, because from February 1989 no cabs could be sold in London that did not have this facility. Over at Carbodies Sales and Service at Torrington Avenue, the latest of Roger Ponticelli's wheelchair conversions caught Ed Osmond's eye. It had a fixed dog-leg partition, a lifting back seat, and the floor sloped at the rear to allow the wheelchair to be turned around more easily. The doors were hinged on the C-posts, on throw-back hinges, demanding that the door be secured flat against the rear wing when the wheelchair ramps were in use. The conversion became an option for the Plus, at £998.

A better design of door was needed for production, however, a door that would open adequately through 90 degrees to allow full wheelchair access. Within six months a swan-neck hinge was designed, using MIRA's facilities to select the best sections for the design of the hinge and the best material for it. This left only six months to put it into production, although at the time there were no test requirements for impact tests for wheelchair fittings in vehicles, which would speed things up. This aspect was worrying Jevon Thorpe, however, who had become senior designer. Working with MIRA, the Department of Transport and the seat-belt manufacturers, a series of tests were carried out at MIRA, which concluded that the safest arrangement was to secure the wheelchair in a rear-facing location, held down by a belt fixed to the partition. By December 1988 it was being built into the new model, code-named Beta.

But Beta was more than just a wheelchair-accessible S-Plus. As early as 1984 Barry Widdowson had asked Ricardo Engineering to look for a new taxi engine. Amongst what was available, one likely contender came from Japan, the Nissan TC series. However, this range was soon to be deleted, and it was decided to wait for the new range to be developed, and the 2.5-litre Land Rover engine was chosen. In early 1988 Nissan had the TD range of engines ready, with a choice between 2.3, 2.5 or 2.7-litre units; LTI selected the 2.7 litre. It came as a complete integrated powertrain, with a choice of either a four-speed automatic or five-speed manual gearbox. Despite the obvious excellence of the engine, it was

An early Fairway for the Danish market.

still a painful decision to install a Japanese engine in such a thoroughly British institution as the London taxi. Nor was it cheap; but the decision was taken, and Ed Osmond's team re-engineered the chassis to take it.

In February 1989 the new model was released. Bobby Jones' favourite name, Fairway, was dug out of the past and given to the new cab, and the choice was highly appropriate, for one of the most popular pastimes in the London cab trade is golf! Marketed in three trim options, bronze, silver and gold, with head-rests and wood-effect door-capping on the top of the range, Fairway was an immediate hit. Criticism about poor visibility was addressed as best as could be done, and the windscreen was slightly enlarged. It was, without doubt, the best version of the FX4 ever to be built, and it showed immediately in sales.

The Fairway's popularity did not allow anyone to sit on their laurels because success in both the provincial and international markets was vital to LTI's prosperity as an independent manufacturer, and in the provincial areas where London cabs were

An extremely pleasing sales success: a cream-coloured left-hand-drive Fairway, at work in Germany.

187

The Overseas Market

Updesh Ramnath had been promoted to director of overseas operations when the Fairway was re-engineered for left-hand drive and the export side of the business, abandoned since the problems in the USA and the Middle East, was started up again. Depending on the needs of the market, both taxis and limousines were offered. Only limousine versions of the Fairway could be sold in Japan, as all their taxis have to run on liquid propane gas, and no petrol engine was ever offered in a production Fairway. Fitted with air conditioning, leather seats and carpets, they are popular with company directors as mobile offices, because Tokyo's 'rush hour' can last two or three hours each way and the locally fitted telephones, fax and telex machines enable the bosses to conduct their business on the move.

Fairways have also proved popular with Far Eastern wedding halls, because the cab's interior allows brides to travel in comfort without spoiling their huge wedding gowns. Taiwan would take a basic cab and fit leather seats and even a massager for the drivers to use after sitting in traffic for two or three hours. In Hong Kong, hotels use limousine taxis to ferry customers to and from the airports. Singapore is the only country in the Far East to buy Fairways for use as taxis. Over a hundred were sold, where visitors from London and Australia break a long journey, and prefer to travel in a London taxi rather than a saloon car. The famous Raffles Hotel bought a few limousines for their own private use.

Nearer to home, Denmark, Switzerland and Portugal have bought Fairways, but the biggest coup was the German market. LTI did not expect success here, the heartland of Mercedes-Benz, but as over a hundred of their colleagues have been murdered, the German drivers feel a lot safer in a London purpose-built taxi. German cities have centres that deal with taxis only, and that includes all makes – Mercedes, Audi and Opel, as well as London taxis, supplied by a main agent in Essen. In Europe, Germany and Spain have been in the forefront of wheelchair accessibility. The Fairway exceeded the requirements set by the Spanish government for wheelchair accessibility, and the Spanish government promised every taxi driver that bought one 2m pesetas, nearly £8,500

It is LTI's pre-requisite for anyone buying a taxi abroad to ensure that proper service facilities are set up, either by the customer or by LTI themselves, because it is no good selling a taxi if there are no parts. Singapore has excellent service facilities, as does Taiwan. In Japan, Nissan themselves of course handle the servicing of the limousines.

There are a few London taxis in use abroad as government vehicles. The governor of the Falklands has one, as does the governor of the Turks and Caicos Islands.

'non-mandatory' i.e. not required by local regulations, sales resistance to the FX4 engendered over the years had to be overcome. In overseas taxi markets, almost exclusively serviced by saloon cars, the hold by Mercedes, Peugeot and the Japanese makes was strong and would take some breaking.

Two factors worked in LTIs favour, and for that matter Metrocab's too, both at home and abroad: driver safety and wheelchair accessibility. Attacks on cab drivers by passengers were on the increase; in Germany, cab drivers had been carrying firearms to defend themselves, as the incidence of murder among their numbers had risen dramatically in recent years, and in the UK, reports of attacks on both taxi and private-hire drivers were growing. Whilst figures did not distinguish between the two categories, drivers of purpose-built cabs were subject to far fewer attacks, because

KPM-UK PLC

'You can't be competitive without competition'. Barry Widdowson's expression would not only apply to LTI sharing the market with Metrocab: Mann and Overton, long castigated over their complacency, would be facing competition too. A search was begun in the late 1980s to find an organization within the London cab trade to locate a suitable second dealership. The company chosen was KPM-UK PLC, a conglomerate of two long-standing companies, KPM and UK Taxi Services.

KPM was started in 1975 by three men, Keith Marder, Peter da Costa and Michael Troullis, the name coming from the initials of their first names. Da Costa was a London cab driver, whilst Marder and Troullis were both time-served apprentices in the motor trade. They felt that the mush was given second-best treatment by service garages, who would give priority to their own fleet cabs. They also believed that more and more cabmen would buy their own cabs in the future, a prediction that proved to be correct. With these factors in mind, they started up in business in Brady Street, Bethnal Green, in London's East End with the intention of becoming, in Peter da Costa's words, 'the best cab garage in London'. In 1976, in the best cab-trade tradition, they moved the business to some railway arches in Dunbridge Street.

UK Taxi Services was formed in 1978 to meet the need for finance for cab drivers who wanted to buy their own vehicles. In 1988, the two companies merged to form KPM-UK PLC. Three factors led to the choice of KPM-UK in October 1989 as the second LTI dealer in London: one was their

track record in giving first-class service; the second was their location, at the other end of London to Mann and Overton's West London premises; and the third was that not only could they offer a first-class service, but it was a complete service. Even in the newly built Carnwath Road premises, Mann and Overton had no body shop or taximeter hire and maintenance facilities, whereas KPM-UK had them all on site.

Andrew Overton, right, congratulates Peter da Costa at the Café Royal, on the announcement that KPM-UK PLC had been appointed as LTI's second London dealership.

only in a vehicle with a solid partition does the driver have a great degree of safety from any potential assailant.

CUSTOMER RESISTANCE

Regulations governing wheelchair accessibility were to open up the market gradually for both manufacturers – although buyers were not going to purchase any vehicle available simply because it complied with those regulations. Provincial operators put up great resistance to buying a vehicle some three decades out of date, which would involve a great deal of what they saw as unnecessary capital investment, whether the cab was driver-safe and wheelchair accessible or not. They would argue that the number of wheelchair-bound passengers in provincial towns was too small to justify such an investment, and in any case, some had been offering what amounted to personal service to such customers, often using a swivelling front seat in their saloon cars. The government's attitude was that wheelchair-bound passengers were few in number because their condition simply prevented them from travelling, and this type of work would increase with improved accessibility to all transport and public buildings. Besides, new purpose-built cabs would be adapted to take people with a wide range of disabilities, not just the wheelchair-bound.

The Fairway's archaic bodywork was a source of controversy. Poor visibility, water-leaks and its inherent rattles and squeaks came in for much criticism. But there was no doubt about the new cab's recognizability; and many provincial drivers who had swapped over to a Fairway from a saloon car had noticed that their street hirings had increased. There was something about the

shape that made people hail it, where they would not hail a distinctively coloured saloon-car taxi. However, the only true solution would be a completely new body, but in 1990, the possibility of this was not imminent.

But before any work was done on developing a new body, LTI had to know exactly what their customers wanted, and in late 1990 an independent consultant, John Wragg, was commissioned to look at the product. Wragg was working at the European Commission in Brussels representing car manufacturers. His expertise was in product definition and development, with experience in both the Rover group and Ford. Wragg's first report, which came out in February 1991, was the first independent look at the business strategy that LTI had faced, and its message was quite clear: it said 'Look out, life's going to change'. It was shown to Peter Wildgoose, Mann and Overton's managing director, and he recalls his first reaction:

The Zeus disc brake conversion, offered on the last of the original Fairways in late 1992.

The report was rather narrow, because it only addressed disability in the UK, which had been on the agenda for ten years, and didn't look at a European dimension; the purpose-built taxi industry only existed in the UK. In the summer of 1991 I was invited to head up Carbodies sales and marketing; this was a much wider brief than London, and I began working with John Wragg, looking at the product and where we should go.

AN MPV CONVERSION?

Within LTI, Wildgoose's work included looking at what other manufacturers were doing in the taxi line. These included vehicle projects by specialist vehicle designers as well as the Renault Espace, then the only European multi-purpose vehicle. It would not be inconceivable to adapt a future MPV into a taxi. Thinking at Holyhead Road turned in this direction, to investigate costs and what such a conversion would involve. But from Paris, where there was an attempt to introduce the Espace as a taxi, there were already signs of resistance from both the drivers and the public. Moreover one lesson had been learned with CR6: don't depend on another manufacturer's donor vehicle. The study confirmed LTI's belief that they were on the right track with their own, original, purpose-built vehicle.

GAMMA: NEW RUNNING GEAR FOR THE FAIRWAY

Fairway's Nissan engine had proved itself as a first-class unit. Next up for attention was the running gear, under the banner of the Gamma project. It was recognized that

The late Peter Wildgoose, LTI's sales and marketing director for most of the 1990s.

the development of this had long been a specialist operation. For the suspension system LTI called in GKN, now part of the Dana Corporation of the USA. At their Johnston Product Development Centre in Wolverhampton they set about re-engineering the chassis package, the design being exclusive to Gamma, with LTI owning the rights to it. New wishbones were designed with ball joints replacing the old fulcrum pins, and mounted within the coil springs, telescopic dampers were fitted on the front to match those already fitted on the rear. The Salisbury 'Drew's Lane' axle, left over from the Austin Westminster, was replaced by a new GKN light commercial

The Fairway Driver, identified by its domed wheel covers.

unit, hung on the now proven composite springs.

The braking system had for a long time lagged behind contemporary practice, relying on drums all round. The major concern for the cab was that the brakes had to be so mounted on the suspension as to allow the full 25ft(7.6m) turning circle to be made. The development of both front suspension and disc brakes together gave AP Lockheed, the opportunity to liaise with GKN. AP Lockheed had a long track record in work with hydraulic brakes, and at their centre in Leamington Spa they had developed a system with four pot callipers and vented discs. New drums with self-

Demonstration driver Russ Swift puts the new Fairway Driver through its paces for a publicity shot and for a promotional video. Don't try this at work!

Updesh Ramnath, with buttonhole, shows off a chrome-bumpered Fairway limousine in Malaysia.

adjusters were developed for the back, and new six-stud hubs with wider offset wheels were developed to clear the bigger units.

Exhaustive tests were carried out at MIRA's development track, including work on the punishing pavé surface, a rough cobblestone surface which condenses the time-scale of punishment that a vehicle receives into a more manageable level. The new model was named the Fairway Driver, and was released in February 1993. Thus another of Ed Osmond's 'bite-sized chunks' had now been taken, on top of build quality, the new interior and a new engine. Not only was it an improved vehicle for London, but a better cab for Peter Wildgoose's team to sell, both in the rest of the UK and abroad.

The Crown Prince of Tonga was a cadet at Sandhurst and knew about London taxis. He wanted to know if one could be customized with all he wanted, to replace his Mercedes. The shop floor workers put the final polish on a special taxi for him.

DELTA, A NEW CAB AT LAST

The world population is ageing, and as a result becoming less mobile. In 1993 a seminar of European Ministers of Transport in Seville, Spain, recognized this and recommended that public transport world-wide needed to be more accessible, and in particular that public-hire taxis would have to be wheelchair-accessible; this long-term view would create more overseas markets. LTI needed to come up with the right package, so they had to ask, 'What does "accessible" mean, in terms of floor height, door width and door height? Is it just about a cab being wheelchair accessible, or should it cater for the partially sighted? And does it include people who are hard of hearing?' What would legislators and governments want?

The British government was clear, and the 1995 Disability Discrimination Act, the DDA, was to spell out quite clearly in a consultative document, due to be published in July 1997, the dimension required for a wheelchair-accessible taxi. The Act would also require all purpose-built taxis in the UK to be wheelchair-accessible by the millennium, subject to a small number of exemptions. The principles behind this legislation were well known, but they overrode the previous requirements for London. Fierce resistance to legislation of this type was put up by the taxi trade in many parts of the country, especially when local licensing authorities imposed a mandatory requirement for London-type taxis. The old argument – that LTI's cab was unsuitable, unreliable and poorly supplied with service facilities – was put forward again, plus new ones – that there was little demand for wheelchair-accessible taxis, and that most elderly people had difficulty in getting into a Fairway. As far as serviceability was concerned, LTI's quality control had vastly

AP Lockheed ventilated disc brakes on the GKN front suspension. Note the shape of the lower wishbone, curved inwards to clear the wheels. A tight turning circle is not impossible to engineer; it just requires a little application . . .

improved the cab, and UK marketing manager Terry Fryer had worked equally hard on the supply of spare parts: LTI now linked up with the Unipart spares network, ensuring an overnight supply of any component on the Fairway and older models. Furthermore experience with London's Taxicard system for the disabled countered the accessibility argument. Only the point about a high financial entry cost was valid with the government.

In the midst of recession, three years were

spent on customer research in the home market. It was a difficult job to get involvement from the cab trade, now such a familiar source of information to LTI, without them guessing why they were being asked so many pertinent questions; with a single product market, the customer can't be allowed to discover what was behind those questions. In a 1993 Customer Satisfaction Index survey, cab drivers were asked if they wanted a cheap, light, throwaway taxi, or a robust one with high resale values and long life. Next to a house, a taxi is usually the second largest purchase a cab driver makes, so the answer was plain: a high value vehicle. One point that screamed out was the importance of instant recognition – 'don't lose the icon'. But LTI also received some revealing and quite frightening information, that hit home painfully; basically it said, 'We like purpose-built cabs, but the improvements you have made to the old cab, no matter how welcome, are still no substitute for a modern vehicle.'

DELTA, ETA

In conjunction with Roy Axe of Design Research Ltd of Warwick, Jim Randle, the director of the Automotive Engineering Centre of Birmingham University had started the Hermes project, a luxury vehicle with a hybrid gas-turbine electric-power unit. LTI went to Design Research and spent two weeks with Axe and his clay modellers, talking to them about what they thought the purpose-built cab of the future should look like. They produced interior sketches, and a quarter-scale clay model of the hybrid-powered taxi.

The model, originally christened Delta, was unveiled at the Autotech exhibition at the NEC in November 1993. As soon as the project had moved from a luxury car concept to a taxi, what had been largely unnoticed became news. The shape of the model, as well as its proposed powerplant, attracted media attention. But for LTI the technology was too advanced and too complicated, and such a

LTI uses the Cathodic electrophoretic deposition process at Motor Panels (Coventry) Limited. This ensures uniform paint coverage over every part of the body-shell and inside box sections. It significantly extends the corrosion resistance of the Fairway body. The process is followed by a sealer primer coat and an anti-chip spray on the front panel, greatly improving stone-chip resistance.

195

The 'Delta' (later named 'Eta') cab, unveiled at the Autotech exhibition.

powerplant could not be easily maintained in the small, railway-arch garages that are the bedrock of the cab trade.

A year after Gamma went into production, LTI sent Jevon Thorpe to Warwick University, and the project he selected for his final year was a product-development plan for LTI. From the work on the Hermes/Eta he produced a combination of ideas such as front-and rear-end face-lifts; but in the knowledge that new legislation was looming, he also published a book called *Nothing but Safe, Accessible Blue Skies*, focusing on safety, accessibility and environmental friendliness. LTI immediately took the product-development programme on board and the whole team, under Barry

Widdowson, Ed Osmond, Jevon Thorpe and Peter Wildgoose, started to investigate what the new product should be.

Apart from having to comply with ECWVTA (European Community Whole Vehicle Type Approval) regulations, three main imperatives would govern its design: one was the DDA regulations, the second concerned the Conditions of Fitness, and the third was what the customers demanded, both in front of the cab and in the back. Should LTI update the old cab, or build a complete new body? Project leader Jevon Thorpe looked at restyling the old body, even at putting on a fibreglass front and rear end to alter the tooling cost; and he also considered doing a cheap job just to meet the

The Plasma cutter. This remarkable machine uses a fine stream of gas to cut panels to shape with extraordinary accuracy. It was used most effectively to trim the body panels for Thrust SSC, the car in which Squadron Leader Andy Green OBE set the first supersonic land-speed record. Carbodies was one of a number of Coventry companies which helped with the Thrust project.

forthcoming legislation for an M1 (European private car regulations) category vehicle that demanded that all doors should hinge forwards. In a section of the old trim shop, christened the 'skunk engineering department', Delta II evolved into a restyle of the front end, with modern headlights and a big windscreen. The team had listened to some cab drivers who had said they'd like a Mercedes or a BMW – so they tried to make one, even getting a running prototype. But it was scrapped: first, the doors would likely not be big enough for the impending wheelchair regulations, which had still not been finalized, but most importantly, they listened to what most cab drivers had told them, that their greatest asset was the icon value of the London cab. Features such as the

front and rear-end signature, the 'Coke bottle' line and the hire sign, said that they should be *evolving* the shape, rather than looking at a complete revolution. Jim Randle's Delta had that icon value – although having been publicized, attention needed to be diverted from the actual new project. The hybrid cab was renamed Eta 2000, to give the impression that it was a futuristic project, and the code-name Delta applied to what was really going to be built.

Delta would be a vehicle to meet all the requirements until the next century and beyond. It would not be a stop-gap – the London cab trade had had enough of them! There should be a complete new body, built to modern industry standards and acceptable as a vehicle around the world. The design team – and although Jevon Thorpe was design director and Ed Osmond the engineering director, it is important to say that the whole of Delta's work was a team effort, with everyone involved in the decision-making – followed the spirit of the DDA's requirements as well as the letter of that law. Delta would be the vehicle that everybody could hail, a social vehicle which all could use – young mothers with baby buggies, the athritic, and people in wheelchairs.

SIMULTANEOUS ENGINEERING

Simultaneous engineering is the close liaison of different project teams, with one of each team working in another department, rather than passing work from one department to the next. To get Delta from an idea into reality, all departments such as purchasing and material control had to work like this, and a small company such as LTI Carbodies could offer this sort of flexibility. And although Carbodies had specialist knowledge of the taxi industry, a partner with body-making expertise, now absent at Holyhead Road after so many years, would be needed. That partner was NGA of Coventry, and it was arranged that for the first part of the contract Carbodies' people would work at NGA, and for the next part NGA would work at Carbodies. Ed Osmond recalls that in the end it was almost impossible to remember who worked for whom.

Once the decision had been made to build a cab with evolutionary 'retro' styling, the DDA requirements were fed into the design. These requirements demanded a 53in

Barry Widdowson, promoted from LTI Carbodies managing director to MBH Vehicles Group managing director.

(1,350mm) door height – Fairway was only just under 47in (1,200mm) – but this extra could not be added onto the whole vehicle, and so the doors were set into the roof, in modern practice, and only 3in (75mm) was added to the overall height. A much larger windscreen was a vital part of the brief, as was greater driver headroom. The increase in rear headroom demanded by DDA took care of the latter, and allowed for both the extra screen size and a much larger cabin for the driver. With the design parameters accommodated, clay models were made. Data was taken straight from the final model, and put into a surfacing programme in NGA's computer facilities. A full-sized foam model was cut from the CAD data, brought up to showroom standards and signed off.

By modern standards rigidity was lacking in the Fairway. Most of the new body's rigidity was designed in from the start. The A-posts were put in a line direct from the point of the chassis which takes the load from the suspension. A bonded windscreen added to that strength, as well as doing away with leaks! A full steel floor was welded in place. The whole body was designed to be non-handed, package-protected for left-hand drive, which simply meant putting holes in the appropriate side of the vehicle as the panels were made and trimmed. Tooling, once such a vital part of Carbodies' core skills, was farmed out to Coventry-based companies. For the interior, everything from the base upwards on Delta would be brand new: the seats, the dashboard, all the fixings, and all the trim hardware.

CHASSIS IMPROVEMENTS

The Fairway Driver chassis was a proven base for Delta; the design team didn't want to change too many things at one point, or compromise the reliability or service back-up. DDA requirements demanded that the wheelbase be lengthened by 3in(75mm) and the track increased by 2½in(60mm). The Nissan engine, an outstanding success in all respects, received a new fuel pump to improve exhaust emissions. The ball joints on the front suspension and the steering box were uprated; the composite springs were also to be used again.

With the requirement to comply with drive-by noise levels of 74dba, the facilities at Leyland Technical Centre were used to study NVH – noise, vibration and harshness. The chassis was isolated from the body, something not done with Fairway, and the body drumming was virtually eliminated by 'deadpan' material, adhered to the surface of the body-shell.

THE GENESIS PROJECT

FX5 and CR6 had foundered, and it was absolutely vital that Delta became reality. The positive attitude of Ed Osmond, Jevon Thorpe and Barry Widdowson was an essential component in moving it towards production, but a new, revolutionary method of working was to ensure that the new vehicle would be owned by everyone who worked on it: Genesis.

Industrial strife between the workers and management in Coventry is legendary, and the history of the city's motor industry is littered with casualties; but gradually over the years those barriers have been eroded, and replaced by an attitude of co-operation. Barry Widdowson had been working with Terry Kellard of Warwick University to co-ordinate a method for directors of the company to work in harmony. From this grew the idea in Widdowson's mind that the shop floor would feel more confident in a similarly harmonious atmosphere. He contacted the unions, including Roy Howell, the Coventry district official of the Transport and General Workers Union, the largest represented in the company, and openly explained what he wanted to do: to work with the shop floor to make a better future, to give security to employees, and by building confidence in the business, to make a better product. He told Howell he wanted to form a partnership with Warwick University, to work together to make a better future for the whole company. Howell agreed, and with Kellard and Widdowson, signed the Genesis Agreement.

Widdowson then went on to explain to the shop floor what was happening. In groups of no more than ten to fifteen people, at a 'skip lunch' meeting, they identified the most important concerns, namely the future of the company, and when, if the rumours were true, the company would move, whether

The TX1. The headlights demonstrate the dilemma facing LTI's design team: how to give a modern image but still have a vehicle that is economical to repair. The headlights are simple, round items behind a smooth plastic cover, and are considerably cheaper to replace than most private car units.

there would be a new product, and how regulations governing exhaust emissions would affect it. Human resources and quality director Mike Edwards handled the basic organisation of the initiative, including how the employees themselves would fit into Genesis. The principle was simple: people build quality, and if you can get them into teams where they own the work, working within boundaries which actually encourage initiative, the product will improve, and the employees' involvement, their 'ownership' of

the product, will blossom. Here would be the great contrast between Delta and CR6: few people had faith in CR6, whereas everyone believed wholeheartedly in Delta.

INSTALLING PRODUCTION LINES

Genesis proved to be essential in getting the new cab into production. Carbodies as a small company making one product could not

The unique tail-lights of the TX1 echo the FX4's 1967 items. The moulded plastic bumpers are in three pieces with separate ends, to make replacement more economical.

TX1's interior features a child safety-seat, to a design taken from Volvo. The bright flashes on the seat edges are for the benefit of the poorly sighted.

afford the luxury a big company enjoyed, of shutting down a line to install a new model: it had, like the FX4R, to be done alongside the Fairway. However, the new thirty-seven hour working week had reached a stage where the week's work was done in four days. New plant and working practices were started on the Friday, beginning with six weeks of induction so that all understood what was to happen. During the following Fridays, the new lines were installed along-side the old. On Fridays the new cab was worked on: problems were recorded, and on the following Friday they were solved. Barry Widdowson recalls a 'tremendous buzz' in the factory, as PCRs – product change requests – came from the production team leaders (each elected by their teams with no influence from management) working around the clock, with the lights never off in the factory.

Jevon Thorpe endorsed the change in the atmosphere. He says:

I like some measures in business, and one is smiles per minute. If you've got a happy workforce, the chances are that they'll build a quality product. You go around the factory now and you can talk to anyone; they'll talk to you, and they'll *want* to talk to you. If you'd gone out there a few years ago they'd have just ignored you.

From signing off the original clay model to the release date of the new cab took a remarkably tight twenty-eight months. Nostalgia plays no part in business: Historians might have liked to have seen the old FX4 reach its fortieth birthday, but the London cab trade certainly wouldn't have wanted to wait that long, but more importantly, neither would the government nor the EC. Fairway would not have met new European Whole Vehicle Type Approval regulations, due to be introduced on 1 January 1998, and it had to go.

But was Delta a good product? And did it look like a taxi, as the survey results had demanded? Initial tests at MIRA showed up some shortcomings in the chassis, but with the teams working together these were soon put right. Jevon Thorpe took a prototype home and asked his three young sons about it. They recognized it immediately as a taxi, but when the middle lad, nine-year-old Oliver, was asked exactly what he thought, he said 'Well, it's different, but it's the same . . .': recognition indeed. When the first prototype was driven out into Holyhead Road and off the infamous ring road into the city centre, this brand-new vehicle, never before seen in public, was hailed by somebody wanting a cab. This, as Jevon Thorpe said, 'is the moment when the fist punches the air – yes! We got it right!'

At the end of March 1997 the vehicle was clinicked in London before a group of taxi drivers, the hardest customers to please. Plenty of comments were made, but significantly they were all about details. Nobody said they didn't like it, which was quite a contrast to when the FX4 was originally shown to cab proprietors in 1958!

Now there was the matter of a name to be decided. Jamie Borwick wanted to call the new cab the 'Fairmile', a name apparently analogous with the cab trade, but harking back to the factory near Brooklands where Noel Macklin had built his Invictas and Railtons. Jevon Thorpe and the rest of the design team were not convinced. In a lengthy meeting they persuaded Borwick to change his mind. They wanted to get back to how all the old Austins were named, and after a brainstorming session taking just about every option, Thorpe wrote on the flip chart, 'TAXI'. He then crossed out the 'A', and the name jumped off the paper: TX1.

The last Fairway came off the tracks on 7 November 1997, destined for the National Motor Museum, with the registration number R1 PFX. From that point on, the TX1's production began to build up steadily, ensuring along the way that each problem was nipped in the bud. Overall reaction was excellent. After such a long time a new cab from the same stable as the FX3 and FX4 had to be right. On the road, one has to look to notice that it is different, so readily does it blend in among, the hordes of FX4s. Curiously, if any other manufacturer had spent the £20m that TX1 had cost, and it hardly stood out, they would not be pleased. For LTI, it was yet another indication that they had got it right.

And for the future? The TX1 will be available as a left-hand drive model, for the world market is ripe for exploring. Trials with a dedicated Iveco LPG-fuelled spark-ignition engine began in mid-1996, and if successful, will be available to markets where such requirements are mandatory. From November 1997 Barry Widdowson was promoted to Vehicle Group managing director. Jevon Thorpe was promoted in his place, and at the same time the name 'Carbodies' was dropped from the company title. With legislation in place for the next few years, TX1 will undoubtedly be the most popular option in the UK where London cabs are mandatory, and will sell on its own merits where there is a choice of vehicles. The only part of the business where LTI do not have control, the political field, will still remain a potential minefield, but the manufacturing side is safe in LTI's hands.

And what would Bobby Jones would have made of his company today? His portrait hangs in the boardroom, and looking down at a successful, profitable business with an excellent future, one cannot help but think he would raise a smile of satisfaction.

Index

Abbey Panels, 103, 117, 126
Adkins-Soobroy, Tooby, 14
AEC, 38, 109, 112
Aircraft drop tanks, 44
Airflow Streamline, 85, 116, 137, 149
Allingham, Henry, 27, 28
Alpha project, 182
Alvis, company, 15, 30, 42, 55
   10/30, 15
   11/40, 15
   12/50, 15, 18, 19, 27
   12/75, 15
   FA 8/15, 15
   14.75, 18
   Silver Eagle, 21, 27
   12/60, 27
   Speed 20, 27
   TA14 , 53, 56
   TA14 Sports Saloon, 54
'Alvista' body, 22
Armstrong Whitworth, Wigston, 44
Whitley bomber, 39
Asquith taxi, 74
Aston, Stanley, 93
Atlantic saloon body, 21, 23, 30, 31, 32, 33
Austin, Herbert, 67, 68
Austin Motor Company, 38, 57, 58, 67, 69,98, 105, 107, 124
   Redditch Sales Dept, 69, 78, 143
   K6 lorry, RAF office body, 46
   K8 'Three-Way' van, 51, 69
   A70 Hereford Coupé, 56, 59
   A40 Devon, 70
   A40 Devon Countryman, 64
   A40 Somerset Coupé, 59, 61
   Pathfinder pedal car, 64
   J40 pedal car, 64
   Healey 100, 64
   Westminster, 105
   Gypsy gearbox 108
Taxis, early
   Heavy 12/4, 66
   FX, (14hp) 66, 68
   FX2 , 68-71
FX3 taxi, 56 et seq, 98
FL1 hire car, 56, 59 et seq

FX4 taxi, 75, 97, 117, 122, 183
   early development, 98 et seq
   facelift, 123
   sales to New York, 129, 139-40
   LPG conversion, see Cook, W. H. & Sons
   crash test, 137
   brake modifications, 138-9
   Plastic over-riders, 148
   leasing deals, 150
   improved trim specification, 150
   FX4Q, 181, 184
   see also Carbodies FX4 & LTI FX4, Fairway, FX5, CR6 & TX1
Austin FL2 Hire Car
   early development, 98 et seq
   end of use as hire car, 143
   as passenger ambulance, 151
   see also Carbodies London Limousine
Austin-Morris, 128, 130
   JU250 van, 123
   LM11 prototype taxi, 123, 128
   Courthouse Green engine plant, 146
Automatic gearboxes, see Borg-Warner
Autotech Exhibition, 195
Auxiliary Fire Service, 42, 43
Avro Lancaster bomber, 39, 45, 116
Axe, Roy, 195

Bache, David, 123
Bailey, Bill, 124
Bailey, Eric, 98
Baginton Airport, 116
Baldwin, Sir Peter, 156
Ballard, Arthur, 120, 122
Bambers of Southport, 24
Barkers, coachbuilders, 87
Bateman, Bill, 173
Bates, Bernard, 139, 140, 143
Bayer Plastics, 165
Beardmore, 66, 74, 78, 122
Beale, Stan, 130
Bean 14hp Doctor's Coupé, 16
Bedford TK lorry body, 113
Beebe, Walter 'Snowy', 62, 163

Bell, Jimmy, 14
Benlow, Charles, 98
Benn, Anthony Wedgewood (Tony), 136
Bentley, 3-Litre, 4.5 litre & Speed Six, 21
Berkeley, coachbuilders, 32
Beta project, see LTI Fairway
Bessoneau, Maurice, 34, 35
Betford, Billy, 48, 106
Bevin, Bernard, 113
Birch Brothers, and taxi, 73, 75, 99
Blackburn Aircraft Company, 112
Blackburn Eric, 116, 124, 131
Blackshaw, Doug, 124
Bland, R. G., 45
Blitz (Coventry), 40, 43, 44
Borgward Hansa diesel engine, 73
Borg-Warner, 76, 166
   Automatic gearboxes:
   DG150M, 76, 99, 107
   Model 35, 108
   Model 40, 166, 178, 184
Borwick, Jamie, 185, 200
Boulton & Paul, 45
Bridge Clock Motors, 86
Briggs Bodies, 127
Bristol Siddeley, 39, 113
British Light Steel Pressings, 116
British Motor Corporation, 72
Broughton, Bob, 119
Bruce, Dickie, 63
BSA group, 62, 63, 83, 89, 111, 114, 128, 93, 134
   history, 84
   take-over of Carbodies, 64-5, 83-4
   Birtley Engineering, 135
   heating, 109, 111
   guns, 135
   metal components, 135
   Group News, 118, 130
   Sunbeam scooter, 110
   Beagle motorcycle, 118
   Ladybird 3-wheeler, 114
Burton, Arthur, 105, 112, 117
Burzi, Dick, 98

Cadogan, coachbuilders, 31

Carbodies
  founding, 13
  fire at West Orchard, 11, 16
  formation of limited company, 45
  take-over by BSA, 63, 65
  take-over by Manganese Bronze
    plc, 135-6, 137
  factory, 167
  as part of LTI,
  dropping of name, 204
Carbodies Sales & Service, 142 *et
  seq*, 170, 186
Carbodies taxis:
  FX4, 187
    European Type Approval, 158-7
    'Glider' 174-4
  FX4R, 178, 184, 200
    development & introduction,
      166-8
    automatic door locks, 168
    provincial & export sales, 170-9
    London Limousine, 175
  FX5 taxi, 144 *et seq*, 147
    chassis adapted for CR6, 152
  CR6, 166, 174, 178, 183, 184, 191
    early development, 151-157
    wheelchair accessibility, 155-5
    wheelchair trials, 158, 159, 171
    final prototype, 172, 173
    plastic front wings, 172
    delay of release date, 173
    scrapping, 179-8
Carrier Engineers Ltd, 57, 65
Central Autos, Chelsea, 71
Chapman, Colin, 135, 136
Charlesworth, coachbuilders, 12, 27,
  28
Chataway, Christopher, MP, 135
Chater, Geoff, 174
Clarke, Kenneth, 156
Coachcraft, coachbuilders, 32, 33
Cobb, Don, 45, 70, 99
Coleman Milne FX4S limousine, 180
Colston dishwashers, 111
Commer
  N-Type van, 51, 52
  TS2 Crew cab 124
  Superpoise van, 126
Commercial Motor Exhibition/Show,
  71, 73, 110, 109, 118, 130
Communist influence in British
  motor industry, 92
Comparative Dimensions Plan, 37
Conditions of Fitness, Metropolitan
  Police, 67, 74-75, 76, 98, 99, 135,
  159
Connolly, F, 54, 96
Cook, Christopher, 181

Cook, W. H. & Sons, taxi
  proprietors, 71
  LPG conversions, 128 *et seq*
Costa, Peter da, 189
Coventry:
  Broadgate, 169
  Cathedral, 13, 42, 169
  Economic Building Society, 20
  Evening Telegraph, 93
Coventry Climax fire pump trailer,
  42
Cowlishaw Walker presses, 62, 118
Crayford, vehicle conversions, 160
Cripps, Derek, 166, 174
Cross & Ellis, 15, 16, 22, 27
Crossland, Sir Leonard, 127
Crouch, car mfrs., 14, 15,
Crouch E. A., Taxi proprietors, 184
Cushman, Leon, 33
Customs & Excise, HM, 163-2

Daimler, company, 58, 62, 83
  Radford factory, 83, 96, 114
  Brown's Lane factory, 114
  1950 'Pacific' saloon, 25
  Conquest, 86
  Conquest Century saloon, 86
  Conquest Century coupé, 87
  Conquest Century Roadster, 87
  Conquest Century Roadster Fixed
    Head Coupé, 87
  Conquest Century Roadster
    Drophead Coupé, 87
  DK400 Limousine, 87-8
  Regency, 87, 94
  Empress, 94
  One-0-Four, 94, 95
  Majestic, 94-6, 113, 118
  Majestic Major, 96, 113, 115
  Majestic & Major limousines, 96-7
  DN250, 96
Dana Corporation, 191
Davis, Barney, Felday Cabs, 101
Dawson, Bill, 13, 113
Dawson Mick, 14, 113
Dawson Peter, 60, 113, 129, 130,
  131, 144
Disability Discrimination Act, 194,
  196, 197, 199
Delage, 1952 D6, 22
Delta/TX1, *see* LTI taxis
Design Research Ltd., 195
Docker, Sir Bernard, 83, 93
Docker, Lady Norah, 83, 85, 86, 87,
  93
Dodson, George, 103
Donoghue, Joe, 93
Donaldson, Jake, 57, 59, 83, 87, 88,
  94, 99, 113, 121-3, 126, 127,

130, 133, 137, 139, 140, 144-4,
  147, 153-2, 160-9, 173
Drew, Bill, 144, 166

Earl's Court Motor Exhibition/Show,
  34, 35, 55, 56, 57, 90, 97, 101,
  102, 108, 115, 116, 117, 118, 121
Edwards, Joe, 48, 64, 69
Edwards, Mike, 200
Edwardes, Michael, (Sir) 146, 152
Ellinghouse, Frederick, 65, 85, 94
English Rose kitchens, 111
Enigma code, 40
Eta project, 195, 196, 197
European Commission, 190
European Community Whole
  Vehicle Type Approval, 196, 203
European Common Market, 137
European Ministers of Transport,
  conference in Spain, 194
Evans, Brian, 63, 93
Everitt, Jack, 66, 75, 146
Everitt, Ken, 45

Fairbrother, Derek, 77
Fairway bodies:
  Rover, 28
  Morris, 28
Fairway patent power head, 34
Fairway taxi, *see* LTI
Faulkner, Horace, 147, 166
Ferguson diesel, *see* Standard
Fletcher, George, 109, 124, 130
Fletcher, Rivers, 87
Fogg, Dr Bertie, 157
Follet, Charles, 27
Ford Motor Company, 12, 38, 58, 59,
  117, 127
  Consul, Zephyr Six MkI coupés,
    57-60, 89
  Zephyr Zodiac, MkI, 58
  Consul, Zephyr & Zodiac MkII
    coupés, 89-91, 114
  MkIII Zephyr & Zodiac coupés,
    117
  MkI Capri coupé, 127
  Diesel engines, 147, 166
  Cortina Coupé, 159-162, 178, 184
  US Ford engine in London cab,
    175
Fowler, (Sir) Norman, 156
Frye, Ann, 155, 157, 181
Fryer, Terry, 194

Genesis Project, 199-7
Girling, brake mfrs., 99
GKN, 191 *see also* Sankey and Dana
  Corporation
Gotla, Michael, 142

Gooderhams, timber merchants, 13
Gould, H. 70, 99, 103-4
Grace, HSH Princess of Monaco, 81
Greater London Council, 172, 181

Habbits, Frederick, 110, 111, 112, 114
Hancock & Warman, coachbuilders, 23
Handley Page Halifax bomber, 45
Happich, lock mfrs, 137
Harper, Joan, 35 *see also* Swaine
Heath, Bert, 63, 93
Heinz, Arthur, 121
Hellberg, C. J. (Jack), 83, 84, 85, 86, 92-3, 98, 99, 102, 113, 114
Hennessey, Patrick, 57
Hermes, *see* Eta project
Hillman, 57, 58
    Wizard, 29
    Aero Minx, 30
    Hawk, 30, 31, 33
    Twenty/Seventy, 30, 31
    Minx, pre-war, 28, 29, 30, 31
    Minx, post-war, 54, 55, 56, 59, 82, 116
    Super Minx, 115
Hobbs Mecha-matic transmission, 78
Hodgkinson, Michael, 153-2, 179
Holbrook, coachbuilders, 30
Holland, Freddie, 45
Hollick & Pratt, 12-13, 17
Home Guard, 42, 43
Hoopers, coachbuilders, 87, 96
Howell, Roy, 200
Hudson Terraplane, 31, 32
Hughes of Birmingham, 17
Humber, Beeston Notts, 11
    Snipe, 29
    Super Snipe, pre-war, 34
    Twelve, 29, 30, 31
    Super Snipe, Hawk estate, 116-8

IBCAM, coachwork medals, 116, 123
International Year of the Disabled, 155, 157
Iveco LPG engine, tests in TX1, 204
Invicta, company, 31, 33, 204
    4-Litre, 30
    Low Chassis S-Type, 31, 32
Issigonis, Alec, 123

Jaguar, 94, 114, 126
    E-Type, 126
    MkX, 126
    XJ6, 126

James, Peter, 94, 121, 123, 139, 144-4, 153-3, 160-9, 162, 168, 177, 178, 181, 182, 183-2
James, Joe, 103
James, Sid, 108
Jofeh, Lionel, 134
John, T. G., 15, 18
Johnson, 'Ack', 130
Johnson, Ben, 14, 58, 63, 70, 124
Jones, Dorothy (*née* Aikin), 25, 54
Jones, Ernest, 22, 47
    birth and early life 11, 13,
    joins company, 17
    marriage, and builds house, 25, 26
    letters to strikers, 40
    AFS service, 42, 43
    made managing director, 45
    excess profits tax, 50
    arguments with Bobby, 50, 61, 62
    BSA take-over, 65
    Austin taxi contract, 69, 71
    Bridge Clock Motors, 86
    illness and subsequent death, 96
Jones, Lillie, 13, 22, 47
Jones, Robert 'Bobby', 204
    anecdotes, 36
    early life and career, 11-13
    and Lillie move house, 25
    forms limited company, 45
    daily routine, 50
    arguments with Jack Orr and Ernest, 50, 60, 62
    BSA take-over, 63, 65
    industrial relations, 92
    death and memorial service, 96
Keller die machine, 48, 61, 64
Kimber, Cecil, 17, 18, 19, 20, 21, 26
King, Spen, 163, 177, 178, 180-8
Kirksite, 44, 45, 48, 50, 63, 69, 94, 95, 100, 102, 126
Knight, Bill, 42-44
KPM-UK Ltd, 189
Kraus, Ziggy, 140

Lagonda 3-litre, 22
Lanchester
    40hp six-light saloon, 17
    Fourteen DHC, 35
    Fourteen/Leda, 57, 86, 87
    Sprite, 83, 94
Landers, D. F., 174
Land Rover, *see* Rover
Lawton, carriage makers, Manchester, 11
Lawton, Frank, 140
Lea Francis, 34, 117-8
    Ace of Spades, 23
    12/40, 23
    Lynx, 118

Lend-Lease, 45
Levy's, cab proprietors, 76
Lewis, J. R., 140
Leyland
    15 & 20 van, 118 *et seq*, 146
    Speke factory, 118
    Stampro, Indian subsid., 119
Leyland Technical Centre, 199
Lloyd, Percy, 124, 130
Lloyds & Scottish, Bowmaker, 148, 174
Lockhart, Grant, 177
    joins company, 150
    improving spec. on FX4, 150
    scraps FX5, 152
    struggles with Mann & Overton, 151
    begins CR6, 153 *et seq*
    wheelchair accessibility, CR6, 155
    FX4 European Type Approval, 158
    Cortina Coupé, 159-9
    Land Rover engines, 166-8
    D. F. Landers and 'Glider' taxi, 174-4
    resigns from company, 184-3
Lockheed Lightning fighter, 48
Lockheed, AP, brake mfrs, 192
Lindsay, Mayor of New York, 129
Loewy, Raymond, 55
London Coach Co. Inc, London Sterling, 174-4
London General Cab Company, 67, 73, 101, 123
London Taxis International
    formation, 174
    Customer Satisfaction Index, 195
LTI taxis:
    FX4S, 178-7
    FX4W, 182
    FX4S Plus, 182-1, 186
    Beta/ Fairway, 186 *et seq*, 203
    Gamma/Fairway Driver, 192, 195
    last example to National Motor Museum 204
    Delta/TX1, 193 *et seq*
Lord, (Sir)Leonard, 64, 68, 72
Lucas, Bill, 128, 133, 138, 140, 160, 163
    joins Carbodies, 44
    on dispute between Bobby and Ernest, 61
    leaves on BSA take-over, 63, 83, 84
    FX4 early involvement, 99 *et seq*
    rejoins company, 110, 113
    industrial relations, 132
    Rootes estate cars, 116 *et seq*
    Leyland 20 van, 118 *et seq*
    Triumph 2040 estate, 119 *et seq*

discussions with PCO, 122
LM11, 123
promotion to director and general
    manager, 125
acquisition of chassis plant, 130 *et
    seq*
MBH take-over: retention as
    managing director, 135-6
creation of Carbodies Sales &
    Service, 143
development of FX5, 144-4
search for new FX4 engine, 146 *et
    seq*
attempt to buy Mann & Overton,
    148
retirement, 148-7
Lucas, Mrs. Doris, 149
Lucas, Joseph, Electrical, 38, 45
    Limpet indicators, 76, 108
Ludford, Peter, 97
Lyons, Sir William (Bill), 114, 126

Mackay, Alistair, 93, 113
Macklin, Noel, 30, 31, 32, 33, 204
Maddox, coachbuilders, 39
Manganese Bronze Holdings plc,
    134-7, 144, 149, 185
    purchase of Mann & Overton
Mann, J. J., 67
Mann Egerton, 13
Mann & Overton, 66, 67, 68, 69, 70,
    71, 72, 73, 78, 82, 98, 100, 104,
    106, 122, 123, 124, 135, 137,
    139, 144, 146, 148, 151, 155,
    173-2, 179, 184, 189, 190
Mansfield, Jayne, 102
Marrs, Jimmy, 45
Martin Walter, coachbuilders, 30
Mary, HM Queen 25
Massey, Bert, 156
McLaughlin, Derek, 127
McMullan, David, 160
McNally, Percy, 92, 94, 95, 99, 101,
    103, 105, 110, 113
Mercedes-Benz diesel, in FX3, 73
Meriden, 125, 134, 136-7
MCW Metrocab
    early prototype, 74, 128
    production model, 174, 182
'Midget Shop', 21
Midland Motor Body Company, 23
Minicabs, 142-2
Ministry of Aircraft Production, 50
Ministry of Manpower, 44, 45
MIRA, (Motor Industry Research
    Association) 137, 186, 192, 203
MG, 30
    Factory, Abingdon, 20
    Sports Special, 17

'Old No. One', 18
14/28, 14/40, 17, 18, 19, 20, 21
18/80, 20, 21, 22
18/100 Tigress, 21, 23
M- Type Midget, 19, 20, 21, 26
C-Type Midget 'Montléry', 21
D-Type Midget, 25, 26
Magna, 25, 26
K-Type Magnette, 26
J-Type Midgets, 26
Airline Coupés, 28
Molesworth
    Mr., Senior, 14
    Harry, 14
    Len, 14, 40
Montgomery, Field Marshal,
    wartime caravans, 41
Moore, Albert, 98
Morris Motors, 53
Morris Bodies, 26
Morris Commercial Adderley Park,
    130
Morris Garages, 17
Morris, William, 12, 17, 26
    Minor, 19
    10/6 'Fairway', 28
Morrison Electricar, 51
Moss, Stirling, 156
Motor Bodies, coachbuilders, 32
Motor Packing Company, 52, 59
Motor Panels, 94, 97, 110, 195
Motor Show, NEC, 161
Mulliner, 30, 53
Munday, Jim, 112, 113, 116, 125
'Mush' (taxicab owner-driver), 67

National Exhibition Centre, (NEC)
    195
National Motor Museum, 204
Neville, John 136, 138, 143, 144-4,
    150
NGA, 197
Nicholls, Herbert, 70
Nissan diesel engines, 186, 191, 199
Norton Villiers, 134, 135
Norton-Villiers-Triumph (NVT),
    135-7

Olivier, Sir Laurence, 133
Olympia Motor Exhibition, 16, 21,
    25, 26, 27, 28, 30, 31, 33, 34
Orr, John Hewitt (Jack), 34, 40, 42,
    43, 50, 51, 53, 55, 57, 58, 60, 62,
    64, 69, 70, 81, 83, 85, 86, 89, 92,
    99, 173
Osmond, Ed, 193, 196, 199
    appointment as engineering
        director, 177
    FX4S, 178

FX4S Plus, 182-1
Beta/Fairway, 186-5
Gamma/Fairway Driver, 193
Delta/TX1, 196-6, 200-9
Overton, Andrew, 155, 173, 183, 189
Overton, J. T. 'Tom', 67
Overton, Robert, 69, 70, 73, 133,
    138, 173
Overton, William, 67
Oxford (Nuffield) taxi, 66, 69, 71, 72,
    81

Pacific saloon, 21, 23, 24
Panhard, 83
Pass, Thomas & Sons, 14
Paton, John, 144, 170
PCR (Product Change
    Requirements), 200
Penrose, J. W. R., 68
Perkins diesel engines
    P4C , 73, 76
    4.99, 147
    3-litre, 147, 166
Peugeot, 129
    Diesel engines, 147, 154, 166
Ponticelli, Roger, 181, 186
Poore, Dennis, 134, 136, 144-4, 149,
    150, 151, 157-6, 178, 182, 184
Pressed Steel Company, 87
Public Carriage Office, (PCO) 67, 68,
    70, 74, 76, 78, 80,81, 101, 104,
    108, 109, 129, 151, 159

Q-cabs, *see* Rebuilt Taxis Ltd
Railton, Reid, 32
Railton, Tim, 33
Railton company, 31, 204
    Carbodies saloon, 31, 32
    Cobham, 32
    Claremont, 33, 34
    Sandown, 33, 34
    Tourer, 33
Ramnath, Updesh K., and LTI
    overseas sales, 188, 193
Randle, Jim, 195, 197
Raworth, coachbuilders 17
Ray, Mike, 173
Rebuilt Taxis Ltd, 184
Reeves, Cissy, 14
Renault Espace, 191
Ricardo Engineering, 186
Riley Stelvio, 23
Robinson, Alf, 57
Rogers, Jim, 87, 88
Rolls-Royce:
    20/25 tourer, 24
    20/25 'Pacific' Saloon, 24
    Phantom II 'Pacific' Saloon, 24

Rolls-Royce:
  Mérlin aero engine, 39
  Silver Shadow LWB, 137
Rootes Group, 29, 51, 53, 54, 55,
    113, 115, 116,117, 126
Rothschild, Lord, 23
Rover company, 27
  12hp Nizam, 27
  12hp Speed Pilot, 27
  Streamline coupé & saloon, 28
  SD1 estate, 152
  Land Rover, 153
  Land Rover diesel engine, 147,
    152, 154, 166
  Range Rover, 153
  as taxi base, 144, 153
  Unitruck, 162-3, 178, 184
  'City Rover' (CR6) 153
  5-speed gearbox, 166
Rowe, John, 63, 65
Runciman Committee, 73

St Denise yacht, 52
Salmons, coachbuilders, 30
Salmons, Geoff, 48, 106
Samuels, Ronnie, 107
Sangster, J. Y. 'Jack', 93, 110, 111
Sankey, suspension mfrs, 99
Scott, Jan, 142, 174
Scottish Motor Show, 21
Shawcross, Lord, 134, 135
Sheet Metal Workers' Union, 39,
  92-3
Shufflebotham, Fred, 124
'Skunk engineering dept.', 197
Singer
  Birmingham factory, 116
  Twelve coupé, 34, 35
  Vogue, 115
  Vogue estate, 116, 117, 118
  Gazelle, 116
Smith, Freddie, 58
Smith, Geoffrey, 160
Smith, Richard, 62, 65, 83, 84, 92-3
Society of Motor Manufacturers &
  Traders, 33, 118, 159
Southwell David, 76, 98, 99, 103-4,
  105, 139, 146, 173
Standard Triumph, company,
  118-120, 130
Standard Motor Company, 34
  Flying Eight, 34

Flying Fourteen, 34, 35
diesel engine (Ferguson) 73, 75, 76
Atlas Major van, 118
Stansfield, Keith, 119
Steering Wheel magazine, 68
Stevens, G. A. 'Steve', 25, 35, 45, 62,
  63, 64, 65, 85, 86, 92, 94, 111,
  113, 126, 138
Stirk planers, 45, 48
Sunbeam;
  3-litre, 14
  16hp, 21
  Talbot coupé
  Alpine, 113
Supermarine
  Sea Otter, 49
  Spitfire, 45, 48
Swaine, Stan, 60, 105, 130
Swaine, Joan, 60
Swift, Russ, 192

Taxicard, London, 194
Taxi Driver of the Year Show, 182
Taxis, *see* Asquith, Austin,
  Austin-Morris, Beardmore,
  Carbodies, LTI, MCW, Morris,
  Oxford (Nuffield), Unic,
  Winchester,
Taylor, George, 130
Thorpe, Jevon, 199
  interior re-design on FX4, 182
  joins LTI, 182
  becomes design director, work on
    Beta/Fairway, 186
  Author, *Nothing but Safe
    Accessible Blue Skies*, 196
  Delta/TX1, 196-204
Thompson, Jack, 62
Thomson & Taylor, 32
Thrupp & Maberly, 29, 30, 55, 59,
  137
Tickford, 35, 53
stretch FX4, 177
Tokyo Arms Company, 144
Tomin, Frank, 45, 52
Tonga, Crown Prince of, 193
Toolmakers & Design, company, 44
Trade and Industry, dept of, (DTI),
  134
Transport, Department of, 155, 159,
  171-70, 186,
  Accessibility Unit, 171, 181

Transport & General Workers
  Union, 200
Transport Road Research
  Laboratory:
  Road Transport Study group, 158
Triumph cars
  1300 estate, 125
  2040 MkI estate & hatchback, 119
    et seq
  2040 MkII estate, 125, 140-1
Triumph motorcycles, 93-4
  Tigress scooter, 110
Troman, Brenda, 168
Troman, Stan, 138, 168
Trotter, Geoffrey, 73, 101, 104, 107,
  128, 140
Troughton, Frank, 124
Turnbull, George, 118, 120, 130,
  131, 140
Turner, Edward, 93, 114
Turner, Eric, 112, 113, 125, 134

Unic taxi, 67
Unipart, 194
Unitruck, *see* Range Rover

Vanden Plas, 21, 27, 30
Volvo, child seat in TX1, 204

Wales, HRH the Prince of, 140
Walker, George Tweedie, 21
Warwick University, 195, 200
Watson, William, 13, 28, 66
West Orchard, 11
Whitehead, Graham, 129
Whybrow, Peter, 107
Widdowson, Barry
  joins company, 157-6
  FX4R development, 166-6
  promotion to managing director,
    176
  Beta/Fairway, 186
  Delta/TX1, 196-6
  Genesis Project, 199
Wildgoose, Peter, 173, 190, 196
Wilmot Breeden, 137
Winchester taxi, 74, 122, 123
Wragg, John, 190-9

York Way Motors, 101

Zeus disc brake conversion, 190